Epistemic Instrumentalism Explained

Do epistemic requirements vary along with facts about what promotes agents' well-being? Epistemic instrumentalists say "yes" and thereby earn a lot of contempt. This contempt is a mistake on two counts. First, it is incorrectly based: the reasons typically given for it are misguided. Second, it fails to distinguish between first- and second-order epistemic instrumentalism, and it happens that only the former is contemptible.

In this book, Nathaniel P. Sharadin argues for rejecting epistemic instrumentalism as a first-order view not because it suffers extensional failures but because it suffers explanatory ones. By contrast, he argues that epistemic instrumentalism offers a natural, straightforward explanation of why being epistemically correct matters. What emerges is a second-order instrumentalist explanation for epistemic authority that is neutral between competing first-order epistemic theories. This neutrality is an advantage. But, drawing on work from cognitive science and psychology, Sharadin argues that instrumentalists can abandon that neutrality in order to adopt a view he calls epistemic ecologism.

Epistemic Instrumentalism Explained will be of interest to researchers and advanced students working in epistemology, ethics, and philosophy of mind.

Nathaniel P. Sharadin is an assistant professor of philosophy at the University of Hong Kong. He is the author of numerous articles on epistemology and ethics.

Routledge Studies in Epistemology
Edited by Kevin McCain, *University of Alabama at Birmingham, USA* and Scott Stapleford, *St. Thomas University, Canada*

The Epistemology of Group Disagreement
Edited by Fernando Broncano-Berrocal and J. Adam Carter

The Philosophy of Group Polarization
Epistemology, Metaphysics, Psychology
Fernando Broncano-Berrocal and J. Adam Carter

The Social Epistemology of Legal Trials
Edited by Zachary Hoskins and Jon Robson

Intellectual Dependability
A Virtue Theory of the Epistemic and Educational Ideal
T. Ryan Byerly

Skeptical Invariantism Reconsidered
Edited by Christos Kyriacou and Kevin Wallbridge

Epistemic Autonomy
Edited by Jonathan Matheson and Kirk Lougheed

Epistemic Dilemmas
New Arguments, New Angles
Edited by Kevin McCain, Scott Stapleford and Matthias Steup

Proposition and Doxastic Justification
New Essays on Their Nature and Significance
Edited by Paul Silva Jr. and Luis R.G. Oliveira

Epistemic Instrumentalism Explained
Nathaniel Sharadin

For more information about this series, please visit: https://www.routledge.com/Routledge-Studies-in-Epistemology/book-series/RSIE

Epistemic Instrumentalism Explained

Nathaniel P. Sharadin

NEW YORK AND LONDON

First published 2023
by Routledge
605 Third Avenue, New York, NY 10158

and by Routledge
4 Park Square, Milton Park, Abingdon, Oxon, OX14 4RN

Routledge is an imprint of the Taylor & Francis Group, an informa business

© 2023 Nathaniel P. Sharadin

The right of Nathaniel P. Sharadin to be identified as author of this work has been asserted in accordance with sections 77 and 78 of the Copyright, Designs and Patents Act 1988.

All rights reserved. No part of this book may be reprinted or reproduced or utilised in any form or by any electronic, mechanical, or other means, now known or hereafter invented, including photocopying and recording, or in any information storage or retrieval system, without permission in writing from the publishers.

Trademark notice: Product or corporate names may be trademarks or registered trademarks, and are used only for identification and explanation without intent to infringe.

Library of Congress Cataloging-in-Publication Data
A catalog record for this title has been requested

ISBN: 978-0-367-55880-2 (hbk)
ISBN: 978-0-367-56183-3 (pbk)
ISBN: 978-1-003-09672-6 (ebk)

DOI: 10.4324/9781003096726

Typeset in Sabon
by SPi Technologies India Pvt Ltd (Straive)

Contents

Acknowledgements   *vi*

1 Introduction   1

2 Preliminaries   9

3 First-Order Epistemic Theory   32

4 Epistemic Correctness and the Minimal Functional Criterion   49

5 First-Order Epistemic Instrumentalism   69

6 The Functionalist Challenge   84

7 Second-Order Epistemic Theory   99

8 Second-Order Epistemic Instrumentalism   126

9 The Content Constraint   139

10 Bespoke Explanations   154

11 New View, Old Problems   176

12 Going Further   182

Index   198

Acknowledgements

I'm grateful to many people for their comments, feedback, and suggestions both on earlier drafts of written material and on the broader ideas that appear in this book. I'll forget some; but I'd especially like to thank Jamin Asay, Derek Baker, Adam Bradley, Lindsay Brainaird, Ethan Brauer, Simon Blackburn, Finnur Dellsén, Luke Elson, James Fanciullo, Daniel Fogal, Holly Haynes, Zoë A. Johnson King, John Lawless, Daniel Layman, Errol Lord, Ram Neta, Kate Nolfi, Geoff Sayre-McCord, Daniel Singer, Keshav Singh, James Stacey Taylor, and Daniel Wodak. I'm also grateful to members of the Cottage Group; participants in Daniel Singer's 2020 graduate seminar on epistemic consequentialism; and audiences at the University of Chicago, Virginia Tech, Syracuse University, Ohio State University, Cardiff University, and a 2021 symposium on epistemic normativity at the Central APA.

1 Introduction

1.1 Introduction

Here is some pablum. It is epistemically correct to believe some things and epistemically incorrect to believe others. For instance, it is epistemically correct to believe that the earth goes around the sun, that 2 and 2 is 4, and that electrons have a negative charge; it is epistemically incorrect to believe the negations of these claims.

These claims about epistemic correctness are not brute. They do not sit, unexplained, at the bottom of our epistemic theorizing. So we shall want to know what explains them: Why is it that it is epistemically correct to believe some things and it is not epistemically correct to believe other things? At least part of what first-order epistemic theory is in the business of doing is offering a satisfactory *explanation* for why it is that some things are epistemically correct to believe and others are not epistemically correct to believe.

There are many familiar first-order epistemic theories. Evidentialism is the view that says what explains epistemic correctness are facts about evidential support. Epistemic neo-Aristotelianism is the view that says what explains epistemic correctness are facts about intellectual excellence, or what it takes to exhibit certain competencies. Coherentism is the view that says what explains epistemic correctness are facts about coherence among agents' doxastic attitudes. And so on for other first-order epistemic theories. There are many such views, and the debates among them are relatively mature. The view I call *first-order epistemic instrumentalism* is the view that says that what explains epistemic correctness are facts about what would make agents better off – what would promote agential well-being. First-order epistemic instrumentalism is largely reviled.

Here is some more pablum. Whether something is epistemically correct or not *matters*. It is really quite important that agents do what is epistemically correct and not do what is epistemically incorrect. Epistemic correctness is, as I put it, *authoritative*. This claim is also not brute. And so, just as we shall want to know what explains why the things that are

DOI: 10.4324/9781003096726-1

epistemically correct are epistemically correct, we shall also want to know what explains why it is that epistemic correctness matters or is authoritative. At least part of what second-order epistemic theory is in the business of doing is offering a satisfactory *explanation* for why it is that epistemic correctness is authoritative.

There are many much less familiar second-order epistemic theories. *Sui generis* evidentialism is the view that says what explains epistemic authority are facts about the *sui generis* authoritative nature of evidence. Veritistic evidentialism is the view that says what explains epistemic authority are facts about promoting the fundamental epistemic values of truth. Constitutivist evidentialism is the view that says what explains epistemic authority are facts about *what it is* to be an epistemic agent or, perhaps, *what it is* to be a belief. And so on for other second-order epistemic theories. There are many such views, although the debates between them are relatively immature. The view I will call *second-order epistemic instrumentalism* is the view that says what explains epistemic authority are facts about what would make agents better off – what would promote agential well-being. Second-order epistemic instrumentalism, like its first-order counterpart, is largely reviled.

This is a book about both first- and second-order epistemic instrumentalism. I have three aims. First, I aim to show that we should, in fact, reject first-order epistemic instrumentalism – it is rightly reviled, however, importantly, not for the reasons typically given. Critics of first-order epistemic instrumentalism typically complain that first-order epistemic instrumentalism yields systematically incorrect predictions about the extension of epistemic correctness. First-order epistemic instrumentalists then offer more or less ameliorative replies, critics remain unconvinced, and all parties retreat to their corners. Stalemate. I aim to break the stalemate on behalf of the critics but not for the reasons they suggest. We should reject first-order epistemic instrumentalism. But this is not because of an extensional failure on the part of first-order epistemic instrumentalism. Instead, it is, much more importantly, because of an explanatory failure.

Second, I aim to show that, despite being widely reviled, second-order epistemic instrumentalism actually offers an appealing, natural, straightforward explanation for epistemic authority. Doing so will require saying something more – although not *much* more – specific about what, precisely, epistemic authority is supposed to be and what an adequate explanation of it looks like.

Finally, I aim to diagnose the relative unpopularity of second-order epistemic instrumentalism in a way that explains why it has been so long reviled. I argue that evaluating the quality of second-order explanations for epistemic authority requires antecedently accepting some first-order epistemic theory. As it happens, the most natural methodology that arises out of attempting to respect this constraint on our theorizing makes second-order epistemic instrumentalism look like an absolute non-starter. But, as I explain, this methodology is not obligatory; moreover, we have no reason to expect that the second-order explanations for epistemic authority it yields are any better than those, such as second-order epistemic instrumentalism, that it does not.

This book, then, is largely programmatic. I think that, in effect, second-order epistemic instrumentalism has been blamed for first-order epistemic instrumentalism's failures. In this way, it has gotten an unfair shake. I think we should shake it more fairly. I am happy to say that we should reject first-order epistemic instrumentalism. (However, again, I think that the traditional case against first-order epistemic instrumentalism is misguided.) But this does not mean we have any reason for being suspicious of second-order epistemic instrumentalism. Or so I think. And while an admittedly natural methodology one might employ does make second-order epistemic instrumentalism relatively hard to come by as a second-order epistemic theory, as it happens that too does not tell us anything at all about whether we should accept it. Given how appealing the view is as an explanation for epistemic authority, I think it deserves to be taken much more seriously than it has been taken.

In the remainder of this brief introduction, I outline the argument in more detail and say a bit more about how different readers can think about reading the book.

1.2 Overview of Argument

My first aim is to convince you to give up first-order epistemic instrumentalism. I do this by dealing with preliminaries (Chapters 1–4), laying out the view (Chapter 5), and then articulating the central problems for the view (Chapters 5–6). In more detail, here is how this goes.

In Chapter 2, I deal with preliminaries concerning epistemic – and other kinds of – correctness. My view is that there are maximally many (or, at least, many, many) different kinds of correctness and that different kinds of correctness are conventionally, rather than in some way naturally, determined. This will turn out to matter later on, since it turns out that first-order epistemic instrumentalism might well be a theory of one kind of correctness or another, but it is not plausibly a theory of *epistemic* correctness.

In Chapter 3, I explain how to think about what first-order theories of epistemic correctness are in the business of doing. Such theories are attempts at articulating the *explanatory grounds* of epistemic correctness: they do not just content themselves with saying *when* things are epistemically correct, but they also purport to tell us *why* those things are epistemically correct.

In Chapter 4, I consider how to mark out *epistemic* correctness from the maximally many other kinds of correctness there are (Chapter 2). As I explain, it is neither possible to carve the epistemic from the non-epistemic in terms of the *objects* that can be epistemically correct nor in terms of the *content* of epistemic correctness without begging the question against particular first-order epistemic theories. Instead, the way to do it is via what I call the *minimal functional criteria*: what marks off epistemic correctness as a distinctive kind of correctness is its functional role in our evaluative thought and talk, namely, flagging reliable informants.

With this framework in place, in Chapter 5, I lay out what first-order epistemic instrumentalism actually says about how to explain epistemic correctness. Here I also outline the traditional objection to first-order epistemic instrumentalism and explain why pressing that objection leads to theoretical stalemate between first-order epistemic instrumentalism and its critics.

In Chapter 6, I break the stalemate. I argue that we should reject first-order epistemic instrumentalism because, very roughly, accepting it would involve accepting an account of epistemic correctness that would disable epistemic correctness from doing what it is for, namely, flagging reliable informants. This is what I call the Functionalist Challenge for first-order epistemic instrumentalism.

My second aim is to convince you that *second*-order epistemic instrumentalism is in fact a natural, straightforward view. To do this, I first lay out the aims and objectives of second-order epistemic theorizing (Chapter 7) and then say a bit more about the details of second-order epistemic instrumentalism (Chapter 8). In more detail, here is how that goes.

In Chapter 7, I explain the intuitive difference between *authoritative* and *formal* correctness. I lay out what I dub the *minimal conception* of epistemic authority and identify two characteristics thereof, corresponding to which are two criteria of adequacy for any second-order explanation of epistemic authority.

In Chapter 8, I lay out second-order epistemic instrumentalism as an explanation for epistemic authority. I explain why it (easily) meets the two criteria of adequacy identified in Chapter 7 and illustrate why it is a natural, appealing view to accept. Importantly, my aims here are relatively modest. I do not take myself to be offering anything like a strong positive argument in favor of second-order epistemic instrumentalism. Instead, I aim simply to explain clearly what the relatively neglected view says about how to explain epistemic authority and exhibit several of its virtues.

My next aim is to diagnose the relative, and in my view lamentable, unpopularity of second-order epistemic instrumentalism. My idea is that we correctly view ourselves as under a particular constraint in our theorizing about second-order explanations for epistemic authority, and the natural methodology that arises out of an attempt to respect that constraint makes second-order epistemic instrumentalism look wildly unappealing – perhaps even simply unavailable. In more detail, here is how that goes.

In Chapter 9, I articulate and argue for what I call the Content Constraint. According to the Content Constraint, in order to evaluate a second-order epistemic theory – that is, an *explanation* for the authority of epistemic correctness, we must antecedently accept some *extension* for epistemic correctness. And that, in turn, requires accepting a complete first-order epistemic theory (since explanation precedes extension in first-order epistemic theorizing). I consider several ways of resisting the Content Constraint – including by appeal to an analogy with ethics – and argue that either they are unsuccessful on their merits or they are theoretically unmotivated.

In Chapter 10, I explain the natural, commonplace methodology that arises out of the need to respect the Content Constraint. As I explain, the most natural thing to do if you have to accept some first-order epistemic theory prior to evaluating your second-order epistemic theory is to *tailor* your second-order epistemic theory to *match* your first-order epistemic theory. And that, in fact, is what we see. Evidentialists about the explanation for epistemic *correctness* tailor their second-order explanation for the *authority* of epistemic correctness by passing through evidentialist materials to their second-order theory. Other first-order views do the same. Given this methodology, it is *no surprise at all* that second-order epistemic instrumentalism is (almost) never in the offing. After all, as I argued in Chapter 6, we have decisive reason to reject first-order epistemic instrumentalism, and so you will not ever get (something like) second-order epistemic instrumentalism via this tailoring process. But, as I argue, this tailoring methodology is not obligatory. And, moreover, there is no reason to think that the *bespoke explanations* we get as a result of it are better, *qua* second-order epistemic theories, than ones that arise out of some different process.

In Chapter 11, I consider whether second-order epistemic instrumentalism will face a variant on either the traditional problem with first-order epistemic instrumentalism or my new Functionalist Challenge for first-order epistemic instrumentalism. I argue that it will not: it is immune to both worries.

In the final chapter, Chapter 12, I consider whether second-order epistemic instrumentalists might want to make themselves less agreeable. The most promising way of doing this, I argue, is by becoming *epistemic ecologists*.

If I am successful in my aims, my hope is that second-order epistemic instrumentalism has some room to breathe. It is not to be confused with first-order epistemic instrumentalism (Chapters 2–5), which we should reject on its merits (Chapter 6). It represents a plausible view about an importantly different, although obviously related, subject matter (Chapters 7–8). And despite a very real constraint on our theorizing (Chapter 9) that has systematically failed to deliver it up as a contender view, that is no reason to be suspicious of second-order epistemic instrumentalism as an explanation for epistemic authority (Chapter 10). Moreover, the reasons we had for worrying about *first*-order epistemic instrumentalism do not reappear (Chapter 11). Finally (Chapter 12), we can think about second-order epistemic instrumentalism as adopting an *ecological* account of epistemic correctness; as we'll see, doing so has some advantages.

1.3 Avoiding Reading the Entire Book

I often want to know which parts of a book I can get away with not reading. So let me say a bit about potential ways you might get away with not reading different parts of the book, depending on what you are interested in.

One way you can do this is by reading only half the book.

The first half of the book (Chapters 2–6) comprises a new argument against first-order epistemic instrumentalism. If you are not interested in *second*-order epistemic theory or the idea of epistemic authority, you can safely *stop* after Chapter 6.

Correspondingly, the second half of the book (Chapters 7–12) lays out second-order epistemic instrumentalism and argues that it is unfairly neglected. If you are not interested in *first*-order epistemic theory or the idea of epistemic correctness *per se*, you can safely *begin* at Chapter 7.

A different way you can avoid reading the entire book is by skipping certain chapters. I think you can under certain conditions safely skip quite a few of the chapters.

Chapters 2 through 4 all involve ground clearing and terminological stipulation. The important upshots of those chapters can be easily and quickly summarized like so:

> Chapter 2: There are many different *kinds* of correctness, no kind of which is somehow more "natural" or "genuine" than another.
>
> Chapter 3: First-order epistemic theory aims to explain, rather than just account for the intuitive extension of, epistemic correctness. It does so by articulating principles specifying the explanatory grounds of epistemic correctness. We cannot know which things epistemic correctness applies to antecedently to deciding on a first-order epistemic theory.
>
> Chapter 4: The earmark of the kind of correctness that is epistemic correctness – as compared to a kind of correctness that is some kind of correctness other than epistemic correctness – is that our thought and talk in terms of epistemic correctness serves a particular function: it serves to flag reliable informants.

If you are willing to simply accept these claims and feel like you understand what they mean without further comment, you can skip to Chapter 5. You could read even less. Chapter 5 is a statement of a familiar, if again as I have mentioned largely reviled, view in first-order epistemic theory, namely, first-order epistemic instrumentalism, together with a statement of a familiar, if ultimately as I argue stalemate-inducing, objection to that view. The main claims can be summarized like so:

> Chapter 5: First-order epistemic instrumentalists claim that epistemic correctness is explained by the fact that being epistemically correct promotes agents' well-being. But critics argue that there are cases where being epistemically correct does not promote agential well-being. Instrumentalists deny this or shrug their theory's shoulders. Stalemate results.

You probably have to read Chapter 6; there is just no getting around it. But we are back to potential laziness with Chapter 7. Here is everything you need:

> Chapter 7: Epistemic correctness seems to *matter*: it is *authoritative*. At the very least, this means it has a *potential psychological impact*. Moreover, epistemic correctness is *usually* authoritative in this way. An adequate explanation of epistemic authority must account for these two facts.

Chapter 8 is not surprising given what comes before (especially in Chapter 5), but it is required reading. You can skip Chapters 9 and 10 if you do not care about why it is that second-order epistemic instrumentalism has been (unfairly, in my view) neglected. Here is a summary:

> Chapter 9: If you want to explain why it is that epistemic correctness is authoritative, you first have to say what the extension of epistemic correctness comprises. This is the Content Constraint. There is no avoiding the Content Constraint.
>
> Chapter 10: Given the Content Constraint, the natural way to generate a second-order epistemic theory is by taking one's first-order epistemic theory and tailoring a second-order epistemic theory to match. If you do this, then, given the failure of *first*-order epistemic instrumentalism, you will almost never end up with second-order epistemic instrumentalism. Happily, you do not *have* to do things in this way, and you do not necessarily end up with better second-order views if you do.

Chapters 11 and 12 show that *second*-order epistemic instrumentalism is not liable to variants on the problems facing first-order epistemic instrumentalism and that it might helpfully be understood as an ecological view of matters. They are not, strictly speaking, required reading:

> Chapter 11: There are no analogues of the problems facing first-order epistemic instrumentalism for second-order epistemic instrumentalism, and this is largely because of the subject matter of that view.

Chapter 12: There's a clear route from second-order epistemic instrumentalism to epistemic ecologism; whatever theoretical advantages ecologism has when it comes to the authority of deliberative correctness, it has them here, too.

In sum, then, if you are as lazy as I am allegedly but never decisively shown to be, you could potentially get away with reading just Chapter 6 (the novel argument against first-order epistemic instrumentalism) and Chapter 8 (the bit where I articulate and then extol the virtues of second-order epistemic instrumentalism). Doing that would leave you with a good sense of why I think we should reject first-order epistemic instrumentalism and why I think we should accept second-order epistemic instrumentalism. Of course, I think you would be missing a lot if that was all that you did. That is why I wrote the other chapters.

2 Preliminaries

2.1 Introduction

To begin, here is a familiar way to think about our thinking.

On one hand, we can describe the way the world is. Doing that involves, among other things, issuing descriptive judgments about how things actually are in the world. Those judgments employ descriptive concepts. There are a *lot* of descriptive concepts. For example, there are the descriptive concepts CHAIR, POLITICIAN, WATER, H_2O.[1] We can probably modify some of our descriptive concepts to make them in some ways better (Cappelen 2020). We can try to analyze them (Jackson 1998). Or maybe we cannot, or should not, or simply do not regularly, or do not with much success (Schroeter 2004; Papineau 2009; Johnston and Leslie 2012; Deutsch 2020). It might be that the meaning of our descriptive concepts is in some part and manner determined by the world rather than exclusively by ourselves (Putnam 1975; Kripke 1980). Or it might not (Millikan 1984; Papineau 1993; Horowitz 2001). These are fraught issues. And there are plenty more where those came from.

On the other hand, here is something else we can do: we can evaluate how the world is. Doing that involves, among other things, issuing evaluative judgments about how well things are going in the world. Those judgments employ evaluative concepts.[2] There are a *lot* of evaluative concepts. For example, there are the evaluative concepts VICIOUS, HONEST, GOOD, BAD, DISGUSTING. Whatever you think about the huge range of fraught issues that come up for descriptive concepts, there is an intimidatingly huger range of issues that arise in the case of evaluative concepts. I will not even begin to iterate them.

Instead, I direct your attention to a particular evaluative concept that will be my exclusive focus in this book, namely, the generic evaluative concept CORRECT. In fact, as it will emerge, I'm primarily interested in a somewhat more restricted concept, namely, EPISTEMICALLY CORRECT. But it will take a bit to get to that. Right now, I need to say a few things about the assumptions I will be making about the concept CORRECT and related issues in order to set up the issues I *am* interested in.

DOI: 10.4324/9781003096726-2

2.2 Assumptions

Most of these assumptions are uncontroversial, amounting to terminological choices. Some of them are controversial, but they represent simplifying assumptions: my argument does not depend on their being true. One assumption is very controversial, and it will matter very much later on. I devote the bulk of this chapter to defending it. Before that, the terminological choices and simplifying assumptions.

First, I assume that if the concept CORRECT correctly applies to some object of evaluation O, then O has the property of *being correct*.[3] This assumption is a terminological choice. Everything I say is compatible with any view whatsoever about the nature of the relevant properties, ranging from the extremely metaphysically robust (Enoch 2011) to the extremely deflationary (Hofweber 2016). This way of speaking simply enables me to use predicates such as *is correct* or refer to something's *being correct* or talk about *correctness* rather than always everywhere the much more cumbersome: falls under the concept CORRECT or is correctly judged to meet the conditions under which something is conceived of in terms of the concept CORRECT and so on.

Second, despite what I have just said, I assume there is no such thing as the property of *correctness per se* – there is nothing it is to be correct, full stop. Instead, there are many kinds of correctness and, correspondingly, many concepts. For instance, there is the concept MORALLY CORRECT, the concept EPISTEMICALLY CORRECT, the concept PRUDENTIALLY CORRECT, and so on, as I argue later, *ad infinitum*. This is the view I call *maximal pluralism* about kinds of correctness. As I said, I will have a lot more to say about this in not too long. But it is easy to get the intuition that there are at least *some* kinds of correctness up and running by considering cases where kinds of correctness appear to conflict. For example, and quite familiarly, it might be prudentially correct for you to cheat on your taxes but morally incorrect to do so. Less familiarly, and much more controversially, it might be morally correct to believe that your friend did not commit the murder but epistemically correct to believe she did (Stroud 2006; Preston-Roedder 2013).

But I will not rely on your intuitions to defend the thought that there are many (in my view, maximally many) kinds of correctness and no single unified concept CORRECT. Instead, I defend this idea in detail later on in this chapter. Here, I simply assert, without further argument, that correctness is always associated with a kind. There is no such thing as the concept CORRECT, there are only many different concepts of k-LY CORRECT, for some kind k. And so, correspondingly, there is no such thing as the property of *being correct*, there is only such a thing as the property of *being k-ly correct*. As I say, more on this later. But let me head off an immediate concern with this way of speaking.

Committing to the view that there are many, perhaps maximally many, kinds of correctness does not mean committing to a view according to which all kinds of correctness are in all ways on a par. In particular, it definitely does not mean committing to a view that sometimes gets called "normative pluralism" (Tiffany 2007; Sagdahl 2014; Clarke-Doane 2017; Eklund 2020). As it is usually understood, normative pluralism is a view that combines the idea that there are many (perhaps maximally many) kinds of correctness with the view that there are no (important) differences between such kinds – that all kinds of correctness are, for all intents and purposes, on a par. In particular, the thought that they are on a par is usually expressed as the thought that all these kinds of correctness are all "normative." It is predictably fraught what their all being normative is supposed to amount to. But whatever the case, this view has a lot to be said against it (Case 2016). There are delicate issues here, and we will come to some of them later on in this chapter. But I want to avoid talk of what's normative, and I want to make it clear what I'm assuming. So, very briefly, the thing to keep in mind right now is that you can think that there are many kinds of correctness without also thinking that all kinds of correctness are, as I will put it for the time being, *equally important*.

Third, I shall say that something is *k*-ly correct when it conforms to a *k* standard of correctness. A standard of correctness is simply a description of what a thing must be like in order to be correct. I treat standards of correctness as sets of properties; for example,

$$SK : \{p_1, p_2, p_3\}$$

SK is the standard of *k* correctness, and $p_{1...3}$ are the properties that comprise *k* correctness. *K* correctness is a matter of conforming to SK.

Fourth, and relatedly, I assume that correctness can come in degrees. This will happen when it is possible for an object to exhibit more or fewer of the properties that comprise the relevant standard of correctness, or to exhibit (more or fewer of) those properties to a greater or lesser degree. When that happens, we can say generically that an object of *k* evaluation is partly *k*-ly correct or that it is more or less *k*-ly correct than some other object of *k* evaluation. Or, more specifically, we can say that the object is *k*-ly correct in some particular respect (e.g., by being p_1 but not being p_2).

These two assumptions are harmless. They amount to terminological regimentation. Let me emphasize this point. Rather than introducing the language of standards of correctness, objects of evaluation, and so on, I might have talked about *reasons* or *norms* or *fittingness* or … something else. There are ongoing fights between proponents of these different ways of speaking about which if any of these notions is primary, fundamental, or should come "first."[4] But this is not a book about the maximally perspicuous way to frame our evaluative thought and talk or an attempt to try to say what does or should sit unexplained at the bottom of our evaluative theorizing. Maybe that is unfair. What those engaged in such fights would presumably say is that they are attempting to limn the normative bedrock; to be honest, that came out sounding unfair too.[5] Here's a less contentious, more constructive way to put things.

I want to investigate whether a relatively unpopular view – epistemic instrumentalism – has anything to be said in its favor. What I'm going to argue is that epistemic instrumentalism has been misconstrued as a *first-order* epistemic theory and should instead be understood as a *second-*order epistemic theory. This requires me to say something about what both first- and second-order epistemic theories are in the business of doing: I need a way to think and speak about what they are getting up to. Take first-order epistemic theory. One way would be to say that first-order epistemic theory is an attempt to articulate *epistemic norms* or *epistemic obligations*. Another would be to say that first-order epistemic theory is an attempt to specify *epistemic reasons*. A third would be to say that first-order epistemic theory attempts to identify *epistemically fitting* responses. And another – the one I have selected – would be to say that first-order epistemic theory attempts (as we will see, among other things) to articulate the conditions under which things are *epistemically correct*.

Now, there are probably interesting relations between these different ideas. If something is epistemically correct, then it might be epistemically fitting to respond to it in a certain way (McHugh and Way 2016). Reasons might be related to correctness by serving as *evidence* of correctness (Sharadin 2016; Whiting 2018). Fair enough. The point here is that I'm just not interested in the details of these possibilities. And whether or which of them are correct does not bear on what I am interested in. Moving on.

2.3 Kinds of Correctness

2.3.1 Maximal Pluralism about Kinds of Correctness

I have said that I think there are maximally many kinds of correctness. Here, I defend that idea.

Maximal pluralism about kinds of correctness is the view that there are no restrictions on what can count as a genuine kind of correctness. Remember, a kind of correctness is determined by a standard of correctness, which, in turn, comprises some properties. The thought that there are *maximally many* kinds of correctness therefore follows from the thought that *standards* of correctness are themselves extraordinarily cheap – in effect, *free*. Why think *this* is true?

My answer is that the alternative is both mysterious and theoretically unmotivated. It is both unclear what it would mean to think that there are some restrictions on what can count as a standard of correctness, and it is unclear why you be inclined to think such a thing. Let me explain.

We can begin by stating the question to which maximal pluralism is the answer more carefully. It is manifest that we *can* think and speak in terms of maximal kinds of correctness. There are two ways to see this, one abstract and one a bit more concrete. Abstract first: we can, if we want, generate maximally many kinds of standards of correctness. Recall, a standard of correctness is simply a set of properties. So insofar as there are no meaningful restrictions on such sets, there are no meaningful restrictions on the number of different standards of correctness. Since a kind of correctness is simply determined by a standard of correctness, there are no meaningful restrictions on the number of kinds of correctness. Now concrete: it is assassinly correct to sneak up on your victims. It is not morally correct to have victims. It is Trumpily correct to ignore your critics and incite violence. It is 8chanly correct to believe the Storm is coming. It is not epistemically correct to believe any such thing. And so on.

The question, then, is, How many of these kinds of correctness in terms of which we manifestly can think and speak are genuinely ways of thinking and speaking in terms of a kind of correctness? The question is *not* whether some of these ways of speaking in terms of kinds of correctness matter more or less than others or whether we should (or do) care about some and not about others or whether we should go in for some ways of thinking and speaking but not others.

The question is about the meaningfulness of thinking and speaking in these ways *qua* a way of thinking and speaking about (a kind of) correctness. We want to know whether it is possible to have meaningful thought and talk about these kinds of correctness – independently of the question of whether we should go in for such thought and talk. Maximal pluralism about kinds of correctness says: all of these kinds of correctness are on a par with respect to being kinds of correctness. All such ways of thinking and speaking in terms of correctness are genuinely ways of thinking and speaking of things as being (a kind of) correct.

The alternative says that *not* all of these kinds of correctness are on a par with respect to being kinds of correctness. Not all such ways of thinking and speaking in terms of correctness are genuinely ways of thinking and speaking of things as being (a kind of) correct.

There are actually *two* alternatives here: monism and restricted pluralism. According to monists, there is just one kind of correctness that is a genuine kind of correctness. According to restricted pluralism, there are many kinds of correctness that are genuine kinds of correctness, but there are not *maximally* many kinds of correctness that are genuine kinds of correctness.

I said, earlier, that I thought these alternatives were both mysterious and unmotivated. I will now explain why I think that. I take them in reverse order, starting with restricted pluralism.

2.3.2 Restricted Pluralism about Kinds of Correctness

If you are a restricted pluralist about kinds of correctness, then what you think is that there are potentially many kinds of correctness but that there are not maximally many kinds of correctness. As far as I can tell, there is only one thing that could motivate the idea that, given that there is more than one kind of correctness, there are restrictions on how many kinds there are. That idea is that something about the shape of evaluative reality sets a limit to the potential variety of kinds of correctness. In other words, evaluative reality puts limits on what kinds of correctness there can be. But it is utterly mysterious what such limits could be, what they would look like, and what could motivate us to accept the thought that they exist.

What we have, here, is a familiar kind of divide over how to think about the existence of lines in our conceptual apparatus. There are, as there always are in such cases, two possibilities. One is that the lines are entirely down to us – we draw them. The other is that the lines are a reflection of something already there – at most, we trace them. Call the first possibility *conventionalism* about kinds of correctness. Call the second possibility *anti-conventionalism* about kinds of correctness. Maximal pluralism about kinds of correctness follows from conventionalism. The restricted pluralist is therefore an anti-conventionalist about kinds of correctness. But anti-conventionalism is both unmotivated and mysterious. Hence, restricted pluralism is both unmotivated and mysterious. It is easiest to see why this is so when we have its competitor, conventionalism about kinds of correctness, in front of us. So let's start there.

According to conventionalism about kinds of correctness, kinds of correctness – such as ethical, epistemic, Trumpy, assassinly, aesthetic, etiquettical, and so on – should be understood in much the same way we all agree *musical genres* should be understood.

There really are musical genres: there is classical, there is indie pop, there is top 50, there is country-western, there is folk, and so on. But important, the existence of these musical genres is entirely down to us. Or rather, the existence of these musical genres *qua genres* is down to us.[6] They exist as categories because they are for us useful ways of carving up the musical space we occupy. This is not to say there are no facts about that musical space. This is to say that such facts about musical space do not in any way serve to restrict our ability to carve it up in one way or another. And hence there are no principled restrictions on what can count as a musical genre. What musical genres there are in our ordinary musical thought and talk is determined entirely by a series of probably mostly implicit agreements to treat some categories as important and others as unimportant in our musical thought and talk. You will notice, cultural fragmentation notwithstanding, that there is no genre on Spotify corresponding to music-Nate-listens-to-when-sad-or-writing-but-not-both (although there might be such a playlist). This is because we have all by unspoken agreement come – by whatever mechanism – to think that we are not interested in this genre when we are thinking and speaking about music. Fair enough. That does not mean that such a genre is any less a *genre*; it simply means it does not matter to us.

But interests, and so our interest in particular genres, can change along with changes to our environments. I may become through an unlikely series of posts on the Gram a major influence on conventional musical taste and thereby cause my sad-or-writing musical category to take center stage. If I do this, and I will definitely not do this, then Nate's-sad-or-writing-but-not-both music may become a genre of music that matters to us.

Conventionalism about kinds of music – about musical genres – is clearly correct. I am not sure anyone disagrees.[7] Insofar as anyone *does* disagree and does go around saying things that suggest they think some kinds of music are more real *qua kinds* than others, the correct response is to accuse them of thinly veiled parochialism or at the limit of out and out partisanship. Anyway, do not let them near the stereo.

So, too, according to conventionalism about kinds of correctness. There really are kinds of correctness: there is epistemic correctness, ethical correctness, legal correctness, and the like. But importantly, the existence of these kinds of correctness is down to us. They are for us useful ways of carving up the evaluative space we occupy. This is not to say there are no facts about that evaluative space. This is to say that such facts about evaluative space do not in any way serve to restrict our ability to carve it up in one way or another. And hence, there are no principled restrictions on what can count as a kind of correctness. What kinds of correctness there are in our ordinary thought and talk is determined entirely by a series of probably mostly implicit agreements to treat some categories as important and others as unimportant in our evaluative thought and talk.

Unlike conventionalism about kinds of music, conventionalism about kinds of correctness is not entirely uncontroversial. But as I will now explain, it probably should be. The opposing view does not make much sense, and it is not well motivated. Maybe you already accept conventionalism about kinds of correctness. That is great; I think it is the natural and straightforward view to have. Maximal pluralism about kinds of correctness follows directly from conventionalism about kinds of correctness. This is because, according to conventionalism about kinds of correctness, there is nothing to being a "genuine" kind of correctness above and beyond our thinking and speaking in terms of that kind of correctness. Given that we manifestly can think and speak in terms of maximal kinds of correctness, there *really are* maximally many kinds of correctness.

Restricted pluralists – those who think there are some restrictions on what kinds of correctness there "really" are – must therefore reject conventionalism about kinds of correctness: they must be anti-conventionalists. Beyond the fact that conventionalism about kinds of correctness has much to recommend it to intuition (as I have tried to illustrate earlier), there are, as I've said, two broad reasons we should not accept anti-conventionalism about kinds of correctness (and hence also reject restricted pluralism): it is entirely unmotivated, and it is completely mysterious. I take these in turn.

According to anti-conventionalism about kinds of correctness, the lines around kinds of correctness are determined by evaluative reality: evaluative reality, as it were, has *joints*. Of course, this is a metaphor. And it will need to be unpacked. I say more about the prospects for doing this later; to anticipate, they are dim. But set that to one side for a moment. Assume it can be unpacked. The conventionalist and the anti-conventionalist will presumably agree on the existence of *some* range of kinds of correctness. For instance, both will probably think there is a kind of correctness that is ethical correctness. Both will likely think there is a kind of correctness that is epistemic correctness. The conventionalist will then be happy to continue without end: there is assassin correctness, there is Trumpy correctness, and so on. The anti-conventionalist will presumably balk at these – if they do not balk here, then where?

Anyway, let them pick their spot, and then ask: Why balk? It cannot be because there is supposed to be something special about (say) ethical correctness as compared to Trumpy correctness. The conventionalist can happily agree. (There is something "special" about 1960s' rock music as compared to Nate's-sad-writing music.)

Let me emphasize this point. The conventionalist is in no way committed to the thought that all kinds of correctness are on a par in all respects. Their view is that all kinds of correctness are on a par with respect to being genuinely kinds of correctness. Kinds of correctness might then go on to vary in terms of their importance in various ways, in terms of their relationship to one another, and in other ways. This might not sound like the conventionalist is in the end saying all that much. I very much agree; that is why it is so baffling why the *anti*-conventionalist should be made so uncomfortable by their having said it.

Worse and worse, the anti-conventionalist must themselves agree that we are capable of the thing the conventionalist says we actually do in order to give shape to kinds of correctness, namely, drawing lines around different bits of evaluative reality and then going on to baptize and use these bits of evaluative thought and talk in a variety of ways. The anti-conventionalist cannot possibly deny this fact, since it is something we manifestly can do. I will show you how to do it right now. First, think of any two unrelated properties that an action might exhibit. Say, *being done on a Tuesday* and *being done with one's right hand*. Now, baptize a new kind of correctness like so:

Right-Hand-Tuesdayical-Correctness: φ-ing is right-hand-tuesdayically correct iff φ-ing is done on a Tuesday and done with one's right hand.

Now, go about using your new kind of correctness. Everything Tom Seaver did for the Mets for ten long seasons during Tuesday evening games was right-hand-tuesdayically correct. It was not right-hand-tuesdayically correct to wave at Jana last Wednesday and so on. Again, the anti-conventionalist cannot possibly mean to be suggesting that we *cannot* do this: we *just did it*.

What the anti-conventionalist must be meaning to deny is that in doing what we manifestly can do we are – and there are various ways to put this, but I do not know how to put it entirely non-tendentiously – *capturing differences in evaluative reality that are there independently of us*, or *limning the edges of evaluative reality*, or *carving evaluative reality at its joints*. But to borrow a question, What else is added by saying, as the anti-conventionalist insists on saying, that those differences are there independently of us and that some kinds of correctness *carve evaluative reality at its joints*? I simply cannot see the motivation.

Perhaps you think that *failing* to say that the kind of correctness corresponding to *epistemic* correctness represents a joint in evaluative reality whereas the kind of correctness corresponding to *8chan* correctness does not represent a joint in evaluative reality fails to take epistemic correctness sufficiently seriously. On this way of thinking, the motivation for the anti-conventionalist approach to kinds of correctness is to take seriously the importance of certain kinds of correctness. But although I agree that we should take seriously the importance of certain kinds of correctness, I cannot see how this motivates treating certain kinds of correctness as more real *qua kinds of correctness* than other kinds of correctness.

For one thing, as we saw earlier, there are plenty of ways other than in terms of a distinction in the nature of the kind in which we can and do reflect the fact that we take a particular kind of correctness seriously, for instance by giving or withholding from it pride of place in our evaluative thought and talk. This is the case of misfit musical genres such as Nate's-sad-writing music. It is presumably also the case of misfit kinds of correctness, such as right-hand-tuesdayical correctness.

For another, it is unclear why the claim that (say) the epistemic kind of correctness *carves evaluative reality at its joints* is something that would itself explain why we should take the kind thereby carved (more) seriously. Even if it is true that one or another kind of correctness tracks some edge there already independently of us in evaluative reality, there is no reason to think this entails that it should matter all that much to us – that we should take it seriously. Again, as we have already seen, there are plenty of uncontroversially non-jointy distinctions that we all regularly care a lot about – think of the distinction between democratic and nondemocratic societies, or between Euclidean and hyperbolic geometry. And moreover, there are also plenty of at least arguably jointy distinctions that usually do not matter much to most of us most of the time – think of the difference between up and down quarks. Our reasons for taking epistemic correctness seriously and for not taking 8chan correctness seriously have nothing to do with the thought that the kind *epistemic* but not the kind *8chan* is a *natural, jointy* place at which to carve evaluative reality. So, the anti-conventionalist approach is, as far as I can tell, simply unmotivated.

18 Preliminaries

Worse, the anti-conventionalist approach is mysterious. Go back to the guiding anti-conventionalist metaphor: evaluative reality has *joints*. The idea is apparently borrowed from the analogous debate over *natural kinds* in philosophical theorizing about science. In that debate, at least, it is clear what an anti-conventionalist view might look like and, crucially, what evidence one might potentially acquire for that view. One can at least imagine discovering through empirical research that there was something that counted as non-metaphorically constituting "joints" in the fundamental "bones" of reality. Setting aside issues in the special sciences, this might be because one can imagine coming to believe that the best physical theory contains clear, nonoverlapping, empirically verifiable distinctions between kinds of fundamental forces and actually empirically verifying those kinds of forces' existence and nonoverlap.

By contrast, I do not know how to begin to imagine what it would be to acquire analogous evidence for the corresponding idea about kinds of correctness. Such evidence would presumably be acquired from the armchair – this is not the kind of thing concerning which we can run any kind of empirical tests. What could such evidence be except for certain philosophers' amazingly exquisite intuitions? How would we go about acquiring it (beyond polling philosophers)? Anti-conventionalism about evaluative kinds is mysterious. Hence, we should reject restricted pluralism about kinds of correctness, which relied on it. Hence, if we are to be pluralists about kinds of correctness, we should be *maximal* pluralists about kinds of correctness.

2.3.3 Monism about Kinds of Correctness

That argument still leaves open the possibility that we should be *monists* about kinds of correctness: we should think there is just *one* kind of correctness. What's wrong with monism?

One thing that is wrong with monism is that it is clearly false. Here is a Moorean-inspired argument against it:

1. Here is an example of one kind of correctness: Believing in accord with your evidence is *epistemically* correct.
2. And here is an example of a second kind of correctness: Treating persons with respect is *morally* correct.
3. So: monism about kinds of correctness is false.

I myself am perfectly happy with this argument. But this argument is not going to convince a monist. In this section, I aim to address two related questions: First, why might you be a monist? What could motivate the idea that there is just one kind of correctness in the face of what appear to be straightforward arguments, such as the one I just offered, that there is more than one kind of correctness? The second question is this: Assuming monism is true, what kind of correctness is there?

As we will see, these questions are related in interesting ways; most important, the answer to the motivational question shapes the monist's answer to the content question – to the question about what kind of correctness there is. I argue that we should be suspicious of this second answer: I do not think there is the kind of correctness the monist must think exists. My enjoined suspicion might itself appear suspicious: after all, previously I argued that we should be *unrestricted* pluralists about kinds of correctness, yet here I am going to be urging suspicion about a particular kind of correctness. I will attempt to explain myself.

First, why might you be a monist about kinds of correctness? The motivation for the view, I think, is buried in an assumption about correctness, namely, that correctness is always everywhere *authoritative*. We have not said, yet, what the idea of authoritativeness is meant to be. That is something we will come to in much more detail a couple chapters from now. Right now, we can work with an intuitive grip on the notion given by the kinds of illustrative examples that are all too familiar, and that we have already seen a sprinkling of throughout the discussion so far.

Forget for the moment about how many kinds of correctness there are; assume there are a lot of them. Recall our observation, from earlier, that some of these kinds of correctness seem to matter a lot more than others. There are various ways to put this. We can say that some of these kinds of correctness intuitively *really matter*: they are *legitimate* or *forceful* or *normative* or *oomphy* (Finlay 2006; Tiffany 2007; Wedgwood 2007; Southwood 2008; Parfit 2011; Baker 2017; Lord 2018; Bedke 2019). They have a *grip* on agents (Horgan and Timmons 2018). There are *a lot* of different ways to put the italicized notion. Many more than I have just mentioned. The most intuitive way to illustrate what this notion is meant to be is by adverting to a kind of correctness that *is* intuitively oomphy or legitimate or authoritative, at least *some* of the time, and then contrasting it with a kind of correctness that is almost certainly *not* oomphy, legitimate, or authoritative, at least *most* of the time. Here is an illustrative such pairing: moral correctness and table-tennis correctness.

If some action is *morally* correct, this *really matters*: moral correctness is supposed to have a *grip* on agents (Korsgaard 1996; Parfit 2011). If you fail to do what is morally correct, you are *ipso facto* criticizable (Strawson 1962). We do and should enforce conformity to standards of moral correctness coercively. And so on. We can say that moral correctness is *authoritative*. Not so with table-tennis correctness. If some action is table-tennisly correct, this does not (usually) matter: table-tennis correctness does not have a grip on agents. If you fail to do what is table-tennisly correct, it does not follow that you are thereby criticizable. We do not and should not enforce conformity to standards of table-tennis correctness coercively and so on. We can say that table-tennis correctness is *not* authoritative.

This does not mean that table-tennis correctness cannot *inherit* oomphiness or authority from some other authoritative set of standards. Perhaps it can. The point is that it is not authoritative *per se* – that there is some at least intuitive difference between the "grip" that moral standards enjoy on agents and the "grip" (if there is one) that table-tennis standards enjoy. Again, this is just to gesture at the intuitive idea of authoritativeness. Later on, I will have more to say about what authoritativeness – especially *epistemic authoritativeness* – is supposed to be, and how we should think about it. Right now, we just need the intuitive idea of the difference to be getting on with, and I assume it is a familiar one.

Returning to monism about kinds of correctness: monism about kinds of correctness is driven by the assumption that correctness is *always* authoritative together with the claim that there is just one kind of correctness is always authoritative in this sense. In other words:

For any K such that K is a purported kind of correctness:

1. (Correctness–Authoritativeness Connection) If φ-ing is k-ly correct, then φ-ing is authoritatively k-ly correct.
2. (Authoritativeness–Monism Connection) There is only one k such that if φ-ing is k-ly correct, then φ-ing is authoritatively k-ly correct.
3. (Monism) There is only one k such that k is a kind of correctness.

Correctness–Authoritativeness Connection is the assumption about correctness that I said motivated the monist view; it, in effect, rules out the possibility, mentioned before, that there could be a kind of correctness that failed to be authoritative on some occasion or other. Table-tennis correctness, in other words, is not a "genuine" kind of correctness precisely *because* it is not (always) authoritative. Authoritativeness–Monism Connection says that there is just one kind of correctness that meets the constraint introduced by Correctness-Authoritativeness Connection. Monism follows.

The question, then, is whether we should accept Correctness–Authoritativeness Connection and, if so, whether we should go on to accept Authoritativeness–Monism Connection. Assume for the moment that Correctness–Authoritativeness Connection is correct. I will return to it below. Should we accept Authoritativeness–Monism Connection?

2.3.4 *Authoritativeness–Monism Connection and All-Things-Considered Correctness*

Here, I take it, is the best argument in favor of Authoritativeness–Monism Connection. Notice that we regularly encounter conflicts between kinds of correctness. Moreover, sometimes at least, it is entirely clear that there is a correct way to resolve these conflicts. For instance, it is 8chanly correct to believe Nancy is a cannibal. It is epistemically incorrect to believe this. And, it is extraordinarily tempting to add, what it is *really* correct to do in this situation is not believe that Nancy is a cannibal. This last (really) correct is sometimes called *all-things-considered correctness*. All-things-considered correctness, the thought continues, is the only kind of correctness that is *always* authoritative. This, in effect, is what the functional definition of all-things-considered correctness is supposed to be: it is the kind of correctness that takes all the things, considers them, and then spits out an *authoritative* verdict about what it would be (all-things-considered) correct to do.

Put otherwise, all-things-considered correctness is always authoritative as a result of its being the kind of correctness that considers all of the things. It is the kind of correctness that we have precisely because we need a kind of correctness that can do this job for us. And it is a job we apparently definitely need done. Considering the fact that it would be 8chanly correct to believe, and considering the fact that it would be epistemically incorrect to so believe, it turns out that, as a matter of fact, what it is authoritatively all-things-considered correct to do is not to believe. And, the thought goes, we can run this kind of story *every single time* we encounter conflict between different purportedly authoritative kinds of correctness.

That, anyway, is how proponents of the idea usually characterize the notion. For instance, here is a representative passage from a recent discussion by Barry Maguire and Jack Woods:

> The "just plain ought" is itself identifiable by its functional role. It is the second "ought" employed in questions of the form "according to this activity I ought to x, but ought I to x?" ... Sometimes this ought is modified with "all things considered," as in, "I know I morally ought to x, but ought I to x all things considered?" or as in, "I know that I ought, as a ticket inspector, to give this impoverished person a ticket, but is it really the case that I ought to do so?" and "... ought I to do so all things considered?"
>
> (Maguire and Woods 2020, p. 226)

They put the idea in terms of the all-things-considered "ought" rather than in terms of all-things-considered correctness, but the idea is the same.

The thought, then, would be that insofar as we have the intuition that other "kinds" of correctness are *also* authoritative, this is because they are authoritative only in a degenerate sense, or via a kind of confusing synecdoche. We can talk about what it would be authoritatively epistemically correct to do because sometimes what it is all-things-considered correct to do is identical to what it is epistemically correct for you to do. But this does not mean that there is anything that is actually authoritatively epistemically correct for you to do. What it is all-things-considered correct for you to do is what it is authoritatively correct for you to do, and it just so happens in this case that this is the same as what it is epistemically correct for you to do. As we have seen, it can certainly *appear* as if there is something it would be authoritatively epistemically correct for you to do. Presumably, the explanation for this appearance is that in certain cases what it would be epistemically correct to do somehow *contributes* to what it would be all-things-considered correct to do; it is one of the *things* that is *considered*. And so we sometimes say (or think) that it would be authoritatively epistemically correct to do something, but when we do that, we are simply taking the mental shortcut of letting the most salient component ingredient (the epistemic considerations) stand for the whole (what, all things considered, is correct). Anyway, so the story goes.

Let me pause for a moment and remind you why all this matters. This is a book about epistemic correctness. I am interested in epistemic correctness in two different ways. First, I am interested in how to think about first-order accounts of epistemic correctness: What should we think those theories are getting up to, when they get up to giving first-order theories of epistemic correctness? And, relatedly, does epistemic instrumentalism represent a good first-order epistemic theory that we should accept? (Spoiler: it does not, and we should not.)

Second, I am interested in how to think about second-order accounts of the *authority* of epistemic correctness: What should we think *those* theories are getting up to, when they get up to giving second-order theories of the authoritativeness of epistemic correctness? And, relatedly, does epistemic instrumentalism represent a good second-order epistemic theory that we should accept? (Spoiler: it does, and we should.)

But *neither* of those sets of questions makes much sense if you think there is just *one* kind of correctness that is authoritative and that it is not epistemic correctness but is instead all-things-considered correctness.

If it is true that there is just one kind of correctness that is authoritative, this would make investigating explanations of the authority of epistemic correctness *per se* a bit like investigating the finances of Disney by opening an investigation into ESPN's books; it will get you somewhere – it is certainly a contributing factor and sometimes might even determine whether Disney comes up profitable for the quarter. But it is also potentially *very* misleading, so it is probably not where we should be focused.

But I *do* want to focus on epistemic correctness and on epistemic authority *per se*. So I need to say why I do not think the *purported* authority of epistemic correctness can simply be bundled under the *actual* authority of "all-things-considered" correctness. I do not think we can do this because I am skeptical about the very existence of all-things-considered correctness.

This might seem odd. After all, I just got done defending maximal pluralism about kinds of correctness. It is there in the name: *maximal*. So it might seem odd for me to be skeptical about the existence of any particular kind of correctness, namely, all-things-considered correctness. But in fact, it is precisely *because* I am happy to let kinds of correctness proliferate that I think we have reason to be suspicious of the existence of all-things-considered correctness. Let me explain.

Corresponding to each kind of correctness is a domain of first-order theorizing that purports to tell us the substantive content of that kind of correctness – it is the bit of theory that gives an account of the relevant standards of correctness. So we have first-order ethics, first-order epistemic theory, first-order aesthetic theory, and, with enough grant writing, we can probably get some first-order 8chan theory up and running. But given what all-things-considered correctness is supposed to be – correctness that considers all of the things, what is it that first-order all-things-considered theory is supposed to be?

My understanding, from proponents of the idea, is that it is meant to be the first-order theory that tells us *how to consider* all of the kinds of correctness – epistemic correctness, ethical correctness, aesthetic correctness, 8chan correctness, and so on – and then somehow agglomerate them into a single (all-things-considered and, as it happens, authoritative) correctness (Maguire and Woods 2020). My skepticism about the existence of all-things-considered correctness is driven by skepticism about the possibility of always being able to accomplish this last feat in a coherent way: I do not think we have a grip on what it means to say that we ought to agglomerate all the kinds of correctness into a single, univocal authoritative verdict. What this means is that first-order all-things-considered theory is not possible, so I do not think there are any corresponding facts about all-things-considered correctness that are the deliverances of such theory.

As we will see in a moment, it will not be fatal for my argument if authoritative all-things-considered correctness turns out to exist. Remember, monism depends not just on the claim that there is such a thing as authoritative all-things-considered correctness, which is what we are here arguing over. It also depends on the claim that being a genuine kind of correctness requires always being authoritative. I will explain why we should reject that idea later.

But let me briefly try and further motivate my skepticism. All-things-considered first-order theory is *wildly different* from any other kind of first-order theory. Compare first-order ethical theory. We are certainly going to have first-order ethical disputes: we will disagree over what explains why it would be ethically correct for people to φ and so over what, ethically speaking, it would be correct for them to do. But it is at least reasonably clear how to set the bounds around those disputes and how to go about resolving them. If I tell you that what explains why it would be ethically correct for Molly to donate to charity is the fact that chal is a beverage made from camel's milk, you will know I have changed the subject *entirely*. It is not that I am doing *bad* first-order ethical theory. Whatever I am doing, I am simply not doing first-order ethical theory anymore. The same is true in other ordinary first-order domains. You might (incorrectly) think that it would be aesthetically incorrect for Taylor to rerecord her back catalogue, but I will surely be making aesthetic sense to you if I explain why she should do so by appeal to how doing so represents a compelling expression of artistic freedom. You will say it is self-mimicry aimed at profit, and I will say something about artistic intent. And so it goes. We might not agree, but we agree, at least *very broadly*, on what counts as a meaningful attempt to add something to the conversation.

Things are – indeed, *must be* – wildly different when it comes to any alleged first-order *all-things-considered* theory. In first-order all-things-considered theory, there is no way *at all* to set the bounds around disputes, and more important, it is horribly unclear how to go about settling any disagreements. This is precisely because all-things-considered correctness purportedly considers *all of the things*. There are, in effect, no bounds to the kinds of correctness it agglomerates. And there are an infinite number of ways of actually so agglomerating. What this means is that whereas in the case of other first-order theories, we could rule out as simply unresponsive to the question certain first-order views (camel milk ethics), we cannot do that in the present case. We cannot rule out any way of agglomerating the various kinds of correctness into one, all-things-considered, verdict.[8]

On one hand, this means the problem space for first-order all-things-considered theory is *very* big. To give you an idea of how big, consider that my camel milk view from before is a perfectly good kind of correctness, in the sense that I can describe what things would have to be like in order to be correct like that. Of course, it is not a perfectly good kind of correctness in the sense that it is a genuine kind of correctness – the only genuine kind of correctness is all-things-considered correctness, which will agglomerate it. Corresponding to this view, then, will be a view about all-things-considered correctness that says something like: correctness in the camel's milk fashion (whatever this is!) is lexically prior to all other kinds of correctness. There will also be a view that says that camel's milk correctness is lexically prior to all other kinds of correctness *except* for ethical correctness. There will also be a view that says … and so on. And this is just what we get by running out the possibilities on *camel's milk* correctness and the relation of *lexical priority*; wait until we get to *even crazier* kinds of correctness and more bizarre ordering or weighing relations between them. Perhaps the relationship is not hierarchical, but instead perhaps the kinds of correctness *trade off* to generate authoritative all-things-considered correctness. You can see why there'll be a lot of options.

On the other hand, the fact that the problem space for first-order all-things-considered theory is relatively large (to be fair: it is non-relatively *really really big*) does not *itself* entail that there is no such thing as first-order all-things-considered theory, and so no such thing as all-things-considered correctness. But notice that all-things-considered correctness is supposed to be the *authoritative* kind of correctness: it is supposed to be *the* kind of correctness that *really matters* or has *oomph*. So, it *cannot* be the case that every possible way of agglomerating all the kinds of correctness is equally correct – if that were true, there would be a plethora of authoritative all-things-considered, er ..., *correctnesses*. But that, of course, is a misnomer. If there is a kind of correctness that considers all the things by ordering them in some way lexically and a kind of correctness that considers all the things by allowing trade-offs or by adopting a somewhat different lexical ordering, then at best *one* of these is, in fact, authoritative all-things-considered correctness. At worst, none is: they are just further kinds of correctness that must all be considered!

Here is another way to put the same point. According to the present line of thought, there is supposed to be just one authoritative kind of correctness. The idea must be therefore that there is a single way of considering all of the things that is the single way of considering all of those things that it is correct to engage in. Fair enough. But what about this latter kind of correctness: the kind of correctness adverted to in the claim that "there is a single way of considering all of the things that is the single way of considering all of those things that it is correct to engage in"? Is *that* an authoritative kind of correctness? If it is not, then we are back to our plethora of apparently authoritative all-things-considered kinds of correctness, none of which is the one that it is authoritatively correct to adopt.[9] That, forgive the expression, cannot be correct.

So, there must be a single way of agglomerating the various kinds of correctness that it is authoritatively correct to engage in. But only all-things-considered correctness is authoritative. So this claim that it is authoritatively correct to agglomerate in a particular way is elliptical for the claim that it is all-things-considered correct to agglomerate in a particular way. This means we will end up with something like (and this is about to get messy) all-things-considered-as-it-is-all-things-considered-right-to-consider-them correctness should. Regress.

To be as clear as possible, here's how you get the regress going:

1. All-things-considered correctness is the only kind of authoritative correctness.
2. All-things-considered correctness agglomerates all other kinds of correctness.
3. There are myriad possible ways to agglomerate all other kinds of correctness and no way to rule out such ways of agglomerating *a priori*.
4. There is a single way that it is correct to agglomerate all other kinds of correctness into all-things-considered correctness.

5. Either the first instance of "correct" in (4) is meant to be authoritative, or it is not.
6. If it is not meant to be authoritative, then it does not *matter*: it does not tell us anything important about how to agglomerate all other kinds of correctness. We can move on.
7. If instead the first instance of "correct" in (4) is authoritative, then given (1), this kind of correctness is all-things-considered correctness.
8. But then (back to 2): this kind of correctness agglomerates all the different ways of agglomerating all other kinds of correctness.
9. But then (back to 3): There are myriad ways ...

Perhaps there are ways out of this worry. I do not want to press the issue any further here. Instead, I offer an olive branch to fans of all-things-considered correctness.

As we saw earlier, if you think there is a notion of authoritative all-things-considered correctness, the simplest way to think about the relationship between this kind of correctness and other kinds of correctness – take epistemic correctness – is that epistemic correctness (at least sometimes) *contributes* in one way or another to (authoritative) all-things-considered correctness. Perhaps it does not always contribute to all-things-considered correctness, and certainly it does not always uniquely determine it. But epistemic correctness helps play a role in determining what, all things considered, it would be correct for agents to do. With this in mind, here's a way to understand the topic of this book, if you are tempted by the thought that *only* all-things-considered correctness is ever authoritative: what I am interested in investigating are the conditions under which epistemic correctness contributes to authoritative all-things-considered correctness.

Put another way: as we have seen, sometimes, kinds of correctness play a role in helping determine all-things-considered correctness. Plausibly, the ethical correctness is like this, and so, too, is prudential correctness; these kinds of correctness are kinds of correctness that (and we have to go carefully here, given the commitment to thinking that only all-things-considered correctness is authoritative) sometimes *contribute* to what matters (although they are not kinds of correctness that matter, as it were, *all on their own*). Perhaps there are specifiable conditions under which these kinds of correctness contribute to the (all-things-considered) correctness that matters, and perhaps there is something that *explains* their so contributing. That is roughly what I am interested in, in the case of *epistemic* correctness. So, rather than putting my question as the question of what explains *epistemic* authority, we could put the question like so: What explains why epistemic correctness is (sometimes) a contributing factor in determining what is all-things-considered authoritatively correct? Again, I am not going to put things this way, since I do not think that all-things-considered correctness is uniquely authoritative for the reasons outlined above. Instead, I offer this as a way of grasping the question I am interested in here for someone with that commitment.

2.3.5 Correctness–Authoritativeness Connection

I just argued that the best way of making sense out of monism's commitment to a unique kind of authoritative correctness – all-things-considered correctness – was, at best, problematic and, at worst, incoherent. Whatever you think about that argument, we have a good independent reason for rejecting monism in the course of the present debate.

Suppose you thought that all-things-considered correctness existed and that it was always everywhere authoritative. Still, this would not deliver monism about kinds of correctness unless you also thought that *being always authoritative* was a condition of being a kind of correctness. In other words, it will not do simply to point out that *this here* kind of correctness is always authoritative and that no other kind of correctness is. You'd have to think that Correctness–Authoritativeness Connection is true, that is, that the fact that something is k-ly correct entails that it is authoritatively k-ly correct.

But we should not accept this idea prior to an actual substantive account of authoritativeness. And so we should not accept it in the course of theorizing about the authoritativeness of, for example, epistemic correctness. Recall that Correctness–Authoritativeness Connection says that *if* φ-ing is k-ly correct, then φ-ing is *authoritatively* k-ly correct. And we are here working with our intuitive grip on what it means to say something is *authoritatively* (as opposed to *merely*) correct; in effect, authoritative correctness is a kind of correctness that *matters* or that has a *grip* on agents.

But here's the thing: prior to an account that purports to *explain* what it is and what it takes for something to be k-ly correct, we have no reason for thinking, *a priori*, that something's being k-ly correct always everywhere entails that it is authoritatively correct. (This is true even if it is true that *if* there is a unique kind of correctness, e.g., all-things-considered correctness, then we should think that correctness is always authoritative.) And whether particular kinds of correctness are, in fact, authoritative on each and every occasion turns out to be a matter of some dispute.

We do not have to introduce bizarre, baroque kinds of correctness to make the point; forget about right-hand-tuesdayical correctness: famously, there is a live, ongoing dispute about whether *moral* correctness is always authoritative. According to one group of philosophers, moral correctness is the kind of thing that always everywhere has *oomph* (Korsgaard 1996; Enoch 2011; Parfit 2011). According to their opponents, this is not so: whether the fact that something is morally correct *matters* or has "legitimate force" will depend. The most common idea is that whether this is so depends on something about the subjective conative states of the agent over whom correctness is supposed to be authoritative (Blackburn 1998; Schroeder 2007; Sobel 2016). But that is not the only possible view. And here, the details do not matter. What matters is that we are not within our rights, prior to an actual account of what explains the authority of a particular kind of correctness, to assume that this kind of correctness will always everywhere be authoritative.

But if this is correct – and it seems undeniable – then how much more when it comes to correctness *per se*. For Correctness–Authoritativeness Connection does not just say that, for example, *moral* correctness entails authoritativeness. It says that correctness *per se* entails authoritativeness. But again, absent an account that purports to explain why it is that – and what it means to say that – correctness is authoritative, we should not accept this. Later on, I will come to the question of what we should think about the authority of *epistemic* correctness. Here, we can leave it at that. I conclude that we should not accept Correctness–Authoritativeness Connection. And we should not be monists about kinds of correctness.

2.4 Conclusion

This chapter involved preliminaries. I outlined several assumptions about the notion of correctness that I am using. I also defended, at length, what I take to be the most controversial of these assumptions, namely, that there are a maximally many *kinds* of correctness, all of which are on a par when it comes to being kinds of correctness. This is the view I called maximal pluralism about kinds of correctness. There are two alternatives to this view: restricted pluralism and monism. Restricted pluralism is unmotivated and mysterious. Monism either faces a troubling regress (if it requires a notion of all-things-considered correctness) or requires an illicit theoretical assumption about the nature of authoritativeness. Either way, we should reject it.

I have spent a lot of time on the idea that correctness comes in (maximally many) different kinds. In later chapters, this idea will turn out to matter quite a bit. But strictly speaking, you do not have to accept my *maximalist* position in order to follow the upcoming arguments. What you have to accept is that there are many (perhaps, many, many) kinds of correctness, that some of them may be authoritative and others not, and that, in principle, we can simply stipulate a kind of correctness by stipulating a standard of correctness the meeting of which entails being that kind of correct. Maximal pluralism about kinds of correctness entails these claims. But if it is possible to accept them without also committing to maximal pluralism, that is fine too. As we will see, the thing that matters is that, because of the plethora of different possible kinds of correctness, our first-order epistemic theorizing is constrained in the following way: whatever first-order epistemic theory we accept, it must plausibly be an account of *epistemic* (as compared to some other kind of) correctness. And we cannot simply pick out what we mean by "epistemic" (as compared to some other kind of) correctness by pointing, as it were, at evaluative reality. More on this shortly.

Notes

1 Here and in what follows I use small capitals to refer explicitly to concepts.
2 A terminological note. Sometimes, this broad category of thought is referred to as "normative" thought and talk rather than, as I have it here, "evaluative" thought and talk. Authors who do this typically reserve "evaluative" for contrasting concepts such as good, bad, better than, and so on with so-called deontic concepts such as right, wrong, obligatory, permissible, and the like. For example, see Berker (n.d.), and Tappolet (2013, 2014). Here, I avoid this way of speaking for two reasons. First, the idea of a kind of thought and talk being "normative" carries some associations I want to avoid. Most important, it is typically assumed that normative thought and talk carry a kind of authority or importance. But I want to leave open the possibility that some kinds of evaluative thought and talk do not carry authority.
3 Here and in what follows I use italics to refer to properties.
4 For just a few examples, see Chappell (2012), Hieronymi (n.d.), Rowland (2017), McHugh and Way (2016), and Schroeder (2022).
5 Although in my defense, see Gert (2012).
6 This is completely compatible with the widespread thought that there are restrictions on which genres we are inclined to think and speak about. Similar remarks go for, for example, accounts of "style" in fiction and art, such as (Walton 1983) that might apply more broadly than "genre." For helpful discussion, see Gracyk (2016).
7 I should hedge: I am not sure anyone would, in a cool and collected moment, disagree. You can, of course, find people saying, in a particular tone of voice and usually breathlessly, that there is no such thing as a particular genre of music or style of art. But what they mean to be saying is presumably that we should not think or speak in terms of that style or that it is uninteresting or whatever. They do not mean to be denying the possibility of so thinking and speaking.
8 Maybe that is too strong: maybe we can rule out *internally incoherent* ways of doing so. I am not sure that is correct, but it would still leave a completely unmanageable problem space.
9 For similar skepticism similarly based, see Baker (2018).

References

Baker, Derek Clayton. 2017. "The Varieties of Normativity." In *The Routledge Handbook of Metaethics*, edited by Tristram McPherson and David Plunkett, 567–581. New York: Routledge.
———. 2018. "Skepticism about Ought Simpliciter." *Oxford Studies in Metaethics* 13: 230–252.
Bedke, Matthew. 2019. "Practical Oomph: A Case for Subjectivism." *Philosophical Quarterly* 69 (277): 657–677. https://doi.org/10.1093/pq/pqz024.
Berker, Selim. n.d. "The Deontic, the Evaluative, and the Fitting."
Blackburn, Simon. 1998. *Ruling Passions: A Theory of Practical Reasoning*. Oxford: Oxford University Press.
Cappelen, Herman. 2020. "Conceptual Engineering: The Master Argument." In *Conceptual Engineering and Conceptual Ethics*, edited by Herman Cappelen, David Plunkett, and Alexis Burgess, 132–151. Oxford: Oxford University Press.

Case, Spencer. 2016. "Normative Pluralism Worthy of the Name Is False." *Journal of Ethics and Social Philosophy* 11 (1): 1–20. https://doi.org/10.26556/jesp.v11i1.107.

Chappell, Richard Yetter. 2012. "Fittingness: The Sole Normative Primitive." *Philosophical Quarterly* 62 (249): 684–704. https://doi.org/10.1111/j.1467-9213.2012.00075.x.

Clarke-Doane, Justin. 2017. "Objectivity and Reliability." *Canadian Journal of Philosophy* 47 (6): 841–855. https://doi.org/10.1080/00455091.2017.1315289.

Deutsch, Max. 2020. "Conceptual Analysis without Concepts." *Synthese* 198 (11): 11125–11157. https://doi.org/10.1007/s11229-020-02775-0.

Eklund, Matti. 2020. "The Normative Pluriverse." *Journal of Ethics and Social Philosophy* 18 (2). https://doi.org/10.26556/jesp.v18i2.652.

Enoch, David. 2011. *Taking Morality Seriously: A Defense of Robust Realism*. Oxford: Oxford University Press.

Finlay, Stephen. 2006. "The Reasons That Matter." *Australasian Journal of Philosophy* 84 (1): 1–20. https://doi.org/10.1080/00048400600571661.

Gert, Joshua. 2012. *Normative Bedrock: Response-Dependence, Rationality, and Reasons*. Oxford: Oxford University Press.

Gracyk, Theodore. 2016. "Heavy Metal: Genre? Style? Subculture?" *Philosophy Compass* 11 (12): 775–785. https://doi.org/10.1111/phc3.12386.

Hieronymi, Pamela. 2021 "Reasoning First." In *Routledge Handbook of Practical Reasoning*, edited by Ruth Chang and Kurt Sylvan, 349–365. Abingdon, UK: Routledge.

Hofweber, Thomas. 2016. *Ontology and the Ambitions of Metaphysics*. Oxford: Oxford University Press.

Horgan, Terry, and Mark Timmons. 2018. "Gripped by Authority." *Canadian Journal of Philosophy* 48 (3–4): 313–336. https://doi.org/10.1080/00455091.2018.1432393.

Horowitz, Amir. 2001. "Contents Just Are in the Head." *Erkenntnis* 54 (3): 321–344. https://doi.org/10.1023/A:1010747032196.

Jackson, Frank. 1998. *From Metaphysics to Ethics: A Defence of Conceptual Analysis*. Oxford: Oxford University Press.

Johnston, Mark, and Sarah-Jane Leslie. 2012. "Concepts, Analysis, Generics and the Canberra Plan." *Philosophical Perspectives* 26 (1): 113–171. https://doi.org/10.1111/phpe.12015.

Korsgaard, Christine M. 1996. *The Sources of Normativity*. Cambridge, UK: Cambridge University Press.

Kripke, Saul A. 1980. *Naming and Necessity*. Cambridge, MA: Harvard University Press.

Lord, Errol. 2018. *The Importance of Being Rational*. Oxford: Oxford University Press.

Maguire, Barry, and Jack Woods. 2020. "The Game of Belief." *Philosophical Review* 129 (2): 211–249. https://doi.org/10.1215/00318108-8012843.

McHugh, Conor, and Jonathan Way. 2016. "Fittingness First." *Ethics* 126 (3): 575–606. https://doi.org/10.1086/684712.

Millikan, Ruth Garrett. 1984. *Language, Thought, and Other Biological Categories: New Foundations for Realism*. Cambridge, MA: MIT Press.

Papineau, David. 1993. *Philosophical Naturalism*. Oxford: Blackwell.

———. 2009. "The Poverty of Analysis." *Aristotelian Society Supplementary Volume* 83 (1): 1–30. https://doi.org/10.1111/j.1467-8349.2009.00170.x.

Parfit, Derek. 2011. *On What Matters: Two-Volume Set*. Oxford: Oxford University Press.
Preston-Roedder, Ryan. 2013. "Faith in Humanity." *Philosophy and Phenomenological Research* 87 (3): 664–687. https://doi.org/10.1111/phpr.12024.
Putnam, Hillary. 1975. "The Meaning of 'Meaning'." *Minnesota Studies in the Philosophy of Science* 7: 131–193.
Rowland, Richard. 2017. "Reasons or Fittingness First?" *Ethics* 128 (1): 212–229. https://doi.org/10.1086/692949.
Sagdahl, Mathias Slåttholm. 2014. "The Argument from Nominal–Notable Comparisons, 'Ought All Things Considered', and Normative Pluralism." *The Journal of Ethics* 18 (4): 405–425. https://doi.org/10.1007/s10892-014-9179-9.
Schroeder, Mark. 2007. *Slaves of the Passions*. Oxford: Oxford University Press.
———. 2022. *Reasons First*. Oxford: Oxford University Press.
Schroeter, Laura. 2004. "The Limits of Conceptual Analysis." *Pacific Philosophical Quarterly* 85 (4): 425–453. https://doi.org/10.1111/j.1468-0114.2004.00209.x.
Sharadin, Nathaniel. 2016. "Reasons Wrong and Right." *Pacific Philosophical Quarterly* 97 (3): 371–399. https://doi.org/10.1111/papq.12089.
Sobel, David. 2016. *From Valuing to Value: A Defense of Subjectivism*. Oxford: Oxford University Press.
Southwood, Nicholas. 2008. "Vindicating the Normativity of Rationality." *Ethics* 119 (1): 9–30. https://doi.org/10.1086/592586.
Strawson, Peter. 1962. "Freedom and Resentment." In *Proceedings of the British Academy*, Volume 48: *1962*, 1–25.
Stroud, Sarah. 2006. "Epistemic Partiality in Friendship." *Ethics* 116 (3): 498–524. https://doi.org/10.1086/500337.
Tappolet, Christine. 2013. "Evaluative vs. Deontic Concepts." In *International Encyclopedia of Ethics*, edited by Hugh Lafollette, 1791–1799. Oxford: Wiley-Blackwell.
———. 2014. "The Normativity of Evaluative Concepts." In *Mind, Values, and Metaphysics. Philosophical Essays in Honor of Kevin Mulligan, Volume 2*, edited by Anne Reboul, 39–54. New York: Springer.
Tiffany, Evan. 2007. "Deflationary Normative Pluralism." *Canadian Journal of Philosophy* 37 (5): 231–262. https://doi.org/10.1353/cjp.0.0076.
Walton, Kendall L. 1983. "Fiction, Fiction-Making, and Styles of Fictionality." *Philosophy and Literature* 7 (1): 78–88. https://doi.org/10.1353/phl.1983.0004.
Wedgwood, Ralph. 2007. *The Nature of Normativity*. Oxford: Oxford University Press. https://doi.org/10.1093/acprof:oso/9780199251315.001.0001.
Whiting, Daniel. 2018. "Right in Some Respects: Reasons as Evidence." *Philosophical Studies* 175 (9): 2191–2208. https://doi.org/10.1007/s11098-017-0954-x.

3 First-Order Epistemic Theory

3.1 Introduction

In the previous chapter, I argued there were maximally many (at the very least, *many, many*) different kinds of correctness. My topic in this book is *epistemic* correctness. In this chapter, I explain in broad terms how to think about *first-order theories* of epistemic correctness. In the next chapter, I explain how to differentiate potential first-order theories of *epistemic* correctness from first-order theories of other kinds of correctness.

This ordering might strike you as exactly backward. If we want to know how to think about first-order theories of epistemic correctness, then you might think we should first have a story about how to think about *epistemic* correctness as differentiated from other kinds of correctness. But that is not right. It is true that making sense of first-order epistemic theorizing as a distinctively *epistemic* enterprise requires some such story. And so I give one in Chapter 4. But it is not true that making sense of first-order epistemic theorizing as a *theoretical* enterprise requires any such story. So that is what I will do, first, here.

Then, together with the view about what makes some potential first-order theory count as a potential view about *epistemic* correctness, I explain (Chapter 5) why a particular first-order epistemic theory, namely, epistemic instrumentalism, has seemed so bad to so many. And then I explain why it *is* actually quite bad but not for the reasons typically assumed (Chapter 6). But first(-order) things first.

3.2 Epistemic Correctness

Consider the question, What is it epistemically correct to believe? There are myriad ways to answer, ranging from commonsense platitudes (it is epistemically correct to believe what is epistemically correct and not what is epistemically incorrect) to formally sophisticated (it is epistemically correct to believe so that your scoring rule is credence-eliciting) to clannish (it is epistemically correct to believe what your peers believe) to nonsensical (it is epistemically correct to believe whatever you want to

DOI: 10.4324/9781003096726-3

believe). As I think of things, first-order epistemic theory is the part of philosophical epistemology that tries to answer this question in a systematic, compelling way.

Maybe you think that first-order epistemic theory is not interested in the concept of EPISTEMICALLY CORRECT but that it is instead interested in other epistemic concepts such as KNOWLEDGE or TESTIMONY or JUSTIFICATION, or ... something else. It is true that a lot of first-order epistemic theory really is interested in these other concepts. I am, too, but not here.

What is the relationship between epistemic correctness and these other interests of first-order epistemic theory? One possibility is that these other areas of first-order epistemic theory are concerned to settle issues that *bear* on epistemic correctness. Another is that they are intended as incomplete accounts *of* epistemic correctness.[1]

Plausibly, discussions of knowledge, testimony, justification, and their ilk are the first sort of area of first-order epistemic inquiry – the sort that bears on epistemic correctness. This is because authors concerned with these issues presumably think of, for example, knowledge and justification as having an evaluative dimension. It is not as if the question of what it takes for a belief to be epistemically justified is somehow *orthogonal* to the question of what it takes for a belief to be epistemically correct. In fact, you might think the two are simply one: epistemic correctness *just is* epistemic justification. If you think that, then you are not going to have any problem at all thinking of first-order epistemic theory as concerned with epistemic correctness, as long as you do not have any problem at all thinking of first-order epistemic theory as concerned with epistemic justification. Just swap in for the latter every time you see me write the former.

But you might *not* think this is true; that is, you might not think that epistemic correctness is exactly the same thing as epistemic justification. I myself do not think they are the same. Here is why. I think it is very easy to imagine a plausible view of epistemic justification and a plausible view of epistemic correctness where the two things – what is epistemically justified and what is epistemically correct – regularly come apart. For instance, suppose you think that what agents are epistemically justified in believing depends entirely on their evidence but that what it is epistemically correct for agents to believe depends also on the practical stakes of their beliefs. That is not a *crazy* view to have. You might not think it is the right view to have, but I submit that it is not somehow conceptually incoherent. And if you have this view, then there will sometimes – perhaps regularly – be cases where what an agent is justified in believing is not the same as what it is epistemically correct for them to believe.

This is not intended to convince you that epistemic justification and epistemic correctness are not the same. If you want to dig in your heels, it is trivial to resist the example I just gave: simply agglomerate features of the practical stakes of an agent's beliefs to features of the agent's evidence or deny the intuitive effect of stakes on correctness or whatever – there are always options. I am not interested in having this argument, here, in this book. Instead, I simply offer it to illustrate the point that it is *possible* to think the two notions come apart and that, if you do think this, then first-order epistemic theorizing will not be *exhausted* by first-order epistemic theorizing about *justification*. Because it will make my view available to a wider audience, going forward I will simply assume epistemic justification and epistemic correctness are not identical. With some range of modifications, I think there is no reason a proponent of collapsing the two couldn't accept everything I say.

In addition to concerning itself with issues that bear on, but are not directly about, epistemic correctness – justification, knowledge, and other epistemic evaluative notions – there is the range of first-order epistemic theory that is, in fact, directly about, although perhaps is not an attempt to completely articulate, an account of epistemic correctness. The clearest illustrations of this kind of first-order epistemic theory are I think drawn from areas of formal epistemology such as, but not exclusively, Bayesian epistemology. Pretty clearly, Bayesians are trying to say *something* about epistemic correctness: they think it is epistemically correct to update on your evidence in accord with Bayes' theorem, that it is epistemically incorrect to have a credence function that violates the axioms of probability, and so on. Similarly, the literature on how it is we should score the accuracy of credence functions seems to presuppose something like the idea that, *ceteris paribus*, it is *epistemically correct* to improve along this or that dimension.[2] Or anyway, that seems pretty plausible.

And as Daniel Singer (2021) points out in a similar context, there are a *lot* of other examples of first-order epistemic theory being interested in partly answering the question about what is epistemically correct. The literature on how to respond to peer disagreement is like this: there, the question is what it would be epistemically correct to do in particular kinds of situations, namely, those situations in which one's epistemic peers disagree with one over what it is epistemically correct to do! Something similar is true of the literature surrounding the role of experts: there, we want, in part, to know whether it is always epistemically correct to defer to domain experts or whether this depends on the domain in question or something else.

So it should not be controversial that first-order epistemic theory is concerned with what is epistemically correct. And this is true even if there is not a lot of literature that speaks, directly, to the question. And – to ward off a certain sort of concern – let me emphasize that accepting this point does not entail anything at all about what other things might fall within the proper scope of first-order epistemic theorizing.

Here is an analogy that can be helpful (although it can also be terribly misleading): ethics. We often wonder, What is it ethically correct to do? There are as before myriad ways to answer. It is ethically correct to act, platitudinously: correctly; formally: so that your maxim is universalizable;

clannishly: in the way your peers do; nonsensically: however you want to act. First-order *ethical* theory is the part of moral philosophy that tries to answer this question in a systematic, compelling way.

Now, unlike their colleagues down the hall, ethicists have been a lot more up front about their interest in ethical concepts such as ETHICALLY CORRECT. Indeed, one common way the topic of moral philosophy is introduced to students is by canvassing different historical and contemporary theories of correct action – by which is usually meant some biconditional statement with "an action is morally correct" on the left-hand side and the substantive moral theory (e.g., Kantianism or consequentialism) on the right-hand side.[3]

And accepting this idea, that part of first-order ethical theory concerns itself with offering an account of evaluative ethical concepts such as ETHICALLY CORRECT does not require accepting anything at all about the proper scope of first-order ethical theorizing. And no one, as far as I know, has ever seriously thought that first-order ethical theory is somehow *restricted* to answering questions about ethical correctness.

And that is not what I have said here, either about first-order epistemic theory or about first-order ethical theory. Of *course* first-order ethical theory is also in addition interested in other questions, such as the questions to do with ethical personhood, free will, responsibility, and so on. Sometimes, answers to those questions connect up with questions about what it would be ethically correct to do, but sometimes – perhaps even quite often – they do not.

The same is true of first-order epistemic theory. First-order epistemic theory is also in addition interested in issues other than epistemic correctness. And the thought that first-order epistemic theory is, in part, in the business of telling us about epistemic correctness in no way entails that first-order epistemic theory is *only* concerned with that issue or that *every* claim in first-order epistemic theory must in some way be connected to settling it. Of *course* first-order epistemic theory is also in addition interested in other questions, such as questions to do with the nature of doxastic states such as suspension of judgment, the possibility of "believing at will," epistemic trustworthiness, and so on. Sometimes, answers to those questions connect up with questions about what it would be epistemically correct to believe, but sometimes – perhaps even quite often – they do not. Perhaps it is even true that some of the debates over what epistemic justification is like, or what epistemic rationality comprises do not themselves connect up with answers to the question about what it would be epistemically correct to believe. I take no stand on those questions here.

So it seems clear that it is appropriate to treat the question of what is epistemically correct as firmly in first-order epistemic theory. But maybe you still disagree. Maybe you think that first-order epistemic theory need not tell us *anything at all* about epistemic correctness. You might be someone who is willing to say, for instance, that an agent's beliefs are justified when such-and-such circumstances hold or who thinks higher-order evidence works like *so* but who is not willing to go on to say anything at all about what it is that it would be epistemically correct for an agent to believe.

There are a few possible *yous* here. One you is a you who is not willing to go on to say things about epistemic correctness because you have other business to attend. Then, we have no quarrel; we should always welcome the division of philosophical labor.

A second you is a you who is not willing to go on to say things about epistemic correctness because you think such things are not the kinds of things first-order epistemic theories *should* be in the business saying. Then, I have three responses.

My first response cajoles: Why *not* say such things? After all, the question concerning what it would be epistemically correct to believe is clearly a meaningful question we can ask. We can ask what it would be epistemically correct to believe in exactly the same tone of voice we can ask what it would be ethically correct to do, what it would be etiquetically correct to do, what stock it would be prudentially correct to purchase, and so on. In fact, we *do* ask instances of this; we ask instances of it *all the time*. I want to know whether it would be correct to believe trivial things (that the store is open until 9), obscure things (that the material components for crafting a mnemonic vestment include a piece of string), and important matters (that the likelihood of asteroid impacts is somewhat higher than I had been told). I do not see any better (or really even alternative) place to ask these questions than first-order epistemic theory. And asking them *just is* asking questions about epistemic correctness.

My second response scolds: As I have just illustrated, it is clear that traditional first-order epistemic theory concerns itself with epistemic evaluative notions such as justification, warrant, knowledge, and the like. There is simply no principled reason to police the boundaries of epistemology such that questions about *those* evaluative notions are *in*, whereas questions about other evaluative notions, such as the notion of epistemic correctness, are *out*.

My final response softens the blow. As I have already indicated, the fact that first-order epistemic theory is in part concerned with offering an account of epistemic correctness does not entail that all parts of first-order epistemic theory must be so concerned. If you do not want to talk about epistemic correctness, no one is holding a methodological gun to your head.

A third possible you is a you that is not willing to say anything about epistemic correctness, despite the manifest *possibility* of doing so, because you think there is no theoretically respectable way of systematically answering questions about, for example, the extension of epistemic correctness. The idea might be something like the epistemic analogue of the particularist position, more familiar from ethical theory, that says, roughly, that the search for fully general principles that deliver verdicts concerning what, ethically speaking, is correct, is hopeless (Dancy 2004). Depending on the version of the particularist view on offer, this can be because of the structure of moral reality (Väyrynen 2014) or the structure of moral judgment (McKeever and Ridge 2006) or something else altogether. Whatever the cause, the idea manifests in a kind of suspicion of ethical theory *qua theory*: the thought is that theorizing about ethical correctness is just the incorrect place to focus our attention, given what moral or ethical reality is like.

Perhaps, then, something similar is true of epistemic correctness: perhaps it is not possible to engage in theorizing of the relevant kind. I think the correct way to think about this worry is as a worry that concerns the *ambitions* of first-order theory. On one hand, you might want a first-order epistemic (or ethical) theory that tells you, under all possible circumstances, what, epistemically (or ethically) it would be correct for an agent to do. I think particularists are right to be suspicious of the possibility of offering any such account.[4]

On the other hand, you might simply want your first-order theory to tell you something about what explains why it is that some beliefs (actions) are epistemically (ethically) correct and others are not. On the assumption that there really can be things that are epistemically and ethically correct, I think it is within our ken to explain at least some of why this is so. (I address a kind of general skepticism about correctness *per se* later on.) And I do not know of any particularists who disagree.[5]

In other words, if the worry here is that all facts about epistemic correctness are *sui generis* facts that stand as brute unexplained explainers about which all theorizing is hopeless, I think this is a mistake. I do not have any new argument against such a view, except to point out the obvious possibility of explaining, in some ways, the existence of at least some of these evaluative epistemic facts.

But I do not think that is something that any particular particularist means to be denying; instead, their worry is, as I have said, a worry about the possibility of giving *particular kinds of first-order theories*, such as ones that purport to give fully general exceptionless principles specifying necessary and sufficient conditions for epistemic (or ethical) correctness that are deployable by agents in their epistemic (or ethical) thinking about what to do.[6] The project I am interested in here will not take a stand, one way or the other, on anything that runs afoul of those concerns.

A fourth and final possible you is a you who thinks first-order epistemic theory does not and shouldn't concern itself with epistemic correctness because questions about epistemic correctness have *trivial answers*. The idea is that epistemic correctness is (*obviously*, it's said as one sighs) a matter of *truth*: a belief is correct when (and only when) it is true (Shah and Velleman 2005; Shah 2006), and if there are such things as *partial* beliefs, then they are epistemically correct when (and only when) and to whatever extent they are whatever way is the partial analogue of truth – perhaps they are correct when and to the extent they are *accurate* (Joyce 1998).

But this will not do. Despite appearances, those answers are not trivial. Instead, they represent substantive views about when it is epistemically correct to believe and when it is not epistemically correct to believe. Sticking to all-out belief for the moment: why not think that, sometimes, it is epistemically correct to (even wittingly) believe something false? The answer cannot be because that would obviously, trivially, uncontroversially be epistemically incorrect. For plenty of people disagree. For instance, epistemic consequentialists will tend to countenance explicit trade-offs between believing truly and believing falsely such that it can be epistemically correct to believe falsely about some propositions, on some occasions (Berker 2013a, 2013b; Ahlstrom-Vij and Dunn 2014; Singer 2018, 2021; Sharadin 2020). Epistemic consequentialists might be wrong about this, but they are not *trivially* wrong about it.

Switching to partial belief, why not think that, sometimes, it is epistemically correct to depart from a credence-function that is accuracy-maximizing? The answer cannot be because that would obviously, trivially, uncontroversially be epistemically incorrect. For, it is possible to disagree. For instance, departing from accuracy-maximization might be required in order to conform one's partial beliefs to the evidence (Easwaran and Fitelson 2012; Meacham 2018). This might be incorrect, or it might be incorrect that partial beliefs *should* so conform, but this is not *trivially* so.

I conclude that epistemic correctness is within the scope of first-order epistemic theorizing. There is no good reason to think otherwise. So let me start to say more about the way I will think of first-order epistemic theories.

3.3 First-Order Theories: Extension and Explanation

One natural idea might be that first-order epistemic theories theorize about epistemic correctness by attempting to give an *extension* for epistemic correctness. But that is not correct. First-order epistemic theory is not, at least not primarily, about the *extension* of epistemic correctness – about what is, in fact, epistemically correct. The easiest way to see this is to notice that two first-order epistemic theories that agree on the extension of epistemic correctness might still intuitively be competitors.

Consider the following scenario:

> Lee's Tea: Lee has just made tea, and it is sitting in his cup. He watches the tea closely and sees steam coming off the top of the cup.

What would it be epistemically correct for Lee to believe in this scenario? Take the first-order epistemic theory – call it *evidentialism* – that says agents' beliefs are epistemically correct when they are supported by, or fit, the evidence. Then, intuitively, it would be epistemically correct for Lee to believe that his tea is hot. This is because Lee's (perceptual) evidence – the steam coming off the cup – strongly supports the belief that his tea is hot. Now take a different first-order epistemic theory – call it *coherentism* – that says agents' beliefs are epistemically correct when they (best) cohere with their other beliefs. Then, intuitively, it would be epistemically correct for Lee to believe his tea is hot. This is because Lee's belief that his tea is hot presumably (best) coheres with his other beliefs, such as his belief that there is steam coming off the cup, that he just made the tea, and so on. Finally, take the first-order epistemic theory – call it *reliabilism* – that says agents' beliefs are epistemically correct when they are formed by a reliable belief-forming mechanism. Then, intuitively, it would be epistemically correct for Lee to believe his tea is hot. This is because Lee's belief that his tea is hot is formed by the (presumably reliable) belief-forming mechanisms associated with ordinary perception, memory, and so on.

So evidentialism, coherentism, and reliabilism all agree about the answer to the question concerning what it is epistemically correct for Lee to believe. Does this mean that these first-order epistemic theories are not competitors? No. Clearly, these three views compete.

You might think this is because although these three theories agree about Lee's Tea, they will disagree over other actual or counterfactual scenarios. For example, it is easy to imagine a variation on Lee's Tea where Lee's belief that his tea is hot does not cohere with his other doxastic attitudes or where the belief is not formed as a result of a reliable process but where it would still conform to his evidence. This would reintroduce competition among the views.

But the fact that the theories might disagree over other actual or counterfactual scenarios is not enough to explain why they should count as competing first-order epistemic theories. For, it is possible to imagine two first-order epistemic theories giving *exactly the same* answer to the question about what beliefs it would be epistemically correct for agents to have in *all possible scenarios* while remaining competitors. This is because first-order epistemic theories do not simply offer principles designed to capture the *extension* of epistemic correctness; they also, and primarily, offer principles designed to *explain* epistemic correctness.

For example, evidentialists will say not just that it is epistemically correct for agents to believe in whatever way their evidence supports. Evidentialists will also say that it is epistemically correct to believe in whatever way is supported by the evidence *in virtue of the fact* that believing in that way is supported by the evidence. Similarly, coherentists will say not just that it is epistemically correct to have coherent beliefs. Coherentists will also say that it is epistemically correct to have coherent beliefs *because* those beliefs are coherent. And reliabilists, in their turn, will not just say that it is epistemically correct to have beliefs formed by reliable processes; they will also say that the reliability of a belief-forming mechanism is what *explains* the epistemic correctness of the relevant beliefs.

This idea, that first-order epistemic theory has an explanatory, as well as extensional, dimension, is not and should not be controversial. Returning to our sometimes misleading analogy: a similar familiar thing is true of first-order ethical theory. There, some philosophers have argued, persuasively in my view, that it is always possible to generate a consequentialist ethical theory that is extensionally equivalent to *any* possible non-consequentialist ethical theory (Dreier 1993, 2011; Portmore 2009). But, of course, this does not mean there is no dispute between ethical consequentialists and ethical non-consequentialists concerning ethical correctness. This is because ethical consequentialists and ethical non-consequentialists disagree over what explains the relevant extension of evaluative ethical properties such as ethical correctness. So, too, in epistemic theory. Even if it turns out to be true that, say, evidentialism and coherentism are or can be made to be extensional equivalents of one another, it is not true that they are thereby in substantial agreement. That is because they disagree over what *explains* the relevant extension of evaluative epistemic properties such as epistemic correctness.

Kurt Sylvan has been, among people working on this issue, the most ardent about insisting on this point (Sylvan 2016, 2018, 2019, 2020). In almost everything he writes on anything even remotely related to the topic, he is at pains to flag the difference between thinking that something is being offered as an account of *which* things are epistemically (or ethically) right, wrong, correct, incorrect, justified, unjustified, and so on and thinking that something is being offered as an account of *why* things are epistemically (or ethically) right, wrong, correct, incorrect, and so on. Following Shelly Kagan (1992), Sylvan identifies the difference as between offering *factoral* and *foundational* theories. The former sort of theory tells us *which factors* (hence factoral) are relevant to various statuses, for example, correctness. The latter sort of theory tells us *why those factors are relevant* to the status (hence foundational; Sylvan 2018).

I very much agree that we be careful about this difference and for exactly the kinds of reasons Sylvan says we should care. But I do not want to adopt what I think is the clunky language of "factoral" and "foundational" theories and, thereby, be forced to say things such as *factorally understood*, theory X is plausible, but *foundationally* understood, it is not (as) plausible (Sylvan 2018). Moreover, it is unclear to me that the way Sylvan wants to frame things leaves room for the distinction between first- and second-order theorizing, which will be crucial later on. In any case, I propose to distinguish between the two ways of thinking about a theory in terms of a theory's *extension* and its *explanation*. A theory's *extension* is the extension of things it says are epistemically correct. A theory's *explanation* is its explanation of why those things that are epistemically correct are so. I take first-order epistemic theories to primarily be concerned with offering *explanations* rather than *extensions*.

Earlier, I put the point about explanations a few different ways. I said that evidentialists think something about what it is *in virtue of which* a belief is epistemically correct, that coherentists say beliefs are epistemically correct *because* they are coherent, and that reliabilists *explain* epistemic correctness in terms of reliability. I might have put the point in other cognate terms too – referring to *truthmakers* or something else. Let me fix terms, in order to begin to fix the idea. I will take first-order epistemic theories to be interested (among other things) in what *explains* epistemic correctness. And I will say that the explanans they cite in their explanations are what they think of as the *explanatory grounds* or just *grounds* of epistemic correctness.

Now the robust philosophical notion of *grounding* is a matter of much dispute. I do not need anything too sophisticated and nothing at all controversial for my purposes here. I make a few assumptions about the relation of grounding in what follows. First, it is explanatory. So, to say that X grounds Y is to say that X explains Y. In recent parlance, this makes me a "unionist" about grounding – someone who thinks grounding just is explanation (Raven 2015). But I have no quarrel with so-called separatists, who think that grounding is not the same thing as explanation. This is because although separatists think it important to treat grounding separately from explanation, they agree that the two are, as Selim Berker (2019) notes in a closely related context, intimately linked. Second, and relatedly, I will assume the relation of grounding is factive. So, to say that X grounds Y entails both X and Y. Third, grounding is gradable. So it is possible for X to be either a partial or a complete ground of Y. Unless I say otherwise, the unmodified "ground" or "grounds" should be read as "complete ground" or "completely grounds." So, if X grounds Y, then X completely grounds Y.

And that is *it*. As I said, there is nothing sophisticated about the notion of grounding I am going to use in what follows. It is effectively a way of thinking about facts that play a particular role in explanation. And it is the explanatory ambitions of first-order epistemic theory that I am interested in here.

3.4 Epistemic Correctness Explanatory Principles

Here, in more detail, is how I will think about the explanatory ambitions of first-order epistemic theory when it comes to epistemic correctness. What we are after, when we are doing first-order epistemic theory concerned with epistemic correctness is a theory that says what *grounds* epistemic correctness. In other words, we want an account of *F* in the generic principle:

> The fact that it is epistemically correct for A to believe that P is grounded by F.*

I will come to the asterisk in a moment. Sticking with the examples of first-order theories we have already put on the table, using this schema, we have all three:

> Evidentialism: The fact that it is epistemically correct for A to believe that P is grounded by the fact that A's believing that P is supported by A's evidence.
>
> Coherentism: The fact that it is epistemically correct for A to believe that P is grounded by the fact that A's believing that P coheres with A's other beliefs.
>
> Reliabilism: The fact that it is epistemically correct for A to believe that P is grounded by the fact that A's belief that P is produced via a reliable mechanism.

These principles are examples of what I will refer to as *epistemic correctness explanatory principles*. With apologies for acronymizing, it will turn out to be occasionally useful to have a way to quickly refer to a theory's epistemic correctness explanatory principle; so, I will call them ECEPs for short. And if I say, e.g., evidentialism's ECEP, then you should think of (something like) the explanatory principle just adduced. When we are fighting over first-order epistemic theory, one thing we are fighting over is which ECEP is correct. Disagreement over what grounds epistemic correctness is, *inter alia*, what puts evidentialists at odds with coherentists, who are at odds with reliabilists, and so on.

Of course, disagreements over the explanatory grounds of epistemic correctness will often lead to disagreements over the *extension* of epistemic correctness. And those disagreements over the extension of epistemic correctness are then sometimes used as the lever for arguing against competing views of the explanatory grounds of epistemic correctness. For instance, someone – an evidentialist, say – will wheel out an example where it appears the reliabilist ECEP apparently delivers the incorrect verdict regarding what it would be epistemically correct to believe in some scenario. The intuitively incorrect verdict is then leveraged by the evidentialist into an argument against the reliabilist account of the ground of epistemic correctness. The reliabilist rejoinder attempts to avoid the problematic extensional difficulty or to rehabilitate it or something else. And so it goes. We will see an instance of this dialectic later on when looking more closely at epistemic instrumentalism's ECEP.

We do not need to say anything else about first-order epistemic theory in order to be getting on with things. In the next chapter, I am going to explain how to think about what it means to say that first-order epistemic theory is concerned with *epistemic* correctness (as compared with some other kind of correctness). Right now, let me address two more issues.

3.5 Ambits and Focal Points

Recall the asterisk in

> The fact that it is epistemically correct for A to believe that *P* is grounded by *F*.*

Thus far, I have been treating epistemic correctness as exclusively a property that can be had an agent's beliefs. But why think the only things that can be epistemically correct are an agent's beliefs? This is clearly false.

At the very least, there are other so-called doxastic attitudes, such as *suspension of judgment* and *disbelief* that, as Errol Lord has recently put it, "compete" to be the epistemically correct doxastic attitude (Lord 2020). Indeed, Lord argues that there are multiple distinct forms of suspension of judgment, each of which might be the attitude that it is epistemically correct. These nonbelief attitudes – and if Lord is correct, there is a bundle of them – are arguably not reducible to belief. Moreover, and perhaps even more obviously, there are intuitively some *gradable* doxastic attitudes, such as "credence" that intuitively can be epistemically correct. And the question of whether these gradable attitudes are reducible to belief is certainly not settled (Foley 2009; Hawthorne 2009; Clarke 2013). So the reach of epistemic correctness at the very least extends beyond mere belief.

Call something an *evaluative focal point* for epistemic correctness when it is something that *can* be evaluated as being epistemically correct. Belief and disbelief are uncontroversially evaluative focal points for epistemic correctness. So, too, is suspension of judgment. Credences also likely make the cut. It will be useful to have a collective noun for the things that are the evaluative focal points for epistemic correctness. Call the collection of all the evaluative focal points for epistemic correctness the *ambit* of epistemic correctness.

Beyond simply adducing plausible candidates, how do we determine the ambit of epistemic correctness? There is one tempting but definitely mistaken way to proceed. It is to consult one's intuitions about what sorts of things we usually go around calling epistemically correct, or usually think about in terms of epistemic correctness, bundle them all up, and call the result the ambit of epistemic correctness. Unsystematic as it might seem, this methodology is pretty common.

Sometimes, it simply lurks in the background; other times, it is explicitly adopted. For example, from Selim Berker (2018, p. 468),

> [e]pistemic and practical normativity are individuated by their objects of assessment: the normative assessment of belief (and other doxastic attitudes) is epistemic normativity, and the normative assessment of action is practical normativity.

In our language, Berker's idea is that the ambit of epistemic correctness (as compared to some other kind of correctness) is given by the bundle of things we usually go about calling epistemically correct, namely, agents' doxastic attitudes. A similar approach is taken by Kurt Sylvan (2016) in his discussion of epistemic reasons. There, Sylvan simply assumes that epistemic reasons, whatever they are, target agents' doxastic attitudes; the difficult question, in his view, is whether there is some "neutral way to explain the difference between epistemic and pragmatic [i.e., non-epistemic] reasons for belief" (2016, p. 371). In our language, Sylvan's thought is that the ambit of epistemic correctness is the bundle of things we usually go about calling epistemically correct, namely, agents' doxastic attitudes, and our question will then be over what makes those focal points, in fact, *epistemically* correct.

One notable exception to this orthodoxy is in work by Daniel Singer and Sara Aronowitz (forthcoming). There, Singer and Aronowitz argue against treating epistemic correctness as importantly different from other kinds of correctness *in virtue of the objects that can possess it*. (I'm translating things into my terms.) I basically agree with Singer and Aronowitz on their conclusion but think it will be helpful to spell out the reasons for accepting it in the context of the debate I'm interested in having.

I think the idea that we can identify the ambit of epistemic correctness simply by glancing around and identifying the kinds of things we usually go around calling epistemically correct and bundling them all together is so widespread because it's not clear to theorists what the alternative could be. But this, I think, is, in turn, because epistemologists have simply failed to recognize that the ambit of epistemic correctness is the *result of* and not an *ingredient in* first-order epistemic theory.

Let me explain. You might think that the way you do first-order epistemic theorizing is that you begin by thinking about which kinds of things can be epistemically correct – beliefs, credences, suspensions of judgment, say. Having decided on that ambit for epistemic correctness, you then craft your first-order epistemic theory: you say something about what facts ground the facts about epistemic correctness as it attaches to the focal points with which you began. That, in effect, is how, for example, Sylvan and Berker think of things.

But while this might sometimes be the order in which things are worked out, this is not the actual order in which they are determined. The ambit of epistemic correctness does not precede the first-order epistemic theory. Instead, the kinds of things that *can* be epistemically correct – the focal points for epistemic correctness – are determined by the epistemic correctness explanatory principles, that is, by the first-order epistemic theory itself.

Think of things like this. Each first-order epistemic theory is (in part) an attempt to tell us how to go about assessing the epistemic correctness of things – in other words, it tells us how to assess things as epistemically correct or incorrect. But *which things*, in fact, can be assessed in this way as (say) epistemically correct will obviously depend on the substantive content of the first-order epistemic theory on offer. So, really, we should think of first-order epistemic theories as attempts to precisify:

The fact that it is epistemically correct for A to φ is grounded by F,

where which kinds of things can be a φ-ing will depend on the particulars of the first-order epistemic theory on offer. This idea is nicely illustrated by contrasting two instances of ECEPs. One we are already familiar with, which is

Evidentialism: The fact that it is epistemically correct for A to φ is grounded by the fact that φ-ing fits A's evidence.

If we are evidentialists, then it turns out that the ambit of the epistemic is restricted to those things that can *fit an agent's evidence*. For, only such entities can be focal points for epistemic correctness. So we end up thinking that *beliefs* and perhaps a few other doxastic attitudes comprise the ambit of epistemic correctness. Maybe we manage to stretch things and squeeze in some not traditionally doxastic attitudes such as the kinds of attitudes Lord argues comprise different forms of suspension of judgment.

Not so if we accept a very different ECEP, such as

Consequentialism: The fact that it is epistemically correct for A to φ is grounded by the fact that A's φ-ing conduces to the best epistemic consequences.[7]

If we are consequentialists of this sort, then we shall think the ambit of the epistemic is *much larger* than the evidentialist thinks it is. This is because almost any φ-ing you like can be something that would conduce to the best epistemic consequences. How in particular this will turn out will depend in part on what we think the best epistemic consequences comprise, and what it takes to "conduce" to them. But to illustrate the idea, take one recent version of the view according to which good epistemic consequences are true beliefs, and the *best* epistemic consequences are the greatest available balance of true beliefs to false beliefs.[8]

If we are consequentialists of this sort, then it can be epistemically correct to believe some proposition. But it can also be epistemically correct to climb a telephone pole, or to exercise more, or … really, anything you like.[9] This is because although these activities cannot "fit the evidence," it might well be the case that that climbing a telephone pole or exercising more or whatever, would conduce to the best available balance of true belief to false belief.

So the evidentialist and the consequentialist will disagree over the ambit of epistemic correctness. But this disagreement over what can and what cannot be epistemically correct is not separable from their more fundamental disagreement over what epistemic correctness explanatory principles are correct – over what, as a matter of fact, grounds epistemic correctness.

3.6 Conclusion

Competing first-order epistemic theories will deliver different verdicts not just about *which* φ-ings are epistemically correct but also about why those φ-ings are epistemically correct. Hence, first-order epistemic theories are, among other things, attempts to precisify the generic:

> The fact that it is epistemically correct for A to φ is grounded by F.

The ambit of epistemic correctness – which kinds of things can be the φ-ings or can be epistemically correct – is determined by the relevant first-order theory on offer. In other words, whether some activity *can* be epistemically correct is not something we can determine prior to accepting some particular first-order epistemic theory.

In the next chapter, I explain how to think about the idea that first-order epistemic theories are in the business of offering us an account of *epistemic* correctness (as compared to some other kind of correctness). Along the way, I identify a minimal criterion of adequacy accounts of epistemic correctness must meet. In the following chapter, I articulate first-order epistemic instrumentalism.

Notes

1 This mirrors the way in which (Singer 2021) understands the relationship between issues in philosophy and what Singer calls "epistemic rightness." Most of what Singer says about the relationship between epistemic rightness and other areas of epistemic inquiry can be said, here, about the relationship between epistemic correctness and those same areas; importantly, I think it can also be said about the relationship between Singer's *own* investigation into epistemic *rightness* and epistemic correctness.
2 For instance, Easwaran and Fitelson (2012), and Joyce (1998).
3 It's trivial to find various examples of moral theories so stated, for instance Korsgaard (1985) Hursthouse (1999), and Feldman (2006).
4 For a recent argument in favor of this view on the epistemic side of things, see Bradley (2019).
5 Even Dancy (2004) himself does not think, for example, that we cannot give explanations of why it is that particular acts are right or wrong, or that there aren't any (defeasible) generalizations about these facts. For more, see Little and Lance (2004), Lance and Little (2008), and Väyrynen (2009, 2006).
6 For example, that is how Dancy (2017) describes the view.
7 Daniel Singer (2021) defends a version of this view. See also Singer (2018) and Ahlstrom-Vij and Dunn (2014). Of course, epistemic consequentialism of this sort is wildly controversial (Berker 2013a, 2013b). The point, here, is that you cannot rule out the possibility that things other than agents' doxastic

attitudes are epistemically correct *prior* to ruling out the possibility that a theory such as this is the correct theory of epistemic correctness.
8 Singer (2021).
9 Singer (2021), and Singer and Aronowitz (Forthcoming)

References

Ahlstrom-Vij, Kristoffer, and Jeffrey Dunn. 2014. "A Defence of Epistemic Consequentialism." *Philosophical Quarterly* 64 (257): 541–551. https://doi.org/10.1093/pq/pqu034.

Berker, Selim. 2013a. "Epistemic Teleology and the Separateness of Propositions." *Philosophical Review* 122 (3): 337–393. https://doi.org/10.1215/00318108-2087645.

———. 2013b. "The Rejection of Epistemic Consequentialism." *Philosophical Issues* 23 (1): 363–387. https://doi.org/10.1111/phis.12019.

———. 2018. "A Combinatorial Argument against Practical Reasons for Belief." *Analytic Philosophy* 59 (4): 427–470. https://doi.org/10.1111/phib.12140.

———. 2019. "The Explanatory Ambitions of Moral Principles." *Noûs* 53 (4): 904–936. https://doi.org/10.1111/nous.12246.

Bradley, Darren. 2019. "Are There Indefeasible Epistemic Rules?" *Philosophers' Imprint* 19: 1–9.

Clarke, Roger. 2013. "Belief Is Credence One (in Context)." *Philosophers' Imprint* 13: 1–18.

Dancy, Jonathan. 2004. *Ethics Without Principles*. Oxford: Oxford University Press.

———. 2017. "Moral Particularism." In *The Stanford Encyclopedia of Philosophy*, edited by Edward N. Zalta, Winter 2017. Metaphysics Research Lab, Stanford University. https://plato.stanford.edu/archives/win2017/entries/moral-particularism/.

Dreier, James. 1993. "Structures of Normative Theories." *The Monist* 76 (1): 22–40. https://doi.org/10.5840/monist19937616.

———. 2011. "In Defense of Consequentializing." In *Oxford Studies in Normative Ethics, Volume 1*, edited by Mark Timmons. Oxford: Oxford University Press.

Easwaran, Kenny, and Branden Fitelson. 2012. "An 'Evidentialist' Worry about Joyce's Argument for Probabilism." *Dialectica* 66 (3): 425–433. https://doi.org/10.1111/j.1746-8361.2012.01311.x.

Feldman, Fred. 2006. "Actual Utility, the Objection From Impracticality, and the Move to Expected Utility." *Philosophical Studies* 129 (1): 49–79. https://doi.org/10.1007/s11098-005-3021-y.

Foley, Richard. 2009. "Beliefs, Degrees of Belief, and the Lockean Thesis." In *Degrees of Belief*, edited by Franz Huber and Christoph Schmidt-Petri, 37–47. Dordrecht and Heidelberg: Springer.

Hawthorne, James. 2009. "The Lockean Thesis and the Logic of Belief." In *Degrees of Belief*, edited by Franz Huber and Christoph Schmidt-Petri, 49–74. Dordrecht and Heidelberg: Springer.

Hursthouse, Rosalind. 1999. *On Virtue Ethics*. Oxford: Oxford University Press.

Joyce, James M. 1998. "A Nonpragmatic Vindication of Probabilism." *Philosophy of Science* 65 (4): 575–603. https://doi.org/10.1086/392661.

Kagan, Shelly. 1992. "The Structure of Normative Ethics." *Philosophical Perspectives* 6: 223–242. https://doi.org/10.2307/2214246.

Korsgaard, Christine M. 1985. "Kant's Formula of Universal Law." *Pacific Philosophical Quarterly* 66 (1–2): 24–47.

Lance, Mark, and Margaret Little. 2008. "From Particularism to Defeasibility in Ethics." In *Challenging Moral Particularism*, edited by Vojko Strahovnik, Matjaz Potrc, and Mark Norris Lance, 53–74. New York: Routledge.

Little, Margaret, and Mark Lance. 2004. "Defeasibility and the Normative Grasp of Context." *Erkenntnis* 61 (2–3): 435–455. https://doi.org/10.1007/s10670-004-9286-2.

Lord, Errol. 2020. "Suspension of Judgment, Rationality's Competition, and the Reach of the Epistemic." In *The Ethics of Belief and Beyond. Understanding Mental Normativity*, edited by Sebastian Schmidt and Gerhard Ernst, 126–145. Abingdon: Routledge.

McKeever, Sean, and Michael Ridge. 2006. *Principled Ethics: Generalism as a Regulative Ideal*. Oxford: Oxford University Press.

Meacham, Christopher J. G. 2018 "Can All-Accuracy Accounts Justify Evidential Norms?" In *Epistemic Consequentialism*, edited by Kristoffer Ahlstrom-Vij and Jeff Dunn, 149–181. Oxford: Oxford University Press.

Portmore, Douglas W. 2009. "Consequentializing." *Philosophy Compass* 4 (2): 329–347. https://doi.org/10.1111/j.1747-9991.2009.00198.x.

Raven, Michael J. 2015. "Ground." *Philosophy Compass* 10 (5): 322–333. https://doi.org/10.1111/phc3.12220.

Shah, Nishi. 2006. "A New Argument for Evidentialism." *Philosophical Quarterly* 56 (225): 481–498. https://doi.org/10.1111/j.1467-9213.2006.454.x.

Shah, Nishi, and J. David Velleman. 2005. "Doxastic Deliberation." *Philosophical Review* 114 (4): 497–534. https://doi.org/10.1215/00318108-114-4-497.

Sharadin, Nathaniel. 2020. "Kristoffer Ahlstrom-Vij and Jeffrey Dunn (Eds.), Epistemic Consequentialism (Oxford: Oxford University Press, 2018), Pp. 352. $77.00." *Utilitas* 32 (2): 256–260. https://doi.org/10.1017/s0953820819000505.

Singer, Daniel. 2021. "Right Belief." Unpublished manuscript.

Singer, Daniel J. 2018. "How to Be an Epistemic Consequentialist." *Philosophical Quarterly* 68 (272): 580–602. https://doi.org/10.1093/pq/pqx056.

Singer, Daniel J., and Sara Aronowitz. Forthcoming "What Epistemic Reasons Are for: Against the Belief-Sandwich Distinction." In *Meaning, Decision, and Norms: Themes from the Work of Allan Gibbard*, edited by Billy Dunaway and David Plunkett. Ann Arbor: Michigan Publishing Services.

Sylvan, Kurt. 2016. "Epistemic Reasons I: Normativity." *Philosophy Compass* 11 (7): 364–376.

———. 2019. "Epistemic Consequentialism and Its Aftermath." *Analysis* 79 (4): 773–783. https://doi.org/10.1093/analys/anz073.

Sylvan, Kurt L. 2018. "Reliabilism without Epistemic Consequentialism." *Philosophy and Phenomenological Research* 3: 525–555. https://doi.org/10.1111/phpr.12560.

———. 2020. "An Epistemic Non-Consequentialism." *The Philosophical Review* 129 (1): 1–51. https://doi.org/10.1215/00318108-7890455.

Väyrynen, Pekka. 2006. "Ethical Theories and Moral Guidance." *Utilitas* 18 (3): 291–309. https://doi.org/10.1017/s0953820806002056.

———. 2009. "A Theory of Hedged Moral Principles." *Oxford Studies in Metaethics* 4: 91–132.

———. 2014. "Shapelessness in Context." *Noûs* 48 (3): 573–593. https://doi.org/10.1111/j.1468-0068.2012.00877.x.

4 Epistemic Correctness and the Minimal Functional Criterion

4.1 Introduction

In the last chapter, I laid out an approach to thinking about first-order theorizing about epistemic correctness. But given what I have said about the plethora of different kinds of correctness there are, and the fact that all are on a par with respect to being kinds of correctness, you might fairly be wondering: Which kind of correctness is the kind of correctness that is *epistemic* correctness? In this chapter, I aim to answer that question.

4.2 The Question

To see how pressing the question is, recall our model for thinking about first-order epistemic theorizing: first-order epistemic theory is an attempt to specify the explanatory grounds of epistemic correctness.

For instance, evidentialists say:

> Evidentialism: The fact that it is epistemically correct for A to φ is grounded by the fact that φ-ing fits A's evidence.

And coherentists, in their turn, tell us:

> Coherentism: The fact that it is epistemically correct for A to φ is grounded by the fact that φ-ing coheres with A's other doxastic attitudes.

Epistemic virtue theorists arrive on the scene:

> Epistemic Neo-Aristotelianism: The fact that it is epistemically correct for A to φ is grounded by the fact that φ-ing manifests an intellectual excellence.

And so on, for a whole host of familiar first-order epistemic theories. Do not sweat the details of these views. What's crucial correct now is the fact

DOI: 10.4324/9781003096726-4

that, given what I said in Chapter 2 about the existence of maximally different kinds of correctness, it is possible to think that, despite appearances, first-order epistemic theories of this sort do not, in fact, share a single subject matter, namely, epistemic correctness. And so, despite initial appearances, *they do not disagree over anything*.

In other words, it is perfectly intelligible to understand each of these three views as articulating the explanatory grounds of some particular, but not the same, kind of correctness. It is trivial: just swap in "epistemically correct" for some unique term referring to a unique kind of correctness. And so we have the following:

> Evidentialist Correctness: The fact that it is evidentially correct for A to φ is grounded by the fact that φ-ing fits A's evidence.
>
> Coherentist Correctness: The fact that it is coherently correct for A to φ is grounded by the fact that φ-ing coheres with A's other doxastic attitudes.
>
> Epistemic Neo-Aristotelian Correctness: The fact that it is neo-Aristotelian correct for A to φ is grounded by the fact that φ-ing manifests an intellectual excellence.

This is clearly *not* what first-order epistemic theories take themselves to be doing when they are in the business of articulating their theories. Decisive evidence of this fact is that the proponents of the views *take themselves to be in disagreement*. What they take themselves to be in disagreement over, I assume, is the correct account of *epistemic correctness*.

What people take to be the case is not always decisive for what we should think is actually the case. That is true even when we are talking about people who at least seem to be experts in their field. The correct way to treat culinary experts who take themselves to be disagreeing over whether hummus requires cumin[1] is as talking about two different things: hummus-with-cumin and hummus-without-cumin. And you can probably get them to agree on this fact, if they are reasonable. The same is sometimes also true in philosophy. For example, it is not clear that it makes sense to have a knock-down fight over what counts as *the* causal relation, or *the* grounding relation.[2]

But this divide-and-conquer approach is an appetizing solution only in some cases. It would not only be extremely difficult to get epistemologists to agree on such a reconciliation; it would also probably be a mistake to try and do so. In the case of epistemic correctness, we are not interested in having a variety of recipes: what we want is to know the ingredients for epistemic correctness – not for evidentialist-epistemic-correctness and for coherentist-evidentialist-correctness and so on.

Maybe you think, despite our interest, this really *is* a mistake. So while it might be true that, as a matter of fact, we are interested in knowing the ingredients for epistemic correctness, rather than generating a variety of recipes for different kinds of correctness, we *shouldn't* be so interested. We should simply be *pluralists* about the relevant notion, in much the same way as some have argued that we should be pluralists about, for example, the notion of grounding.

I have two replies, neither of which are going to be all that convincing to someone who is strongly attracted to this line of thought. But I will give them anyway. The first reply has two steps. The first step can be summarized in the slogan *mattering motivates monism*. Here's the idea: when and to the extent that a kind of correctness appears to be deeply important, or to *matter* to us, the pluralist approach to that kind of correctness will be less appealing, less plausible. For, insofar as we appear to care about being k-ly correct, we shall *really* want to know what being k-ly correct comprises – not what being k_1-ly correct comprises, and what k_2-ly correct comprises, etc. This does not mean pluralism about k-correctness is somehow impossible under circumstances where we appear to care about k-correctness, just that it won't be very attractive.

The second step, then, is to point out that *epistemic correctness* appears to be deeply important or to matter to us in exactly this way. I have a lot more to say about this later on, but right now, just notice that, much of the time, we really care about whether we ourselves or other agents are doing what is epistemically correct. I want to believe what's epistemically correct, I want my interlocutors to be largely epistemically correct about matters of mutual concern, and so on.

Putting these together, the fact that epistemic correctness matters (so much) to us motivates monism about epistemic correctness. This does not mean pluralism about epistemic correctness is somehow impossible, just that it won't be very attractive.

My second reply, which will be even *less* convincing to the pluralist, is to gesture, again, at our actual practice of theorizing about epistemic correctness, which does *not* appear to be a practice compatible with a thousand-flowers attitude toward the subject matter. It is not as if the evidentialist makes peace with the epistemic consequentialist, who, in turn, makes peace with the epistemic Kantian. The committed pluralist, of course, will remain unimpressed, for their view is that this war is unjust, based as it is on false pretenses. There are deep methodological issues lurking in the background here. I do not have anything novel to say about those issues, nor is this the place, if I did, to say it. Going forward, I'm going to assume we are interested in theorizing about a single notion, namely, epistemic correctness, rather than a multitude of notions.

That does not mean I'm dodging all responsibility for saying more about what precisely this notion is supposed to be. Quite the contrary. This idea, that we are interested in a single notion of *epistemic* correctness and that this single notion of *epistemic* correctness is something first-order *epistemic* theories disagree over (as compared to simply offering culinary tweaks on it), presupposes some pre-theoretical independent notion of what kind of correctness *epistemic* correctness is, as compared with other kinds of correctness. Hence, our present question: Which kind of correctness is the kind of correctness that is epistemic correctness?

In fact, the question is even more pressing than I just made it appear. After all, as I have said, we all presumably agree that various familiar first-order epistemic theories such as evidentialism and coherentism are not talking past one another: they are attempting to talk about the same thing, namely, epistemic correctness. And maybe you think it is pretty obvious that, despite their disagreements on the grubby details, they are in pretty wide agreement over what kind of thing epistemic correctness is, as compared with other kinds of correctness. And so maybe we do not need to worry, all that much, about saying anything about the kind of correctness epistemic correctness is. Not so fast. Here is a view:

> Tuesdayism: The fact that it is epistemically correct for A to φ is grounded by the fact that A's φ-ing is done on a Tuesday.

What should we say about tuesdayism as a first-order epistemic theory? One thing we might want to say is that tuesdayism is a *very bad* first-order epistemic theory. Maybe that is correct – as we will see, I do think we should say that tuesdayism considered as a first-order epistemic theory is very bad indeed. But whatever you think of the relative merits of (say) evidentialism and reliabilism, there is a sense in which those two theories appear to be, as we might put it, *in the running* as accounts of what epistemic correctness comprises, whereas tuesdayism does not appear to be in the running. Proponents of tuesdayism seem to have tried to change the subject. It is mashed peas with mint and lemon being sold as "spring hummus": culinary (epistemic) fraud. So, it seems perfectly fine to take the rhetorical tack with tuesdayism that I said, above, we should *not* take with respect to our familiar first-order epistemic theories; we should reframe it as something like:

> Tuesdayical Correctness: The fact that it is *tuesdayically correct* for A to φ is grounded by the fact that A's φ-ing is done on a Tuesday.

But again, why is this? Why is it obvious that tuesdayism is *not*, and evidentialism and coherentism *are* in the running to be accounts of epistemic correctness? Put otherwise, what makes evidentialism and coherentism count, and tuesdayism *not* count, as competing accounts of the standard of epistemic correctness?

This is an instance of a more general question about distinguishing kinds of correctness from one another. It has nothing to do, in particular, with the idea that what we are talking about here is *epistemic* correctness. To see this, set aside epistemic correctness for the moment and focus, instead, on etiquette.

Epistemic Correctness and the Minimal Functional Criterion 53

Suppose you, our recent acquaintance Tom, and I are wondering how to treat our server at a restaurant. I propose that the polite thing to do is to avoid eye contact, rarely ask for drink refills, and to tip generously. You propose engaging them in lively conversation, waving them down for more bread, and, thankfully, tipping generously. Tom suggests asking them to do long division on napkins, measuring their hair with the breadsticks, and helping them with their taxes.

What's going on here? The intuitive thing to say is that you and I are engaged in a substantive, though perhaps not all that important or trenchant, disagreement over the standards of polite patron behavior – over what it would be etiquettically correct to do –whereas Tom is, well, it is a bit difficult to say what Tom is doing. Tom appears to be having a different conversation entirely. His proposal does not even appear to count as a proposal for the standard of *etiquettical* correctness; whatever he is proposing appears to be a *non-etiquettical* standard.

But if that is correct, and it certainly seems like the intuitively correct thing to say about the case, then there must be a single subject matter on which you and I both mean to be disagreeing and about which we think Tom is not even talking. And the same is true in the epistemic case. There appears to be some single subject matter about which our familiar first-order epistemic theories are all trying to talk and about which tuesdayism is probably not even trying to speak (and if counterintuitively it is, it is doing a *terrible* job).

The single subject matter of first-order epistemic theory is epistemic correctness. But our first-order epistemic theories tell us what epistemic correctness comprises. And there are in principle infinitely many ways of articulating various such first-order epistemic theories. So how do we pick OUT this single subject matter prior to accepting a first-order epistemic theory?

4.3 Earmarks of the Epistemic

Our situation is unstable. There is a single subject matter we want all to be talking about in our first-order epistemic theorizing, namely, epistemic correctness. This is on pain of talking past one another. But what we end up saying about that subject matter in our first-order epistemic theorizing will determine, in large part, what it is correct to say about it.

This is a problem familiar in a range of disputes. It arises whenever we have some phenomena or concept we all intuitively agree exists about which we want some theoretical account and concerning which there might be disagreement. Take away any one of these features, and it becomes rather easier to put one's finger on the relevant explanandum. Happily, we know what to do in such cases. What we need to do is identify the earmarks of the relevant phenomena to be explained and then treat accounts as (more or less adequate) theories of the phenomena insofar as they (more or less adequately) capture those earmarks.

For instance, that is what we do when we want to distinguish, say, *intentional* from *nonintentional* actions. We all intuitively agree there exists some distinction here about which we want some theory and concerning which there will probably be disagreement; in particular, which things end up counting as intentional actions will depend, largely, on the account we end up accepting about the nature of intention. So what we do is identify the earmarks of intentional action – for instance, that intentional actions are done wittingly – and treat accounts as (more or less adequate) theories of intentional action (as opposed to theories of *something else*) insofar as they (more or less adequately) capture those earmarks.

So, too, in the present case. What we want to do is to identify, pretheoretically, some features that characterize the difference between standards that are plausibly epistemic from those that are intuitively nowhere in the neighborhood of the epistemic. Those are the earmarks of the distinction we are after. In the next section, I consider two natural but ultimately mistaken sets of earmarks of the epistemic: object- and content-based earmarks. Given the failure of these earmarks to adequately pick out the phenomena we are interested in, I offer an alternative: a function-based earmark. We can neither pick out an epistemic evaluation from a non-epistemic evaluation in terms of epistemic evaluation's special objects of evaluation nor can we pick it out in terms of some special content of epistemic as compared to non-epistemic evaluations. Instead, we pick out evaluation in terms of epistemic correctness from evaluation in terms of different kinds of non-epistemic correctness in terms of the functional role of the former kinds of evaluation. More on this later; first, the two blind alleys: object- and content-based earmarks.

4.4 Blind Alleys

There are a couple promising, but ultimately blind, alleys when it comes to answering our question. I quickly canvass them here, since their failures are instructive. Later on, I explain how the view I favor can capture the insights of these views.

4.4.1 Object-Based Earmarks

One idea might be that the earmarks of the epistemic are object-based. The idea would be that we can pick out epistemic correctness as compared to other kinds of correctness prior to accepting a first-order epistemic theory by picking out a class of distinctive objects to which *epistemic* correctness attaches, that is, by picking out the distinctive *bearers* of epistemic correctness. I will call this the *simple object-based* approach. The basic strategy, briefly, is to look for some kind of unity in

Epistemic Correctness and the Minimal Functional Criterion 55

the potential objects of thought and talk in terms of epistemic correctness, as represented by our familiar first-order epistemic theories. The hope, then, is that we can appeal to that unity – the proposed earmark – in distinguishing competing accounts of *epistemic* correctness from accounts of other kinds of correctness.

Here is an example of how this might go. Take the familiar first-order epistemic theories of evidentialism, reliabilism, and coherentism. Each of these views thinks that the potential bearers of epistemic correctness – the φ-ings that as a matter of fact can be epistemically correct – are, roughly speaking, an agent's doxastic attitudes. After all, it is agents' doxastic attitudes that can fit the evidence or be formed by reliable mechanisms or cohere with agents' other doxastic attitudes. So (the thought goes) *that* is what makes these views count as potential accounts of *epistemic* correctness (as opposed to a different sort of correctness): it is because they each offer views according to which the potential bearers of epistemic correctness are restricted to agents' doxastic attitudes. And that in turn (the thought continues) is what explains why the absurd tuesdayism is ruled out of court; for, tuesdayism allows any sort of φ-ing you like – well, any sort that can happen on a Tuesday – to potentially be epistemically correct. It therefore does not exhibit the requisite unity in the potential bearers of epistemic correctness, and it is therefore not even a *competitor* account of epistemic correctness.

There are three related problems with the simple object-based approach. The first is that it simply pushes the problem back. Now we shall want an account of what the nature of the relevant kind of objects is such that these objects count as the distinctive potential objects of, for example, *epistemic* standards. It is quite plausible that agents' doxastic attitudes can be epistemically correct. And it is much less plausible that agents' hair color can be epistemically correct (rather than correct in some other way). But since the distinction between the epistemic and the non-epistemic is precisely what is currently at issue, we cannot simply appeal to what is intuitively plausible without begging the question. And if we are only adverting to our intuitive sense of the epistemic flavor of things, then we have not made any progress.

In any case, the second problem: my example of doxastic attitudes was carefully chosen to make it seem like there might be some wide agreement over what unifies the potential bearers of epistemic correctness. But as a matter of fact, there is no such agreement among what could plausibly be thought of as potential first-order epistemic theories. This point is related to a point we saw earlier in our discussion of the ambit of epistemic correctness (Section 3.5).

Recall from that discussion that epistemic *consequentialists* think that a host of different kinds of φ-ings that are not doxastic attitudes might be the bearers of epistemic correctness. This is because a host of different φ-ings that are not doxastic attitudes might be φ-ings that produce the best epistemic consequences. Maybe *getting a good night's sleep* is what would be epistemically correct in such-and-such circumstances, or perhaps it is *climbing a telephone pole*. The point, as we saw in that discussion, is that the potential bearers of epistemic correctness will *depend on one's choice of first-order epistemic theory*. But that means it is not an earmark of the distinction – that is, something to which we can appeal *pre-theoretically*. So, it cannot do the work required.

Maybe you think this is unfair. After all, it only seems to be epistemic consequentialists who are so liberal with their understanding of the ambit of the epistemic. And epistemic consequentialism is both a relatively recent arrival on the scene and has a *lot* of critics.[3] So, maybe it does not make sense to appeal to epistemic consequentialism to point out the impossibility of settling on its application to doxastic attitudes as the earmarks of the epistemic. Two points in reply. First, it is not only the recently arrived epistemic consequentialists who are so liberal with their understanding of the ambit of the epistemic. So-called virtue epistemologists do not think it is only agents' doxastic attitudes that can be evaluated as epistemically correct or incorrect. Instead, virtue epistemologists think that, for example, *intellectual competencies* or *agential dispositions* can also be epistemically correct or incorrect (Zagzebski 1996; Sosa 2007). But while those competencies are obviously *related* to doxastic attitudes, they are not identical, and so whatever unity is supposed to be exhibited by the potential objects of epistemic evaluation, it cannot be the unity exhibited by all and only, for example, doxastic attitudes, as the proposal had it. Second, it's neither here nor there whether epistemic consequentialism is a recent arrival; it's clearly a competing view about what explanatorily grounds *epistemic* correctness, as compared to some other kind of correctness.

It's possible to continue to resist in the following way: we are after *earmarks* of the epistemic (you would say), not *necessary and sufficient conditions*. Everyone – epistemic consequentialists, virtue epistemologists, evidentialists, coherentists, reliabilists, *everyone* – agrees that doxastic attitudes have something to do with it – they are either the primary direct object of evaluation in terms of epistemic correctness or a (normal) product of whatever is so evaluated and so on. So (the resistant thought continues), *sure*, it's true that some of these first-order epistemic theories aren't *always primarily* or *directly* concerned with doxastic attitudes – it's not, as it were, a necessary and sufficient condition for counting as epistemic that you so concern yourself – but concern with doxastic attitudes is nevertheless an earmark of the epistemic. The simple object-based approach is *fine*.

This runs headlong into the third problem. The third problem is that, for any proposed object or set of objects that is supposed to be the distinctive object or set of objects of evaluation in terms of epistemic correctness it is trivial to generate a standard of correctness that has only these objects as its potential bearers and still fails to qualify as plausibly an account of *epistemic* as compared to some other kind of correctness. For instance, setting aside the point we just discussed, that there is not in fact agreement on doxastic attitudes as the only possible (or even the primary) bearers of epistemic correctness, suppose we say that *applying to doxastic attitudes* is the mark of epistemic as compared to non-epistemic correctness. Consider the standard:

> Tuesday Evidentialism: The fact that A's φ-ing is epistemically correct is grounded in the fact that A's φ-ing is done on a Tuesday *and* the fact that A's φ-ing fits A's evidence.

You see the problem. It does no good to complain that this standard of correctness is arbitrary or contrived or *ad hoc*. In one sense, *all standards of correctness are arbitrary and contrived*. And anyway, the *ad hoc*-ness presumably means it's a bad *qua* account of epistemic correctness, but the judgment we are after is that it's *not an account of epistemic correctness*. The simple object-based approach will not do.

You might think the problems with the simple object-based approach to the earmarks of the epistemic arise not because it is object-based but because it is *simple*. Perhaps it is not whether an object or set of objects simply *can* be the bearer of epistemic correctness according to some first-order theories but instead whether an object or set of objects are the *typical* bearers of epistemic correctness according to some first-order theories. The basic strategy, then, would be to look for distinctive unity not in what *can* be the potential bearers of correctness according to a range of first-order epistemic theories but in what are *typically* the bearers of epistemic correctness in those theories. Perhaps the *typical* bearers of epistemic correctness are an earmark of the epistemic. I will call this the typical-object-based approach. Unfortunately, it should be clear that the typical-object-based approach faces exactly the same problems as the simple object-based approach. First, it begs the question, because it assumes we know what *typically* bears epistemic correctness. Second, if there is disagreement over how to think about what *can* be epistemically correct, then there is just as much disagreement over how to think about what *typically* is epistemically correct. And finally, it is trivial to generate bizarre alternatives that *typically* apply to certain objects.

One last gasp for the object-based approach to the earmarks of the epistemic. Perhaps we should not look for our earmarks in a unity exhibited by the *possible* or even by the *typical* bearers of epistemic correctness but instead in the *proper* objects of epistemic evaluation, in what *properly* can be said to be epistemically correct. This *proper-object-based* approach is hopeless. The idea that one object or another is or is not the *proper* object of evaluation in terms of epistemic correctness is not something that can be assumed in the present context, pre-theoretically. So, it is entirely unsuitable for serving as an earmark of the epistemic. For what

58 Epistemic Correctness and the Minimal Functional Criterion

is at issue is precisely what counts as *epistemic* as opposed to *non-epistemic* thought and talk. It does no good to add, but among the *possible* bearers of epistemic correctness, these are the *proper* bearers thereof. Maybe that is true – but it is what is at issue.

4.4.2 Content-Based Earmarks

A second idea would be to identify by the earmarks of the epistemic by focusing on the *content* of the relevant standards of correctness rather than on the nature of the objects to which they apply. I will call this the *content-based* approach. In the present case, the content-based approach would say that evidentialism and coherentism count as views about epistemic correctness, whereas tuesdayism does not, because of something distinctive about the content of each of these standards. The idea, then, would be that what makes a particular standard a competitor for being an account of *epistemic* correctness is something distinctively epistemic about the properties that comprise it. Epistemic standards, for instance, might include things about a φ-ing's *evidential support*, or about a φ-ing's *coherence with other doxastic attitudes* – recognizably epistemic properties, these! But epistemic standards will definitely *not* include things about the times or weekdays on which φ-ings happen. Hence, evidentialism and coherentism are plausibly, whereas tuesdayism is not plausibly, views about epistemic correctness.

The problem with the content-based approach is that, like the object-based approach, it clearly runs in place. We began with a question about what pre-theoretically distinguishes accounts of epistemic correctness from accounts of some other kind of correctness: What are the earmarks of the epistemic? The content-based approach answers: the earmark of an epistemic as compared to a non-epistemic standard is having a certain content. Epistemic standards include some, and exclude other, properties. Fair enough, but which properties? Answer: properties such as fitting the evidence, cohering with one's other doxastic attitudes, and their ilk. But this does not help! For now we shall simply want to know what unifies *those properties*. The answer, of course, is that these properties are the intuitively relevant *epistemic* properties. But now we have turned in a *very* small circle.

You might think this dismissal of the content-based approach is too quick. Perhaps we already have or can arrive at some independent grip on what counts as epistemic properties without a prior grip on what counts as an account of epistemic correctness. Unfortunately, I do not think we do or can. Switch domains for a moment. Suppose we are after the earmarks of *moral* as compared to *nonmoral* standards. Take the moral standards:

> No Mere Means: The fact that A's φ-ing is morally correct is grounded in the fact that A's φ-ing does not treat anyone as a mere means.

Epistemic Correctness and the Minimal Functional Criterion 59

Maximize Expected Utility: The fact that A's φ-ing is morally correct is grounded in the fact that A's φ-ing maximizes expected utility.

Tuesday: The fact that A's φ-ing is morally correct is grounded in the fact that A's φ-ing happens on a Tuesday.

Intuitively, No Mere Means and Maximize Expected Utility are in the running to count as views about what is morally correct, whereas Tuesday is not. According to the content-based approach, this is because No Mere Means and Maximize Expected Utility comprise moral properties, namely, treating people as means and maximizing expected utility, respectively, whereas Tuesday does not. The idea is presumably that there is nothing morally interesting *per se* about the property of happening on a Tuesday, but there *is* (or at least might be) something morally interesting *per se* about the properties of (not) maximizing utility and (not) treating people as mere means. Or anyway, so the idea goes.

Unfortunately, but predictably, this intuition obscures the fact that between proponents of No Mere Means and Maximize Expected Utility there is disagreement over whether the properties that comprise their competitors' standard *are* in fact morally interesting *per se*. It is precisely because each accepts a particular first-order moral theory according to which their own preferred standard is the correct substantive account of what morality requires, i.e., the content of the moral standard of correctness, that each will look askance at any suggestion that the properties that comprise their competitors' standards are morally relevant *per se*. Imagine telling a committed proponent of Maximize Expected Utility that some action did not treat anyone as a mere means; anyone who has had conversations with committed act-utilitarians knows how that goes: their reply is the verbal equivalent of a shrug.

The point here is that shrugging is completely aboveboard. There is substantive disagreement between moral philosophers over what properties are the moral properties. So we cannot use the inclusion of some such properties in some particular standard to leverage our way into a view about which standards count as moral. It is a roundabout way of saying that the moral is the earmark of the moral. In one sense, I agree; but in a much more important and in the present context quite salient sense, it does not help to say this.

The same goes for the epistemic side of things. Evidentialists and reliabilists (say) substantively disagree over which properties are epistemic: the former thinks fit with the evidence is an epistemic property, and the latter disagrees. But we have been imagining that there is *agreement* between the two that each is proposing something that is at least in the running to count as an epistemic standard, whereas the proponent of Tuesday is proposing something that is not in the running. And what we are after is some articulation of the earmarks of the epistemic such that this agreement makes sense. It should be clear why we cannot leverage evidentialist and reliabilist's *disagreement* over which properties count as epistemic into an explanation for their apparent *agreement* over which standards count as epistemic. Being epistemic is certainly the best earmark of being epistemic. But if that is the most we can say, we are in trouble.

4.5 Functional Earmarks and the Minimal Functional Criterion

We can't identify the earmarks of the epistemic in terms of a distinctive unity possessed by the objects of epistemic evaluation, and we can't do it in terms of a distinctive unity possessed by the content of epistemic evaluations. What to do?

We could grind away and try to make one of these approaches work. But I do not think there is any way to make any version of the object- or the content-based approaches work. I have tried to explain what I think are the specific problems with each approach. But we can also diagnose the problem in more general terms. The strategy deployed by both approaches is to try to find something that unifies competing accounts of epistemic correctness in the details of the relevant first-order epistemic theories themselves. But given the actual diversity amongst first-order epistemic theories and the looming possibility of generating a basically infinite number of obviously ineligible but nevertheless bona fide competing first-order theories, this strategy is never going to work.

The problem, in short, is that we were trying to look directly at the concept – EPISTEMIC CORRECTNESS – to identify its earmarks. But there is pervasive disagreement over what the concept looks like. So we cannot do that. Remember, I have argued that the shape of kinds of correctness is, like the shape of musical genres, conventionally determined. Imagine there was pervasive disagreement over the boundaries of some musical genre. Then, it would be useless to try and identify the earmarks of that genre by looking directly at it. One party would say that saxophones are the distinctive instrument; another, trombones. Worse: we could pretty well imagine misfit genres that fit the bill.

So how can we make progress? Continuing the metaphor: we want to know what the outline of epistemic correctness looks like – what its *shape* is so that we can compare various ways of filling in the details – that is, various first-order epistemic theories. I propose the way to do that is to look at what *surrounds* epistemic correctness – to look at the role epistemic correctness plays in our evaluative thought and talk.

Dropping the metaphor, what I think is that we should look to the *functional role* of epistemic correctness in order to identify the single subject matter about which first-order epistemic theories all mean to be speaking and over which they substantively disagree. What do I mean by the functional role of epistemic correctness?

Epistemic Correctness and the Minimal Functional Criterion 61

Notice that we do not just go about saying that some things are epistemically correct and others epistemically incorrect, we put these judgments about epistemic correctness and incorrectness to use for us in various ways. Evaluations in terms of epistemic correctness and incorrectness are, as it is sometimes put, *for* something. What, then, are these judgments, and the corresponding concepts they contain, *for*?

I do not have any novel proposal here. Instead, I will adapt a view due to Edward Craig (1990). According to Craig, the point, purpose, role, or function of epistemic evaluative concepts is to *flag reliable informants*. Here's Craig's idea. We – that is, we humans – face a practical problem; there is something that we need. In the first place, what we need is information about our environment. We need that information so that we can successfully pursue what we want. But here's the thing: we can't get all of the information we need on our own – the information space is just too big. So, we need also a way of identifying people who have the relevant information. That, in effect, is what our epistemic evaluative concepts are for: they are for flagging people who (reliably) have the relevant information that we need, and that we cannot, given our limited capacities, be expected to gather on our own (McKenna 2013; Hannon 2019; Kusch and McKenna, n.d.).

The idea, then, is that epistemic evaluative concepts have a particular job to do, and having that job to do is part of what shapes those concepts as the distinctively epistemic concepts they are, since that is why they have come to exist. It is, in the terms I have been putting things, the *earmark* of the epistemic that *epistemic* (rather than some other kind of) correctness plays this particular role in our evaluative thought and talk, namely, the role of enabling us to flag reliable sources of information in our environment.

Now, Craig himself is primarily focused on the epistemic evaluative concept of KNOWLEDGE, rather than EPISTEMICALLY CORRECT. But there is nothing about the genealogical story just told that should encourage us to restrict our attention to the function, purpose, or point of only the epistemic evaluative concept KNOWLEDGE rather than also the concept EPISTEMICALLY CORRECT – or, for that matter, the concepts of EPISTEMIC JUSTIFICATION and EPISTEMICALLY TRUSTWORTHY or … any other distinctively *epistemic* evaluative concept.

Instead, it makes sense to consider the *entire* domain of epistemic evaluative thought and talk and ask ourselves: Why do we go in for *this distinctive* kind of, namely, epistemic evaluative thought and talk? In a related context, Simon Blackburn identifies this as the mark of what he calls a *pragmatist* approach to an area of discourse:

> You will be a pragmatist about an area of discourse if you pose a … question: how does it come about that we go in for this kind of discourse and thought? What is the explanation of this bit of our

> language game? ... [T]he explanation proceeds by talking in different terms of what is done by so talking. It offers a revelatory genealogy or anthropology or even a just-so story about how this mode of talking and thinking and practising might come about, *given in terms of the functions it serves.*
>
> (Blackburn 2013, p. 75, emphasis added)

The revelatory Craigean genealogy, which I'm hereby adapting, is that *this* mode of thinking and talking and practicing has come about because we require a way of flagging reliable sources of information in a complex world where we are cognitively limited in our capacity to learn the things we need to learn about our environments – that is the function it serves. We, in Blackburn's language, *go in* for epistemic evaluative thought and talk because we need a way of flagging reliable sources of information in our environment. Doing the work of flagging reliable informants is, as I put it earlier, the earmark of the epistemic.

This idea, that the epistemic evaluative concepts we have serve a distinctive function in our evaluative thought and talk and that this function is to flag reliable informants, is extremely widely accepted among a range of philosophers with diverse commitments (Neta 2006; Greco 2007; Fricker 2008; Kusch 2009; MacFarlane 2014; Williams 2015). Of course, the Craigean approach has its critics. But that is because Craig himself and some of his more committed followers (e.g., Hannon 2019) go *much further* than the extremely uncontroversial idea that we have epistemic evaluative concepts in part because they *do something* for us. That uncontroversial idea is the genealogy referred to earlier, which I'm busy suggesting we should accept.

The more committed pragmatist – and in the present case, Craig himself – does not stop there. Instead, Craig goes further in two ways. First, he thinks of flagging reliable informants as *the* or at least *the primary* functional role of epistemic evaluative concepts such as KNOWLEDGE and EPISTEMICALLY CORRECT. I am not suggesting we accept anything like that here. It may be that epistemic evaluation is used for a variety of different purposes and that while some of these matter more, it may not be that any one role is "primary" in some to be specified sense. It just will not matter for the uses to which we are putting the idea that epistemic evaluative thought and talk is *for* flagging reliable informants that it is *only* for doing this.

Second, and more important, Craigeans do not just want us to accept what I have said should be a relatively uncontroversial idea about the function role, purpose, or point of epistemic evaluative thought and talk. They also want us to make a methodological turn toward "function-first" epistemology (Craig 1990; Hannon 2019). Function-first epistemology is an approach to epistemology that treats an investigation into the functional role, purpose, or point of epistemic evaluation as the primary methodology for investigating the nature of our epistemic evaluative concepts (such as KNOWLEDGE, EPISTEMICALLY CORRECT, etc.).

This is, in fact, what Blackburn's pragmatist goes in for, too. The pragmatist, of whom Craig is one, goes on to offer an *account* of the particular concepts involved in this "bit of our language game" in terms of which concepts are well- (perhaps best-)suited to doing the job for which we have them. That is what Craig does in the case of the concept KNOWLEDGE. The idea, then, is that we can come to learn precisely what KNOWLEDGE *is* by identifying what KNOWLEDGE is *for*. This so-called function-first epistemology is, unlike the idea that epistemic evaluative concepts, in fact, have a functional role, extremely controversial. And you can I hope easily see why that is. It's one thing to say that the concept of EPISTEMICALLY CORRECT or the concept KNOWLEDGE are concepts we have because in part those concepts do a particular job for us; it's another thing entirely to say that the only way to come to learn about the specific nature of those concepts is by investigating that job.

I should say that I am extremely sympathetic to this methodological approach. I am inclined to think it is correct. But here, I am not signing up for it. Defending a function-first approach to epistemology is a book-length job in itself. I am not signing up for it because we do not need the complete function-first methodology here. Remember, our turn toward function was motivated by trying to get a fix on the *shape* of the epistemic without saying anything controversial about the substantive content thereof. But we can do that without committing to the idea that we can *read off* the content from the function. In particular, what the observation about the function of epistemic evaluative concepts such as EPISTEMICALLY CORRECT enables us to do is to distinguish between potential accounts of epistemic correctness – evidentialism, coherentism, and so on – and accounts that are not even plausibly in the running to count as accounts of epistemic correctness – by thinking about the possibility of these accounts playing the role we should all agree that evaluations in terms of epistemic correctness do, in fact, play.

Back to our analogy, suppose we all agree that some musical genre – call it "indie pop" – plays a distinctive functional role in our musical thought and talk. Say that role is the role of flagging *poseurs*. Part of the purpose, point, or role of thinking and speaking in terms of indie pop is to have a way of identifying people in our environment who are affected aesthetes with poorly refined but extravagantly described tastes. We do not need to think that this functional role *determines* the content of indie pop in order to think that playing this functional role sets a minimal criterion of adequacy on what views count as a competing to be the correct account of what indie pop comprises, namely, that the views must be ones such that the genre they identify is at least capable of playing the functional role thought and talk in terms of indie pop actually plays in our musical thought and talk, namely, flagging poseurs. And that is why, if you say that a sound including Bach comprises indie pop, I will say you have changed the conversation, whereas if you say that indie pop in part comprises twee pop, I will disagree but think that at least you are in the neighborhood.

So it goes with accounts of epistemic correctness. Go back to evidentialism, coherentism, and tuesdayism. Our question was why it is that evidentialism and coherentism plausibly are, and tuesdayism is plausibly not, as we put it, *in the running* as a view about epistemic correctness. We are now in a position to answer this question. It is because evidentialism and coherentism offer us accounts of the content of epistemic correctness that, if they are correct, ensure that it is at least possible for epistemic correctness to play the distinctive functional role it does, in fact, play, namely, flagging reliable informants. Not so with tuesdayism.

To explain, whatever you think about the substantive merits of evidentialism as compared with coherentism, it should be clear that these proposals about epistemic correctness are ones in which, if true, they make sense to think of epistemic correctness as playing its distinctive functional role. If it turns out that being epistemically correct is a matter of conforming to the evidence, then given some plausible assumptions about conforming to the evidence and reliability, it makes sense to think thoughts and talk in terms of which things are epistemically correct as playing the role of flagging reliable informants. If it instead turns out that being epistemically correct is a matter of cohering with one's other doxastic attitudes, then given some plausible assumptions about the relationship between coherence and reliability, this, too, enables the thought that the functional role of such thought and talk in terms is to flag reliable informants. Not so, of course, if it turns out that being epistemically correct is a matter of happening on a Tuesday. There are no plausible assumptions about the relationship between happening on a Tuesday and reliability that would enable us to think that thought and talk in terms of epistemic correctness construed as a tuesdayist do play the functional role of flagging reliable informants. Hence, tuesdayism is not even in the running as an account of epistemic correctness.

The functional role of epistemic evaluative thought and talk in flagging reliable informants, in other words, sets a *minimal criterion of adequacy* on any account of the content of epistemic correctness, that is, on first-order epistemic theories, namely, that they must at least be plausibly accounts of a kind of correctness that plays the relevant role. Else, while they might be an account of *one kind of correctness or another* (that is what our maximal pluralism about evaluative kinds entails), they cannot plausibly count as an account of *epistemic correctness*. It will be helpful, later on, to have a name for this minimal criterion of adequacy. Call it the *minimal functional* criterion of adequacy on accounts of epistemic correctness. The minimal functional criterion of adequacy on accounts of epistemic correctness says that in order to qualify as a potential account of *epistemic* correctness, as compared to an account of *some other kind of correctness*, epistemic correctness as conceived by the proposed account must be one that potentially plays the – or at least *a* – distinctive functional role of epistemic correctness, namely, flagging reliable informants.

Our situation with respect to deciding which first-order theories count as competing to be views about epistemic correctness, then, is somewhat like our situation with respect to deciding which things get to compete to be the department's next hire. There are certain things the competitors must be capable of doing; they must be capable of teaching, of serving on various committees, and so on. Some will, we think, be better or worse than others at doing this, and we can disagree over the details of any particular case. But a candidate is only *excluded* from the competition *ex ante* if there is reason to think that candidate is simply incapable of doing what it is the hire is *for*, namely, being an assistant professor or a colleague or whatever it is we all agree the point of new hires actually is. Stephen Miller is a *no good, very bad, probably disastrous* candidate; he *could* do the job, but we can know with almost complete certainty that, like everything else he is done in his life so far, he would do it both badly and without a shred of human empathy. My phone is not a candidate *at all*; although it can stay quiet in faculty meetings, it is not even capable of pretending to be interested in the vice provost's newest initiative.

4.6 Conclusion

I argued that the object- and content-based approaches to identifying the earmarks of the epistemic were hopeless. But a nice feature of the function-based approach to identifying the earmarks of the epistemic is that it can incorporate some of the intuitively plausible claims of both the object- and content-based views. That is because there is often an important relationship between the functional role epistemic standards play in flagging reliable informants and the objects to which they apply or the content that comprises them. One example of each:

Object-based: a standard of correctness that applied *exclusively* to agents' voluntary ear-wigglings is vanishingly unlikely to capture a kind of correctness that is capable of doing what evaluation in terms of *epistemic* correctness is in the business of doing for us. At least, this is true given some overwhelmingly plausible assumptions about the relationship between ear-wiggling and flagging reliable sources of information in our environments. The thought that epistemic correctness cannot exclusively concern itself with ear-wigglings is therefore overwhelmingly plausible. As a result, it's not surprising that we would think that there's a kind of object-based restriction on accounts of epistemic correctness; after all – here is one! But again, this is not *quite* right; the intuitive plausibility of this idea *derives* from the fact that the application to some particular domain of objects might make it unintelligible that the function of thought and talk in terms of epistemic correctness was to flag reliable informants.

Content-based: a standard of correctness that comprised *exclusively* temporal properties (e.g., tuesdayism) is vanishingly unlikely to capture a kind of correctness capable of doing what evaluation in terms of epistemic correctness is in the business of doing for us. At least, this is true given some overwhelmingly plausible assumptions about the relationship between only temporal properties and flagging reliable sources of information in our environments. The thought that epistemic correctness cannot exclusively concern itself with such properties is therefore overwhelmingly plausible. As a result, it's not surprising that we would think there's a kind of content-based restriction on accounts of epistemic correctness; after all – here is one! But as before, this is not *quite* right; instead, the plausibility of the relevant content-based view derives from the fact that such accounts of epistemic correctness make the function of such thought and talk unintelligible.

This fact, that the function-based approach to the earmarks of the epistemic can eat up the insights of the object- and content-based approaches, should not be too surprising. This is true of our functionalist thinking more broadly. If something is in part functionally defined as a thing that has a particular point, purpose, role, or function, then the ability to serve that function can put restrictions on the nature of the objects that can count as a thing of that kind.

Take knives, for instance, and suppose they are, in part, functionally defined as artifacts that are (broadly) for cutting; cutting, in other words, is what knives are *for*. Then, there are clearly some restrictions on what will be eligible, in our knifely thought and talk, for what can count as a knife and what sorts of things can comprise a knife. This here fifty-milliliter puddle of room-temperature water *is not and cannot be a knife*. It is not a *bad* knife; it is a *non-knife*. And this is true even if we do not have some independent material-based view of what makes a knife a knife according to which knives *must not* be made of water. (And we should not have that view – ice knives can *definitely* be knives.) So, too, with epistemic standards of correctness. This here standard of correctness that applies only to agents' hair color is not and cannot be an account of *epistemic* correctness. It is not a bad account of what epistemic correctness comprises; it is an account of a kind of correctness that is not epistemic. This can be true even without our having some independent object-based view of what distinguishes epistemic from non-epistemic standards according to claims that epistemic correctness *must not* apply to agents' hair color. (And we should not have that view if we are, e.g., epistemic consequentialists.)

In the next chapter, I lay out a particular first-order epistemic theory: epistemic instrumentalism. The typical reasons for rejecting epistemic instrumentalism are that it systematically over- and under-generates cases of epistemic correctness. But as I will explain, this is a mistake. The correct reason for rejecting epistemic instrumentalism is that, given what epistemic correctness is *for*, epistemic instrumentalism cannot be an account of it (Chapter 6).

Notes

1 It does *not*.
2 On the former, see, for example, Hall (2004) and Hitchcock (2007). On the latter, see, for example, Wilson (2014, 2016), Cameron (2014), and Fine (2012).
3 Even the recency of epistemic consequentialism is a matter of some dispute. For competing views, see Berker (2013), Sylvan (2018), Goldman (2015), and Berker (2015).

References

Berker, Selim. 2013. "Epistemic Teleology and the Separateness of Propositions." *Philosophical Review* 122 (3): 337–393. https://doi.org/10.1215/00318108-2087645.
———. 2015. "Reply to Goldman: Cutting up the One to Save the Five in Epistemology." *Episteme* 12 (2): 145–153. https://doi.org/10.1017/epi.2015.3.
Blackburn, Simon. 2013. "Pragmatism: All or Some?" In *Expressivism, Pragmatism, and Representationalism*, edited by Huw Price, 67–84. Cambridge: Cambridge University Press.
Cameron, Margaret Anne. 2014. "Is Ground Said-in-Many-Ways?" *Studia Philosophica Estonica* 7 (2): 29. https://doi.org/10.12697/spe.2014.7.2.03.
Craig, Edward. 1990. *Knowledge and the State of Nature: An Essay in Conceptual Synthesis*. Oxford: Oxford University Press.
Fine, Kit. 2012. "Guide to Ground." In *Metaphysical Grounding*, edited by Fabrice Correia and Benjamin Schnieder, 37–80. Cambridge: Cambridge University Press.
Fricker, Miranda. 2008. "Scepticism and the Genealogy of Knowledge: Situating Epistemology in Time." *Philosophical Papers* 37 (1): 27–50. https://doi.org/10.1080/05568640809485213.
Goldman, Alvin I. 2015. "Reliabilism, Veritism, and Epistemic Consequentialism." *Episteme* 12 (2): 131–143. https://doi.org/10.1017/epi.2015.25.
Greco, John. 2007. "The Nature of Ability and the Purpose of Knowledge." *Philosophical Issues* 17 (1): 57–69. https://doi.org/10.1111/j.1533-6077.2007.00122.x.
Hall, Ned. 2004. "Two Concepts of Causation." In *Causation and Counterfactuals*, edited by John Collins, Ned Hall, and Laurie Paul, 225–276. Cambridge, MA: MIT Press.
Hannon, Michael. 2019. *What's the Point of Knowledge?: A Function-First Epistemology*. New York, NY: Oxford University Press.
Hitchcock, Christopher. 2007. "Three Concepts of Causation." *Philosophy Compass* 2 (3): 508–516. https://doi.org/10.1111/j.1747-9991.2007.00084.x.
Kusch, Martin. 2009. "Testimony and the Value of Knowledge." In *Epistemic Value*, edited by Pritchard, Haddock, and Alan Millar, 60–94. Oxford: Oxford University Press.

Kusch, Martin, and Robin McKenna. n.d. "The Genealogical Method in Epistemology." *Synthese* 197 (3): 1057–1076. https://doi.org/10.1007/s11229-018-1675-1.

MacFarlane, John. 2014. *Assessment Sensitivity: Relative Truth and Its Applications*. Oxford: Oxford University Press.

McKenna, Robin. 2013. "'Knowledge' Ascriptions, Social Roles and Semantics." *Episteme* 10 (4): 335–350. https://doi.org/10.1017/epi.2013.30.

Neta, Ram. 2006. "Epistemology Factualized: New Contractarian Foundations for Epistemology." *Synthese* 150 (2): 247–280. https://doi.org/10.1007/s11229-004-6266-7.

Sosa, Ernest. 2007. *A Virtue Epistemology: Volume I: Apt Belief and Reflective Knowledge*. Oxford: Oxford University Press.

Sylvan, Kurt L. 2018. "Reliabilism without Epistemic Consequentialism." *Philosophy and Phenomenological Research* 3: 525–555. https://doi.org/10.1111/phpr.12560.

Williams, Michael. 2015. "What's so Special about Human Knowledge?" *Episteme* 12 (2): 249–268. https://doi.org/10.1017/epi.2015.14.

Wilson, Jessica M. 2014. "No Work for a Theory of Grounding." *Inquiry: An Interdisciplinary Journal of Philosophy* 57 (5–6): 535–579. https://doi.org/10.1080/0020174x.2014.907542.

———. 2016. "The Unity and Priority Arguments for Grounding." In *Scientific Composition and Metaphysical Ground*, edited by Ken Aizawa and Carl Gillett, 171–204. Basingstoke: Palgrave MacMillan.

Zagzebski, Linda Trinkaus. 1996. *Virtues of the Mind: An Inquiry into the Nature of Virtue and the Ethical Foundations of Knowledge*. Cambridge: Cambridge University Press.

5 First-Order Epistemic Instrumentalism

5.1 Introduction

In Chapter 3, I explained how to think about first-order epistemic theories as accounts of the explanatory grounds of epistemic correctness. Such theories accept particular epistemic correctness explanatory principles, or ECEPs, as I have unprettily called them. I have adduced a few familiar examples of such theories in passing – evidentialism, coherentism, and reliabilism among others. In the last chapter, I then explained how to think about the idea that these first-order theories are theories of *epistemic* correctness, as compared to accounts of some other kind of correctness. We needed that account in order to ward off the thought that such views were simply talking past one another – that they were accounts of, for example, evidentialist correctness or reliabilist correctness or whatever.

In this chapter, I lay out a *very unpopular* first-order epistemic theory, namely, epistemic instrumentalism, by articulating that theory's ECEP and then unpacking it a bit. First-order epistemic instrumentalism has a *few* adherents – including myself in previous time slices. As we will see, proponents of the view differ on the details. But I articulate the central claim that instrumentalists are interested in defending. I then explain how that central claim has given rise to a particular problem that is supposed by first-order instrumentalism's opponents to be particularly pressing.

Unfortunately, the structure of this problem is such that it leads, almost inevitably, to theoretical stalemate; everybody takes their toys and goes home. I explain why this happens, and then, in the next chapter, I explain what to do about it. Hint: it will involve (does this metaphor continue to work?) taking instrumentalists' toys away from them. First, let's get the view on the table.

5.2 The Many Epistemic Instrumentalisms

Let's start by getting the intuitive flavor of the view. The best way to do that is to sample some of the extant instances of it. Now, I have mentioned a few times how unpopular first-order epistemic instrumentalism

DOI: 10.4324/9781003096726-5

is. That's not wrong. But it's potentially a *bit* misleading. I don't mean to suggest that *no one* is a first-order epistemic instrumentalist. There are a few. So, we can look at those instances of the view. We can also look at how *opponents* characterize the position.

What can make things a bit challenging is that both adherents and opponents sometimes use different labels for the view. And they *always* put it in idiosyncratic language. But we can still use those articulations of the view to get a general sense of things before narrowing down to one formulation. And doing so will help us refine the central claims of the view. In each case, I translate the relevant author's formulation of the view into our way of speaking, namely, in terms of a theory's ECEP. Doing this will help with the task of identifying the central instrumentalist claim.

Susanna Rinard is a first-order epistemic instrumentalist; she calls the view "Robust Pragmatism" and says that accepting it means accepting that "C is a reason to believe P if and only if C is a pragmatic consideration in favor of believing P" (Rinard 2015, p. 218).[1] Pragmatic considerations in favor of believing, in turn, are "considerations indicating that doing so would benefit oneself (or others)" (Rinard 2015, p. 217). Rinard is tied to the language of reasons, but it's relatively easy to roughly translate into our talk of explanatory grounds (and to take account of the fact that *belief* is not the only relevant target of epistemic reasons):

> Rinardian Instrumentalism: The fact that it is epistemically correct for A to ϕ is grounded by the fact that A's ϕ-ing would benefit A or someone else.

Thomas Kelly is definitely *not* a first-order epistemic instrumentalist. He puts the view in terms of *rationality*: "epistemic rationality is simply instrumental rationality in the service of one's cognitive goals" (Kelly 2003, p. 618). We can translate that too:

> Kellyish Instrumentalism: The fact that it is epistemically correct for A to ϕ is grounded by the fact that A's ϕ-ing would promote A's cognitive goals.

Matthew Lockard has a similar take: "According to epistemic instrumentalism, epistemically rational beliefs are beliefs that are formed, maintained, and revised in ways that are conducive to the attainment of certain ends that one wants to achieve" (Lockard 2013, p. 1702). Translation:

> Lockardean Instrumentalism: The fact that it is epistemically correct for A to ϕ is grounded by the fact that A's ϕ-ing conduces to the attainment of certain ends A wants to achieve.

First-Order Epistemic Instrumentalism 71

Asbjørn Steglich-Petersen is also an epistemic instrumentalist; he does things in terms of *norms*:

> epistemic instrumentalists claim that epistemic norms concern how one should form and regulate one's beliefs if they are to serve an epistemic aim, for example the aim of believing the truth about some subject matter, which may in turn serve other aims of a more practical nature.
>
> (Steglich-Petersen 2018)

Trickier, but roughly:

> Steglich-Petersenesque Instrumentalism: The fact that it is epistemically correct for A to ɸ is grounded by the fact that A's ɸ-ing serves either an epistemic or a practical aim.

In previous time slices, I myself have said that epistemic instrumentalism amounts to the view that "there is a reason to believe in accord with the evidence because doing so is an instrumentally rational way of achieving the ends, goals, or interests one has" (Sharadin 2018b, p. 3792).[2] This is

> Sharadiny Instrumentalism: The fact that it is epistemically correct for A to ɸ is grounded by the fact that A's ɸ-ing is an instrumentally rational way of achieving A's ends, goals, or interests.

That's enough examples. There are many more. But this suffices to give the intuitive flavor of the instrumentalist approach to epistemic correctness. That approach is one that attempts to ground epistemic correctness in some connection, very roughly, to what is *good* for agents: producing benefit (Rinard), promoting cognitive goals (Kelly), conducing to desired ends (Lockard), serving epistemic or practical aims (Steglich-Petersen), or achieving ends, goals, or interests (Sharadin). What all these different formulations have in common is the thought that what explanatorily grounds epistemic correctness is that being epistemically correct – is a way of *promoting one's well-being*.[3] This is what I think of as the *hard core* of first-order epistemic instrumentalism. If it helps, you can think of this idea, that epistemic correctness is grounded in facts about the promotion of agential well-being, as the instrumentalist version of whatever the hard core of, say, *evidentialist* approaches to first-order epistemic theory is. To explain, there are many evidentialisms, each of which gives a slightly different story about what, precisely, is required in order for an agent's ɸ-ing to be epistemically correct. Perhaps it is *fitting* the evidence or *being supported* by the evidence or *conforming* to the evidence, or maybe it is fitting the *not-misleading evidence* or the *available* evidence. And, of course, variants arise out of different conceptions of what *fit* or *support* or *availability*, in turn, comprise. But each is recognizably an *evidentialist* approach putting, as it does, a particular kind of relation to the evidence at the core of their account of the explanatory grounds of epistemic correctness.

So, too, with first-order epistemic instrumentalism. There are variants, and important differences between these variants, but first-order epistemic instrumentalism at its core is a view that accepts

> Epistemic Instrumentalism: The fact that it is epistemically correct for A to φ is grounded by the fact that A's φ-ing promotes A's well-being.

Or anyway, that is the ECEP I will be working with in what follows. Again, there will be in-house fights about whether this is precisely the right way to state things, but my concern with first-order epistemic instrumentalism here, as we will see, does not depend on settling those fights.

5.3 Unpacking Epistemic Instrumentalism's ECEP

First-order epistemic instrumentalism says that epistemic correctness is grounded by facts about what promotes agential well-being. Obviously, then, "promotion" and "well-being" will need to be unpacked by a complete account of epistemic instrumentalism. This is for exactly the same reason that "reliability" must be unpacked by reliabilists, that "evidence" must be unpacked by evidentialists, "competence" or "virtue" by virtue theorists, and so on.

Here, I do not attempt to explain these notions in detail on behalf of epistemic instrumentalism. Instead, I rely mainly on our intuitive understanding of these ideas, although I do say a *bit* more below. My defense of staying at the mainly intuitive level is that, here, my primary concern here is not to argue that epistemic instrumentalism is true, or even all that plausible as a first-order epistemic theory. Quite the contrary. I agree with its opponents that it fails systematically to constitute a plausible view about what, epistemically speaking, it is correct for agents to do. But I disagree over why this is so. And my reasons for thinking that it fails – unlike the traditional reasons given instrumentalism's opponents – do not depend on any precise understanding of promotion and well-being. More on this in a moment. First, a *bit* more about what well-being and promotion are meant to be.

We saw that various epistemic instrumentalists (and the opponents of instrumentalism) appeal to various notions on the right-hand side of the explanatory grounds, that is, in the place where I have put agential well-being. We have, for example, *ends, interests, goals, aims, desires*, and so on. What these have in common is that they are supposed to be things the achievement or satisfaction of which *makes an agent better off*, or *improves their welfare along some dimension*, hence my use of "well-being"; of course, it's quite controversial what the constituents of agential well-being are.[4] Here, we don't need anything too controversial or sophisticated. To repeat, it will not matter to my argument against first-order epistemic instrumentalism what the constituents of agential well-being are supposed to be. To have something to work with, I will assume that *desire-satisfaction* is a component of agential well-being in the following way: if an agent desires P, then *ceteris paribus*, and very roughly, they are better off when P than when not-P. For instance, if you want right now to eat a taco, then *ceteris paribus*, you are better off when you get to eat a taco right now than when you don't get to eat a taco right now.

That "ceteris paribus, and very roughly," clause is doing *a lot* of work; there are plenty of reasons to think that (merely) satisfying (every one of) one's desires (however strong) does not (always) make one (significantly) better off.[5] And there are *even more* reasons to think that desire-satisfaction is not the only (or perhaps even the most significant) component of agential well-being.[6] For that matter, it's proved difficult even to explain *what it is* for a desire that P to be satisfied. But we can ignore *all of that* for present purposes. Again, that's because my aim here is not to argue against epistemic instrumentalism in a way that depends on settling those issues.

What about "promotes"? What does it take to promote an agent's well-being, for example, by promoting the satisfaction of one of their desires? Here, too, there is controversy, although there is somewhat less. The central controversy concerns whether it's possible to understand promotion in exclusively probabilistic terms, so that, again very roughly, ϕ-ing promotes the satisfaction of an agent's desire when ϕ-ing *makes it more likely* that the desire will be satisfied, relative to some baseline. For example, buying a taco promotes the satisfaction of my desire to right now eat a taco just in case (and because) buying the taco makes it more likely that my desire to right now eat a taco will be satisfied than it would be relative to some baseline likelihood that the desire will be satisfied.

In other work, I have argued against such a probabilistic understanding of promotion.[7] My view, developed along with my coauthor, is that accounts of promotion that focus exclusively on probability-raising suffer a range of difficulties, including the difficulty of identifying a suitable baseline (Sharadin 2015a). Most crucially, I think such *purely probabilistic* views miss an important way agents' behaviors might promote their desires while nevertheless failing to increase the probability that those desires are satisfied by, e.g., making the world more closely *fit* with their desires (Sharadin 2015a, 2016). Hence, according to the view I favor, promotion is somewhat more complicated then (mere) probability-raising (Sharadin and Dellsén 2019). But, as with the case of well-being, the complicated details involved here need not concern us. That's because, as before, it will *not* matter to my arguments against first-order epistemic instrumentalism that we have some precise understanding of what "promotion" is meant to be, so long as we share a plausible first-gloss on that notion. The first gloss I propose we accept, for the sake of getting on with things, is the simple probabilistic view I just said I reject for reasons we are not going to get into here, so, as I will understand things, an agent's ϕ-ing *promotes* their well-being just in case (and because) the likelihood that A's well-being improves given that they φ is greater than the likelihood that A's well-being improves given that they do not φ.

This is pretty sketchy, but you hopefully see the basic ideas of agential well-being and promotion and understand, roughly, how to put them together. Suppose Jon desires a job at an investment bank. Then, wearing a suit to his interview promotes his well-being. This is because (well-being) Jon will be better off if he gets the job, given that he desires it, and (promotion) the likelihood that his well-being will improve (in this case, by getting the job) is greater given that he wears the suit than given that he does not wear the suit. Suppose Mary wants to eat this here piece of chocolate. Then, Mary's eating this here piece of chocolate promotes her well-being. This is because (well-being) Mary will be better off if she eats the chocolate, given that desires to eat it, and (promotion) the likelihood that her well-being will improve (in this case, by eating the chocolate) is greater given that she eats the chocolate than given that she does not eat the chocolate and so on.

So much for well-being and promotion. As I have tried to emphasize, my primary concern, here, is not to argue in favor of first-order epistemic instrumentalism. I agree with its opponents that it fails as a first-order epistemic theory. But I think the traditional problem raised for epistemic instrumentalism is largely unconvincing. At best, it results in an unproductive theoretical stalemate between epistemic instrumentalists and their opponents. In part, this is because the traditional problem opponents of epistemic instrumentalism have raised for the view is sensitive to our take on how, exactly, we should understand well-being and promotion. If we understand these notions in one way, the problem has more (or sharper) teeth, so epistemic instrumentalists tend in response to revise their understandings of promotion or well-being to avoid the problematic result. The opponents of epistemic instrumentalism, in their turn, insist on an alternate conception of promotion or well-being. Back and forth it goes. But we can do better in a way that simultaneously benefits epistemic instrumentalism's opponents *and* its defenders. We can break the stalemate.

Here, very briefly, is the idea: traditionally, the problem with epistemic instrumentalism is supposed to be that it gets the extension of epistemic correctness incorrect. Epistemic instrumentalists, in turn, are largely unimpressed: they dig in their heels in one way or another, and we get our stalemate. But opponents of epistemic instrumentalism are wrong to complain about extensional difficulties. They should complain about *explanatory* difficulties.

Drawing on our observations in the last chapter regarding the earmarks of the epistemic, I am going to argue that the correct way to put the problem to epistemic instrumentalists is not that they get the extension of epistemic correctness incorrect but that they are simply not talking about *epistemic* correctness at all. Given this way of framing the problem, heel-digging is not available. Hence, opponents of instrumentalism should be in favor of this strategy.

But putting the problem in this way also reveals that the initial motivations for epistemic instrumentalism – more on these later – turn out to be extremely poorly served by pitching the view as a first-order epistemic theory in the first place. In response to the idea that they are failing to offer a plausible account of the explanatory grounds of *epistemic* correctness, epistemic instrumentalists should shift tack: they should say that they are offering an account of the explanatory grounds of *authoritative* epistemic correctness. In other words, epistemic instrumentalists should give a *second-order* epistemic theory. I explain what this involves and how it works later on (Chapters 7–8).

Right now, the thing to do is explain the traditional problem with epistemic instrumentalism and the epistemic instrumentalist's traditional replies that generate our theoretical stalemate.

5.4 The Goldilocks Problem

As I have said, epistemic instrumentalism does not have many fans. The typical reaction from epistemologists, assuming you can get them to take the view seriously, has been outright ridicule. Usually, they seem offended by the suggestion that epistemic correctness is grounded in facts about what would promote agents' well-being. The specific charge against epistemic instrumentalism is that it fails systematically to capture the extension of epistemic correctness. The thought, then, is that this indicates that epistemic instrumentalism has systematically failed to identify the explanatory grounds of epistemic correctness. There are actually two variants on this charge.

The first variant on the charge is that there are cases in which an agent's φ-ing is epistemically correct but in which it is not also true that φ-ing promotes that agent's well-being. A paradigm example of the kind of case accusers have in mind is given by Thomas Kelly:

> If, despite my utter lack of interest in the question of whether Bertrand Russell was left-handed, I stumble upon strong evidence that he was, then I have strong epistemic reasons to believe that Bertrand Russell was left-handed. Indeed, my epistemic reasons will be no different than they would be if I had acquired the same evidence deliberately, because I *did* have the goal of finding out whether Russell was left-handed.
>
> (Kelly 2003, p. 625)

76 First-Order Epistemic Instrumentalism

Kelly is no fan of epistemic instrumentalism. His reason is precisely that if epistemic instrumentalism is true then the grounds of its being epistemically correct to believe are not present in cases where, he thinks, it is *manifestly* correct to believe: sure, it would not make you better off in any respect to believe that Bertrand Russell was left-handed, but *nevertheless*, it would be epistemically correct for you to do so. Kelly, again:

> Once I come into possession of evidence which strongly supports that claim that p, then I have epistemic reasons to believe that p, regardless of whether I presently have or previously had the goal of believing the truth about p, or any wider goal which would be better achieved in virtue of my believing the truth about p. The fact that I can have epistemic reasons to believe propositions even though doing so holds no promise of better achieving any of my goals (cognitive or otherwise) fits poorly with the instrumentalist conception of epistemic rationality, since whether it is instrumentally rational to Φ always depends on the contents of one's goals.
> (Kelly 2003, p. 625)

In other words, epistemic instrumentalists have gotten the extension of epistemic correctness incorrect. Hence, they must have gotten the explanatory grounds of epistemic correctness incorrect.

Kelly is not alone; versions of this variant on the challenge to epistemic instrumentalism abound.[8] The structure of the problem, just to repeat, is that there intuitively appear to be cases in which it *is* clearly epistemically correct to do something but in which the explanatory grounds epistemic instrumentalism says ground epistemic correctness aren't present, hence the *too-little-correctness* problem for epistemic instrumentalism.[9]

The second variant on the charge is the complement of the too little correctness problem. Broadly, the structure of this problem is that there intuitively appear to be cases in which ϕ-ing would promote an agent's well-being but in which ϕ-ing is *not* epistemically correct. Cases of this sort are a bit rarer in the literature, but here's the kind of case people usually have in mind:

> Jem desires a new toy and believes in the absence of any kind of evidence at all that he will get that toy as a gift on Friday. This belief makes him better off (it gives him a pleasant anticipatory feeling that contributes to his well-being).

Here, opponents of epistemic instrumentalism think we have the reverse of the situation we faced earlier, in Kelly's case: the purported explanatory grounds of epistemic correctness are present, but it *manifestly is not* epistemically correct to believe: sure, it makes Jem better off to believe he'll get the toy, but *nevertheless*, it is not epistemically correct to do so – it is paradigmatic wishful thinking. Hence, epistemic instrumentalists have (again) gotten the extension of epistemic correctness incorrect. Hence, again, they must have gotten the explanatory grounds of epistemic correctness incorrect. Call this the *too-much-correctness* problem.[10]

So, we have two variants on what amounts to the same kind charge, both of which rely on the thought that epistemic instrumentalism systematically misrepresents the extension of epistemic correctness and so must be failing to be correctly identifying the explanatory grounds of epistemic correctness. I will refer to these two variants jointly as the *Goldilocks Problem* for epistemic instrumentalists: the worry is that they do not get the extension of epistemic correctness *just right*.

5.5 Replying to the Goldilocks Problem

What should instrumentalists say in response to the Goldilocks Problem? Here is what they *have* said. In response to the too-little-correctness version of the problem: as a matter of fact, agents' well-being *is* promoted by believing in cases such as Kelly's. This is because, on investigation, it turns out *either* that agents' well-being, in part, comprises believing in accord with their evidence *or* that, on closer inspection, some other constituent of their well-being is, in fact, promoted by so believing. In previous work (Sharadin 2015b, 2018b), I have called these two strategies of reply the *special interests strategy* and the *modal strategy*, respectively. Both strategies attempt to capture the purportedly correct extension of epistemic correctness within an epistemic instrumentalist framework by uncovering hitherto unnoticed explanatory grounds thereof. Here, in very brief, is how those strategies are supposed to go.

According to the special interests strategy, believing in accord with the evidence (say) turns out, perhaps surprisingly, to itself actually be a constituent of agents' well-being. It turns out to be difficult to say, precisely, what this is supposed to involve: perhaps agents have a dispositional desire of some kind to accord their beliefs to the evidence. Or perhaps they have a "cognitive goal" that is only achieved by so believing.[11] However the details are spelled out, the strategy is the same: uncover the epistemic instrumentalist's explanatory grounds in the relevant problematic cases in order to ameliorate the rhetorical force of those cases against epistemic instrumentalism's account of those grounds.

According to the modal strategy, believing in accord with the evidence (say) turns out, perhaps surprisingly, to actually be a way of increasing agents' well-being, whatever that turns out to comprise. Again, the details turn out to be tricky. But the basic idea is for the epistemic instrumentalist to explain how it is, given her understanding of promotion and well-being, that an agent's well-being might be promoted by always believing in accord with the evidence, *even if there is no particular desire such that it would be promoted by their so doing*. Intuitively, the thought is that believing in accord with the evidence (say) might promote agential well-being, *whatever* the content of one's desires. Or perhaps, cultivating an exceptionless disposition to so believe is the best way to promote one's well-being, *whatever* that turns out to comprise. There are a range of possibilities here.

In either case – whether the agent deploys the special interests or the modal strategy – the thought is that the epistemic instrumentalist will get as a result the intuitively correct extension for epistemic correctness without any serious amendment to first-order epistemic instrumentalism. There are amendments, of course: they are adding special epistemic interests or revising their account of promotion or well-being or whatever. But there aren't meaningful amendments *to the account of the explanatory grounds of epistemic correctness*. Problem solved.

That is too quick. Problem *possibly* solved. The prospects for actually solving the too-little-correctness variant on the Goldilocks Problem either via the special interests or the modal strategies will depend in large part on the plausibility of the accounts of promotion and agential well-being that are required to make each work. For example, one way to make the modal strategy work is by making promotion *very cheap*: the easier it is to promote an agent's well-being, then, *ceteris paribus*, the more likely it is in any given case that we shall have enough explanatory grounds to support the relevant extension for epistemic correctness. Correspondingly, the more capacious the relevant understanding of agential well-being, the easier it will be to pull off the special interests strategy. If it turns out that, say, certain kinds of epistemic achievement make an agent better off, then, plausibly, it will turn out that we have enough explanatory grounds to support the relevant extension for epistemic correctness.[12] Here, I am not interested in investigating the details of what accounts of promotion or well-being could be made to do the work on behalf of the epistemic instrumentalists. As I will shortly explain, this road leads to stalemate.

What about the complementary variant on the problem: too *much* correctness? Here, epistemic instrumentalists' reply has typically had two steps: *reduce* and *shrug*.

Recall, this variant of the problem purports to show that, according to epistemic instrumentalism, there will be cases in which it is epistemically correct for an agent to believe something because the explanatory grounds for epistemic correctness exist but in which, supposedly manifestly, it would *not* be epistemically correct for the agent to so believe. Jem's is a case in point: wishful thinking at its apparently worst. How does the reduce and shrug two-step reply work?

First, *reduce*: epistemic instrumentalists can insist on filling in the details of cases in which it purportedly promotes an agent's well-being to (say) wishfully think. The vast majority of ways of filling in those details in plausible ways, according to the epistemic instrumentalist, will reveal that, as a matter of fact, it *does not* promote the agent's well-being to believe in whatever way is intuitively supposed not to be epistemically correct.

For instance, plausibly, if Jem does not receive the gift on Friday, then he'll feel *horribly* disappointed; moreover, the likelihood of that potential disappointment outweighs any likelihood of potential increase to his well-being caused by his wishful thinking. Hence, it would *not*, in fact, promote his well-being to wishfully think, for it would not increase the likelihood that his well-being would improve were he to believe, in the absence of any kind of evidence, that he'll receive the gift on Friday. Hence, contrary to the problematic result, it would not be epistemically correct – even on epistemic instrumentalist grounds – to wishfully think.

So it goes, according to this strategy, with most such cases.[13] Once we start to fill in the details in plausible ways, it turns out that the epistemic instrumentalist is *not* committed to there being too much correctness. Reduction is a good strategy as far as it goes. But it only goes so far.

This is because the opponent of epistemic instrumentalism interested in pressing the too much correctness variant can simply stipulate all the details in whatever fashion is required in order to generate the purportedly problematic extensional result. "No," they'll say, "Suppose that Jem's belief is *entirely isolated* and will *wink out of existence* before it threatens to cause any disappointment." Annoying but fair enough.

Hence, the second step in the epistemic instrumentalist's reply: *shrug*. Many things are *possible* regarding what it would be epistemically correct for agents to do. Some of these things it is possible under certain conditions for it to be epistemically correct for agents to do might strike us as things it is outlandish to think are things that it is epistemically correct to do. Maybe wishful thinking is like that; it strikes us that, *whatever* the circumstances, it's never epistemically correct to wishfully think. But that is not a decisive reason for rejecting a view that entails it might sometimes be epistemically correct for an agent to wishfully think any more than it is a decisive reason for rejecting, for example, ethical consequentialism that it has what has seemed to some to have the outlandish result that it could in principle be ethically correct to kill a person to prevent some suitably large number of suitably painful headaches (Norcross 1998). You might disagree that this usually happens, and most consequentialists will be at pains to explain why such cases are *extraordinarily* rare.[14] But at a certain point in the argument, suitable details stipulated, ethical consequentialists should simply *shrug*.[15] Epistemic instrumentalists, says this reply, should, at the limit, do the same.[16]

5.6 Stalemate

This dialectic has resulted in theoretical stalemate. Opponents of epistemic instrumentalism pose the Goldilocks Problem in one of its two forms. Epistemic instrumentalists offer special interests and modal strategies in response to the too-little-correctness problem and end up shrugging off charges of too much correctness. Opponents look askance at the strategies and are offended at the shrugging. Instrumentalists look nonplussed. Stalemate.

What to do? I think *both* parties are making crucial mistakes. Let's start with the opponents of epistemic instrumentalism.

Despite what earlier time slices of me appear to have said (Sharadin 2018b, 2019), I do think we should reject first-order epistemic instrumentalism. But I think we can't get an argument for rejecting it via targeting the extension delivered by that view. In other words, the Goldilocks Problem is a red herring. Rather than targeting epistemic instrumentalism's view of *which* φ-ings are epistemically correct (and so opening themselves up to potential stalemate of the sort just described), opponents of epistemic instrumentalism should directly target epistemic instrumentalism's account of *why* various φ-ings are epistemically correct. After all, that is presumably what they think is mistaken. As I explain, the way to do this is to argue that epistemic instrumentalism's view about the explanatory grounds of epistemic correctness makes epistemic correctness as construed by the epistemic instrumentalist unable to play the role distinctive to *epistemic* – as opposed to some other kind of – correctness. This is what I will call the Functionalist Challenge to epistemic instrumentalism. In effect, the Functionalist Challenge to epistemic instrumentalism says that first-order epistemic instrumentalism changes the conversation from one about *epistemic* correctness to … well, something else.

In the face of the Functionalist Challenge, epistemic instrumentalists, in their turn, should give up their first-order explanatory ambitions.[17] What the Goldilocks Problem suggests (although in a way that can be endlessly resisted), and what the Functionalist Challenge reinforces (in a way that I think is decisive), is that epistemic instrumentalists are simply *wrong* about what comprise the grounds (and so, as it happens, the extension) of epistemic correctness.

But as I will go on to explain, this should not worry epistemic instrumentalists *at all*. That is because, despite the way it is regularly understood, epistemic instrumentalism was never intended as a view about the explanatory grounds of epistemic correctness. It was intended as and should be understood as a view about the explanatory grounds of the *authority* of epistemic correctness. Much more on this later. Next, the Functionalist Challenge.

Notes

1 See also Rinard (2017, 2019). For a similar view of what epistemic instrumentalism is committed to, see Côté-Bouchard (2015).
2 See also Sharadin (2019).
3 Rinard's view includes the wrinkle that *other agents'* well-being might also ground facts whether φ-ing is epistemically correct. She's alone in that thought, and I don't take it to comprise the central motivating thought behind first-order epistemic instrumentalism, which is to connect up epistemic correctness to *agents' own well-being*. Of course, this does not mean Rinard is

wrong, but she does not give us any particular reason for the extension to other agents, nor does she explain how it is consonant with the overall instrumentalist project. For discussion, see Rinard (2015).
4 For a nice overview of the various plausible candidates and the relations between them, see Hooker (2015).
5 For discussion, see Heathwood (2019, n.d.), Bruckner (2010, 2019), and Lin (2016, 2017).
6 For relevant discussion, see Bradley (2009), Kraut (2007), Darwall (2002), Lin (2021), Hooker (2015), Hurka (2019), and Pummer (2017).
7 See Sharadin (2015a, 2016) and Sharadin and Dellsén (2019).
8 For a nice overview, see Cowie (2014), Sharadin (2018b), and Côté-Bouchard (2015).
9 This problem mirrors what Mark Schroeder calls the "too few reasons" problem for broadly instrumentalist approaches to kinds of correctness (e.g., moral correctness). See Schroeder (2007). Here, as I've said, I want to avoid talk of "reasons" as much as possible.
10 Cf. Schroeder (2007).
11 For discussion, see Sharadin (2015b, 2018b).
12 Duncan Pritchard (2005, 2009) has argued that *knowledge* is an achievement of this sort; it's not *crazy* that epistemic correctness might also be relevantly similar in this respect. For discussion, see Hooker (2015), and Whiting (2012).
13 For instances of this strategy, see Rinard (2015, 2017) and Sharadin (2015b, 2018b, 2019).
14 Norcross (1997a, 1997b), and Broome (2004).
15 I defend a version of this reply on behalf of *epistemic* consequentialists in Sharadin (2018a).
16 There's a potential *third* step to the reply after *reduce* and *shrug*, namely, *go on offense*. This would involve articulating cases where it *is* plausible that the explanatory grounds epistemic instrumentalists identify give the correct results but where anti-instrumentalist proposals do *not* give plausible results. This is a possibility explored by Rinard (2015), drawing on cases from Marušic (2012), Keller (2004), Stroud (2006), Gendler (2011), and Preston-Roedder (2013).
17 This is the view I failed to articulate in Sharadin (2019).

References

Bradley, Ben. 2009. *Well-Being and Death*. Oxford: Oxford University Press.
Broome, John. 2004. *Weighing Lives*. OxfordOxford University Press.
Bruckner, Donald W. 2010. "Subjective Well-Being and Desire Satisfaction." *Philosophical Papers* 39 (1): 1–28. https://doi.org/10.1080/05568641003669409.
——— 2019. "The Shape of a Life and Desire Satisfaction." *Pacific Philosophical Quarterly* 100 (2): 661–680. https://doi.org/10.1111/papq.12240.
Côté-Bouchard, Charles. 2015. "Epistemic Instrumentalism and the Too Few Reasons Objection." *International Journal of Philosophical Studies* 23 (3): 337–355. https://doi.org/10.1080/09672559.2015.1042007.
Cowie, Christopher. 2014. "In Defence of Instrumentalism about Epistemic Normativity." *Synthese* 191 (16): 4003–4017. https://doi.org/10.1007/s11229-014-0510-6.
Darwall, Stephen. 2002. *Welfare and Rational Care*. Princeton, NJ: Princeton University Press.

Gendler, Tamar Szabó. 2011. "On the Epistemic Costs of Implicit Bias." *Philosophical Studies* 156 (1): 33–63. https://doi.org/10.1007/s11098-011-9801-7.

Heathwood, Chris. 2019. "Which Desires Are Relevant to Well-Being?" *Noûs* 53 (3): 664–688. https://doi.org/10.1111/nous.12232.

———. n.d. "Happiness and Desire Satisfaction." *Noûs*. https://doi.org/10.1111/nous.12347.

Hooker, Brad. 2015. "The Elements of Well-Being." *Journal of Practical Ethics* 3 (1): 15–35.

Hurka, Thomas. 2019. "On 'Hybrid' Theories of Personal Good." *Utilitas* 31 (4): 450–462. https://doi.org/10.1017/s0953820819000256.

Keller, Simon. 2004. "Friendship and Belief." *Philosophical Papers* 33 (3): 329–351. https://doi.org/10.1080/05568640409485146.

Kelly, Thomas. 2003. "Epistemic Rationality as Instrumental Rationality: A Critique." *Philosophy and Phenomenological Research* 66 (3): 612–640. https://doi.org/10.1111/j.1933-1592.2003.tb00281.x.

Kraut, Richard. 2007. *What Is Good and Why: The Ethics of Well-Being*. Cambridge, MA: Harvard University Press.

Lin, Eden. 2016. "The Subjective List Theory of Well-Being." *Australasian Journal of Philosophy* 94 (1): 99–114. https://doi.org/10.1080/00048402.2015.1014926.

———. 2017. "Against Welfare Subjectivism." *Noûs* 51 (2): 354–377. https://doi.org/10.1111/nous.12131.

———. 2021. "The Experience Requirement on Well-Being." *Philosophical Studies* 178 (3): 867–886. https://doi.org/10.1007/s11098-020-01463-6.

Lockard, Matthew. 2013. "Epistemic Instrumentalism." *Synthese* 190 (9): 1701–1718. https://doi.org/10.1007/s11229-011-9932-6.

Marušic, Berislav. 2012. "Belief and Difficult Action." *Philosophers' Imprint* 12: 1–30.

Norcross, Alastair. 1997a. "Comparing Harms: Headaches and Human Lives." *Philosophy and Public Affairs* 26 (2): 135–167. https://doi.org/10.1111/j.1088-4963.1997.tb00079.x.

———. 1997b. "Trading Lives for Convenience: It's Not Just for Consequentialists." *Southwest Philosophy Review* 13 (1): 29–37. https://doi.org/swphilreview19971313.

———. 1998. "Great Harms from Small Benefits Grow: How Death Can Be Outweighed by Headaches." *Analysis* 58 (2): 152–158. https://doi.org/10.1093/analys/58.2.152.

Preston-Roedder, Ryan. 2013. "Faith in Humanity." *Philosophy and Phenomenological Research* 87 (3): 664–687. https://doi.org/10.1111/phpr.12024.

Pritchard, Duncan. 2005. *Epistemic Luck*. Oxford: Oxford University Press.

———. 2009. "Knowledge, Understanding and Epistemic Value." *Royal Institute of Philosophy Supplement* 64: 19–43. https://doi.org/10.1017/s1358246109000046.

Pummer, Theron. 2017. "Lopsided Lives." In *Oxford Studies in Normative Ethics*, edited by Mark Timmons, 275–296. Oxford: Oxford University Press.

Rinard, Susanna. 2015. "Against the New Evidentialists." *Philosophical Issues* 25 (1): 208–223. https://doi.org/10.1111/φs.12061.

———. 2017. "No Exception for Belief." *Philosophy and Phenomenological Research* 94 (1): 121–143. https://doi.org/10.1111/phpr.12229.

———. 2019. "Equal Treatment for Belief." *Philosophical Studies* 176 (7): 1923–1950. https://doi.org/10.1007/s11098-018-1104-9.

Schroeder, Mark. 2007. *Slaves of the Passions*. Oxford: Oxford University Press.
Sharadin, Nathaniel. 2015a. "Problems for Pure Probabilism about Promotion (and a Disjunctive Alternative)." *Philosophical Studies* 172 (5): 1371–1386. https://doi.org/10.1007/s11098-014-0354-4.
———. 2015b. "Reasons and Promotion." *Philosophical Issues* 25 (1): 98–122. https://doi.org/10.1111/phis.12057.
———. 2016. "Checking the Neighborhood: A Reply to DiPaolo & Behrends on Promotion." *Journal of Ethics and Social Philosophy* 1: 1–8. https://doi.org/10.26556/jesp.v10i1.181.
———. 2018a. "Epistemic Consequentialism: Haters Gonna Hate." In *Metaepistemology: Realism & Antirealism*, edited by Christos Kyriacou, and Robin McKenna, 121–143. New York: Palgrave MacMillan.
———. 2018b. "Epistemic Instrumentalism and the Reason to Believe in Accord with the Evidence." *Synthese* 195 (9): 3791–3809. https://doi.org/10.1007/s11229-016-1245-3.
———. 2019. "Ecumenical Epistemic Instrumentalism." *Synthese* 198 (3): 2613–2639. https://doi.org/10.1007/s11229-019-02232-7.
Sharadin, Nathaniel, and Finnur Dellsén. 2019. "Promotion as Contrastive Increase in Expected Fit." *Philosophical Studies* 176 (5): 1263–1290. https://doi.org/10.1007/s11098-018-1062-2.
Steglich-Petersen, Asbjørn. 2018. "Epistemic Instrumentalism, Permissibility, and Reasons for Belief." In *Normativity: Epistemic and Practical*, edited by Conor McHugh, Jonathan Way, and Daniel Whiting, 260–280. Oxford: Oxford University Press.
Stroud, Sarah. 2006. "Epistemic Partiality in Friendship." *Ethics* 116 (3): 498–524. https://doi.org/10.1086/500337.
Whiting, Daniel. 2012. "Epistemic Value and Achievement." *Ratio* 25 (2): 216–230. https://doi.org/10.1111/j.1467-9329.2012.00533.x.

6 The Functionalist Challenge

6.1 Introduction

The Goldilocks Problem targets epistemic instrumentalism's account of the explanatory grounds of epistemic correctness by way of targeting the resulting view about the extension of epistemic correctness. The idea, as we saw, was that there are manifestly cases in which it would (not) be epistemically correct for an agent to behave in some fashion, but given the epistemic instrumentalist's view about the explanatory grounds of epistemic correctness, they must think that it would (not) be epistemically correct to so behave. And as we also saw, the epistemic instrumentalist can then respond to the Goldilocks Problem by uncovering hitherto unnoticed grounds that deliver the requisite intuitively correct extensional result. The anti-instrumentalist can complain about further cases and so on and so on. Hence, we arrive at a stalemate.

On behalf of the *opponent* of epistemic instrumentalism, I suggest the following change in tack: rather than targeting epistemic instrumentalism's view about the explanatory grounds of epistemic correctness by way of the extension those grounds deliver (and so leaving open the various epistemic instrumentalist replies), target those grounds *directly*. In effect, my argument is that given what evaluation in terms of epistemic correctness is *for*, the grounds identified by the epistemic instrumentalist are unsuitable *qua* grounds of epistemic correctness. To see how the argument goes, we are going to need two additional ingredients.

6.2 Explanation–Justification Connection

The first ingredient involves a connection between *explanation* and *justification*. So far, we have been treating first-order theories as offering us accounts of the explanatory grounds of one kind of correctness or another. But in doing so, such theories also, and simultaneously thereby, provide agents with different kinds of *justifications* for what they might be proposing to do. The easiest way to see this is by thinking about particular kinds of correctness, particular potential explanatory grounds, that is,

DOI: 10.4324/9781003096726-6

first-order theories, and the clear connection between justification and explanation that holds in these cases. That'll, I hope, make it clear how the connection is an intuitive one. I then go on to offer an argument in its favor.

Forget about first-order epistemic theory for the moment and consider first-order *moral* theory. Consider the following *moral* correctness explanatory principle:

> Maximizing Hedonistic Act Consequentialism (MHAC): The fact that it is morally correct for A to φ is grounded in the fact that A's φ-ing maximizes expected happiness.

Like the first-order epistemic theories we have been discussing, MHAC purports to give an account of the explanatory grounds of moral correctness. Now, there are a lot of questions we might have about what is involved in accepting MHAC. Some of them parallel questions we have been asking about the epistemic domain – for instance, we might want to know what it is that distinguishes *moral* correctness from other kinds of correctness. Set those issues to one side, and simply suppose we have been convinced that MHAC is true.

Now suppose an agent, Kai, does something about which we morally disapprove – let's say he breaks a promise to a friend – and we ask him why he did what he did in a tone of voice that makes it clear we are looking for a moral *justification* rather than, say, an apology or an excuse. There are plenty of ways Kai might respond. But one way Kai might respond is by citing the consequences of what he did in terms of maximizing expected happiness. And in particular, if what he says is that he did what he did because it maximized expected happiness, and we believe him, then I think we should all agree that our question has been partly answered: Kai has given us a partial moral justification for breaking his promise.

Now, we might not on reflection much care for Kai's moral justification. One thing we might think is that it is in some way insufficient; fair enough – I said that we should think he has at least given us a *partial* justification. I will come to the idea that citing the explanatory grounds of correctness might not comprise a complete justification in a bit more detail later. But notice that we are intuitively not in a position to simply reject Kai's claim as going *any way at all* toward morally justifying what he did. This is because rejecting that moral justification for his having done what he did is tantamount to rejecting MHAC. If we think that what explanatorily grounds the moral correctness of what agents do are the expected consequences in terms of overall happiness, then it appears we must also think that moral *justifications* of what agents do can properly appeal to those explanatory grounds.

This is not just true of Kai and the connection between *moral* explanation and *moral* justification. It appears to be true *whatever* kind of correctness we are considering. Whenever you are trying to *justify* some behavior, attitude, or whatever, citing the *explanatory grounds* of the correctness of that behavior, attitude, or whatever is always permissible. So quite generally, I think we accept the following:

> Explanation–Justification Connection: If G is an explanatory ground of the k correctness of A's φ-ing, then it is always k-ly acceptable to cite G in a k justification of the k correctness of A's φ-ing.

Note a couple of things. First, this principle is relativized to *kinds* of correctness and so to *kinds* of justification and so, too, to what is k-ly acceptable. It does not say that any old explanatory grounds can acceptably be cited in any old justification. It should be clear why this is so. Imagine Kai citing the fact that it maximized his *own* happiness to break his promise. While this might be an explanatory ground of the *prudential* correctness of his breaking his promise, and thereby *prudentially* acceptable to cite in a *prudential* justification of the *prudential* correctness of his breaking the promise, it is not thereby *morally* acceptable to cite this fact in a *moral* justification of the *moral* correctness of breaking the promise.

Second, the principle does not preclude *other* (kinds of) facts from playing a role in k justifications of the k correctness of an agent's φ-ing. We can imagine pressing Kai for the details of his deliberative process, say. It may be that those details are relevant in thinking about the manner and degree to which Kai is morally justified in doing as he did. If he was overly hasty in deciding, perhaps that could impugn his justification. Instead, what the principle says is that the explanatory grounds are always available to serve as part of a justification.

Finally, the principle does not say that citing the explanatory grounds of the k correctness of an agent's φ-ing is always *sufficient* to k-ly justify the agent's φ-ing. Explanation differs in important ways from justification, and there can be reasons for thinking the latter in some sense in some contexts requires more than the former. For instance, as I just suggested, it might be that features of the context that affect our willingness to think Kai was acting with a morally good will affect the shape and content of a complete moral justification for his breaking his promise without also affecting anything about the explanatory grounds of the moral correctness of his doing so.[1]

Given these qualifications, it is hard to make sense of what a denial of Explanation–Justification Connection would look like. Someone who thinks that the explanatory grounds of the moral (or another kind of) correctness of φ-ing are somehow barred from serving as ingredients in a moral (or another kind of) justification of φ-ing appears to me to have changed the topic.

But maybe you disagree. Maybe you think that the explanatory grounds of the *k* correctness of φ-ing are sometimes barred from serving as ingredients in a *k* justification for φ-ing. Then, I have an argument. Here is the argument.

Begin with two commonsense platitudinous observations about the connection between justification and blame. First, the degree to which someone is *k*-ly justified in their φ-ing determines the degree to which they are *k*-ly blameworthy for their φ-ing in at least the following two minimal respects: the more *k*-ly justified the agent is in φ-ing, then, *ceteris paribus*, the less *k*-ly blameworthy they are for φ-ing. And the less *k*-ly justified the agent is in φ-ing, then, *ceteris paribus*, the more *k*-ly blameworthy they are for φ-ing. In other words, the degree to which an agent is *k*-ly blameworthy for φ-ing is an inverse function, *ceteris paribus*, of the degree to which the agent is *k*-ly justified.

Second, one *k* justification is *k*-ly *worse* than another *k* justification when it results in the agent being more *k*-ly blameworthy than the other justification. Correspondingly, a *k* justification is *k*-ly better than another justification when it results in the agent being less *k*-ly blameworthy than the other *k* justification.

These two observations yield the following natural test for whether some fact or set of facts is ever *k*-ly barred from serving in a *k*-justification for φ-ing or whether, by contrast, it is always *k*-ly acceptable to cite those facts or set of facts in a *k* justification: check whether it's ever plausibly true that adding such a fact (or set of facts) to the *k* justification would make the agent *more k-ly blameworthy*. If so, then, sometimes at least, such facts are not acceptably cited in a *k* justification, for they make the *k* justification *k*-ly worse – and we can see this because we can see that the agent whose *k* justification it is, is more *k*-ly blameworthy.

The question, then, is whether an agent's including the explanatory grounds of *k* correctness in a *k* justification of φ-ing ever makes the agent more *k*-ly blameworthy for φ-ing. And the way to test this is to compare cases at the margins. For example, returning to Kai, imagine he cites the following facts in his moral justification of breaking his promise:

> J: My daughter needed emergency dental care, and I was the only available adult.

The quality of J *qua* moral justification for Kai's behavior is, it seems to me, pretty good. Kai seems relatively morally blameless. But whatever you think about the quality of J *qua* moral justification, and however morally blameworthy you think Kai is, suppose that instead of offering J, he cited the following facts in his moral justification of breaking his promise:

> J*: My daughter needed emergency dental care, I was the only available adult, and among the actions available to me at the time,

breaking my promise was the one that maximized expected overall happiness.

Now ask, Is Kai* (whose justification is J*) more blameworthy than Kai (whose justification is J)? No, he is not. They are at least exactly as morally blameworthy as one another. Adding the explanatory grounds of moral correctness (which we are here assuming are facts about maximizing overall expected happiness) to the moral justification does not make a moral justification any morally worse.

Perhaps you disagree because you think that Kai* (but not Kai) has had "one thought too many" and thereby betrayed a morally pernicious lack of concern for his daughter (Williams 1976; Wolf 2012). Maybe that is true; perhaps Kai* is cold and unsympathizing (Williams 1976). But that is neither here nor there when it comes to the quality of Kai*'s justification, *given that the relevant first-order moral theory is true*. Perhaps instead you think that the justification is not *morally* worse, given the relevant first-order moral theory, but it is somehow *interpersonally worse*. Maybe that is true: that does not run afoul of our principle. Perhaps the lesson is that such act-consequentialism is untenable, since it permits (*gasp*: encourages) agents such as Kai* or justifications such as J*. Maybe *that* is true. But that does not tell us anything about the relevant claim here, which, again, is simply that adding the *stipulated to be correct* explanatory grounds of ϕ-ing's being k-ly correct to a k justification for ϕ-ing cannot make the k justification any k-ly worse and that we can see this by noticing that agents don't become more k-ly blameworthy if they add the explanatory grounds of the k correctness of their ϕ-ing to their k justification for ϕ-ing.

Maybe you disagree because you think that this precludes the possibility of so-called government house, or "self-effacing" moral views. Famously, self-effacing moral consequentialists say, roughly, that the morally correct thing to do is whatever results in the best outcome but that simultaneously, as it happens, it's morally correct for agents not do things *on the basis* of the facts that explanatorily ground the moral correctness of what they do, which is to say on the basis of the goodness of the expected outcomes.[2] But I think this is a mistake; the question of whether self-effacing consequentialism is or is not plausible does not bear on the present issue.

Self-effacing views are most naturally understood, as the earlier sketch suggests, as views about the ways in which we morally should want agents to be disposed to go about making moral choices, or, to put things in the language of reasons, as views about the morally correct *motivating reasons* for agents' moral behavior (Sharadin 2019). So understood, such views simply enlarge the scope of their moral attention beyond what we might ordinarily suppose can be evaluated as morally correct, all the way to a wide range of agents' dispositional motivations, and then apply their *very same* view about the explanatory grounds of moral correctness *to that very activity*, perhaps with surprising results.[3] But this – perhaps surprising – enlargement of the moral ambit with perhaps surprising results is neither here nor there with respect to the present issue, which is whether the explanatory grounds of moral correctness could ever be barred from being cited in a moral justification. To see this, notice that we might want a moral justification of, say, being morally motivated in such-and-such fashion (e.g., by having certain dispositions). The claim, here, is that you don't make a moral justification of being morally motivated in that fashion (having those dispositions) any *worse* by adding to it the claim that what explanatorily grounds the moral correctness of being motivated in that way is thus and so. There is no reason to think such explanatory grounds are somehow barred by the structure of a view that takes within its scope questions about the moral status of certain forms of motivation and deliberation! You might *disagree* with self-effacing consequentialism either because you don't like self-effacing views or because you disagree with the relevant consequentialist grounds, but the view is not made conceptually incoherent by insisting that explanatory grounds are always available for justificatory work.[4]

So that is our first ingredient: Explanation–Justification Connection, that is, the view that the explanatory grounds of k correctness are always acceptable in a k justification of the k correctness of ϕ-ing.

6.3 No Interference

Our second ingredient is a bit more subtle. Recall our observation, from the last chapter, that thought and talk in terms of a kind of correctness can be *for* something. There, we discussed the idea that thought and talk in terms of *epistemic* correctness has such a distinctive functional role – it is *for* flagging reliable informants. Now, notice that it is possible for various things to *interfere* with the functional role of a kind of thought and talk. Here, then, is the intuitive idea behind the second ingredient: if a way of thinking and speaking would interfere with the ability of a kind of thought and talk to play its distinctive functional role, then that way of thinking and speaking will be unacceptable *while engaged in that kind of thought and talk*. That is pretty abstract. Let's ease into it in three steps: first an analogy, then a case study with thought and talk in terms of *moral* correctness, and then finally bringing things back to epistemic correctness.

Analogy first. Saws are *for* something: they are for *sawing*. Certain things I might do while using a saw, that is, while sawing, are unacceptable *from the point of view of sawing*, and they are unacceptable precisely because they interfere with the ability of the saw with which I am sawing to play its distinctive functional role, which, as we have said, is to saw. See?

Case study next. You might think that thought and talk in terms of *moral* correctness is also for something. For example, Holly Smith says that a subspecies of thought and talk in terms of moral correctness is *for* guiding choice with respect to choosable events (Smith 1986, 2018). She's focused on *deontic* thought and talk, that is, thought and talk in terms of *moral rightness* and *moral wrongness*:

> Can natural events, such as rainstorms or late frosts, be [morally] right? No: we say that such events and states can be good, but not that they can be [morally] right. The reason for this is that such entities are not voluntary – they are not the objects of effective choice. ... [Moral] Rightness is reserved for entities, namely acts, that are controllable by choosing agents. ... It is precisely because we need some standard of evaluation to serve this function that we have criteria of [moral] rightness in addition to criteria of goodness.
> (Smith, 1986, p. 342)

Suppose that is correct.[5] Then, certain ways I might think or speak while deontically morally evaluating things, are unacceptable *from the point of view of deontic thought and talk*, and they are unacceptable precisely because they interfere with the ability of the moral deontic thought and talk with which I am morally deontically evaluating things to play its distinctive functional role, which, supposing Smith is correct, is to guide choice with respect to choosable events.

What kinds of ways of thinking and speaking might be unacceptable from a moral point of view while using moral deontic concepts to do what they are for, for this very reason, namely, that these ways of thinking and speaking interfere with moral deontic thought and talk's ability to do what it is for? Smith's suggestion is that evaluating the very same action as *right* and *wrong* would count as unacceptable for this reason. The problem, according to her, is that evaluating the very same action as both right and simultaneously as wrong would obviously interfere with the ability of deontic moral thought and talk to play its distinctive role, namely, guiding choice with respect to choosable events. This, in turn, explains why it is that there is a ban on thinking and speaking in moral deontic terms of the very same action as both morally right and morally wrong. If that were permissible, it would interfere with the ability of deontic moral thought and talk to do what it is for. Anyway, so the story goes.

Now, I have issues with Smith's particular story with respect to moral deontic thought and talk. In other work (Sharadin and Greve 2021), I have co-argued that Smith herself cannot get *from* facts about the role, purpose, or point of deontic moral thought and talk *to* any substantive facts about what deontic moral thought and talk is like because, to put it crudely, she cannot get an (interesting) "ought" from an (uncontroversial) "is." But in that same work, my coauthor and I explain why, if you accept a functional criterion for defining the particular domain, then there is no problem *at all* with this style of argument.

In other words, if you think that part of what *defines* a particular set of (say, deontic) concepts is their purpose, role, or point, then *of course* you can move from facts about what kinds of thought and talk would disable those concepts from playing their distinctive functional role to the fact that those ways of thinking and speaking are, from the point of view of those concepts, *banned*.[6]

In other words, if you think that moral rightness *just is* whatever kind of rightness it is that guides agential choice with respect to choosable events, then it makes sense to think that there are some ways of thinking and speaking about moral rightness that do not make any sense at all – they are unacceptable *from the moral point of view*. In particular, if there are ways of thinking and speaking about moral rightness that interfere with the ability of thought and talk about moral rightness to guide agential choice with respect to choosable events, then *those* ways of thinking and speaking about moral rightness are unacceptable from the moral point of view. It turns out that the problem with Smith's view is simply that she does not accept this way of defining the moral deontic concepts in a functionalist way.

But the basic idea to which Smith appeals is exactly correct, given the relevant functionalist assumption. It is the same thing that drives the facts about certain ways of using a saw being unacceptable from the point of view of sawing, namely, that these ways of sawing interfere with the ability of the saw to actually saw. Here is a general version of this idea, with a special focus on the kinds of interference of interest to my argument:

> No Interference: For a kind of correctness k a function of which is F: if citing G in a k justification for φ-ing interferes with the ability of k thought and talk to F, then citing G is k-ly unacceptable in that k justification for φ-ing.

Intuitively, if a point, purpose, or role of a kind of thought and talk k is to F, then it can't be k-ly acceptable to think and speak in ways that interfere with the ability of k thought and talk to as a matter of fact F, that is, in ways that would disable or interfere with k talk's role.

That is our second ingredient: No Interference. We are almost there – we have our two ingredients. In they go into the epistemic hot pot.

6.4 Cooking Up the Challenge

Our first ingredient, recall, says that it is always k-ly *acceptable* to cite the explanatory grounds of the k-correctness of φ-ing in a k-justification for φ-ing. That is Explanation–Justification Connection. No Interference says that, for kinds of correctness that are functionally defined in terms of some distinctive functional role, it is always k-ly *un*acceptable to cite in one's k justifications something that would interfere with the ability of that kind of correctness to play that distinctive role. It should now be clear how we can get ourselves into trouble.

Epistemic correctness is the kind of correctness that is *for* flagging reliable informants. That is how we distinguish a standard of *epistemic* correctness from a standard of some other kind of correctness (Chapter 4), via the minimal functional criterion. The minimal functional criterion of adequacy on accounts of epistemic correctness then says that in order to qualify as a potential account of *epistemic* correctness, as compared to an account of *some other kind of correctness*, epistemic correctness as conceived by the proposed account must be one that plays the – or at least *a* – distinctive functional role of epistemic correctness, namely, flagging reliable informants.

So, if we have some first-order epistemic theory such that the explanatory grounds it identifies are ones where citing them in justifications would interfere with the ability of epistemic correctness to meet this minimal functional criterion, that is, to serve to flag reliable informants, we can know, from the armchair, that this first-order epistemic theory is unacceptable. For such grounds should (per the Explanation–Justification Connection) be acceptable. But (per No Interference) they are not. But they cannot both be acceptable and not acceptable. So the first-order epistemic theory *must* have misidentified the explanatory grounds. Epistemic instrumentalism, I submit, is such a first-order epistemic theory.

Here is why. Epistemic instrumentalism, recall, says the following:

> Epistemic Instrumentalism: The fact that it is epistemically correct for A to φ is grounded by the fact that A's φ-ing promotes A's well-being.

The explanatory grounds of the epistemic correctness of any particular A's particular φ-ing are therefore facts about how and why A's φ-ing promotes A's well-being. According to Explanation–Justification Connection, what this means is that it is always epistemically acceptable to cite such facts in epistemic justifications for φ-ing. Now, this might, by itself, seem peculiar. For what this means is that, if epistemic instrumentalism is the correct first-order epistemic theory, then agents can give epistemic justifications for doing what they do by citing facts about how so doing will make them better off. For instance, suppose you believe it is sunny outside, and I ask you why you believe this, and I ask it in a tone of voice that makes it clear that I am asking for an epistemic justification for your belief. If epistemic instrumentalism is true, then one thing you can cite that at least partially serves to epistemically justify your belief is, say, the fact that believing it is sunny outside makes you happier than believing otherwise and has no ill effects. This is true *even if we are standing outside under the sun with all the evidence that this entails*. Your evidence might *also* help to justify (or it might not, depending on what we think about what epistemic justification requires). The point is that citing the facts about welfare promotion is *in order*, given the truth of epistemic instrumentalism and Explanation–Justification Connection.

As I said, this fact, that someone could in principle cite welfare-promotion facts in epistemic justifications, might by itself seem epistemically peculiar. It is enough to make most epistemologists queasy. But that does not indicate that there is anything wrong with first-order epistemic instrumentalism any more than Kantian's queasiness when confronted with act-consequentialism indicates there is anything wrong with act-consequentialism. Perhaps it is Kantians' – or epistemologists' – stomachs that are the problem.

But we *can* leverage this fact about what it is supposedly acceptable to cite in an epistemic justification into an argument against epistemic instrumentalism. The way to do that is to notice that citing the kinds of things epistemic instrumentalism, if true, entails that it is acceptable to cite, would plausibly interfere with the ability of epistemic evaluative thought and talk to play its distinctive role in flagging reliable informants. But that means those facts are banned from being cited in such justifications, given No Interference. In other words, the explanatory grounds epistemic instrumentalism identifies for epistemic correctness are epistemically acceptable to cite in epistemic justifications, since after all, they are explanatory grounds of epistemic correctness. But they are also *not* epistemically acceptable to cite since they interfere with the ability of epistemic evaluation to flag reliable informants. But they cannot both be acceptable to cite and unacceptable to. So something must have gone wrong. Diagnosis: first-order epistemic instrumentalism has misidentified the explanatory grounds of epistemic correctness.

Why think that citing the explanatory grounds epistemic instrumentalism identifies – facts about agential welfare promotion – will in epistemic justifications interfere with the ability of epistemic evaluation to flag reliable informants? Simple: being reliable is a feature we take informants to have when their, for example, beliefs about P, *are not sensitive to whether believing P promotes their welfare*. So, citing facts about how and to what extent an agent's beliefs promote their welfare (the explanatory grounds of epistemic correctness) in epistemic justifications is going to interfere with the ability of judgments of epistemic correctness to flag who is and who is not reliable.

Here's another way to put the point. The way in which epistemic correctness helps us flag reliable informants is via a kind of epistemic scorekeeping – reliable informants have more, rather than less, epistemically correct beliefs (Rysiew 2012; McKenna 2014; Hannon 2019). Reliability in a domain is a matter of more often than not getting it epistemically correct in that domain. We need to know who to trust (Fricker 2007) and so on. Most of this goes on, as it were, in the background. It is not as if we deploy epistemic correctness *so as* to do these things for us, but it is nevertheless what it does, and indeed, that is what it is for.

But to illustrate the problem for epistemic instrumentalism, take a case of attempting to *deliberately* flag an informant as reliable by thinking and speaking in terms of epistemic correctness. Suppose I tell you that *everything* Matt the used-car salesman believes about used cars is epistemically correct and that you believe me. Then, what I have done is *explicitly* flag Matt as used-car reliable; you should think Matt is a reliable informant with respect to used cars – you can ask him whether this one is a good deal or whether this one needs a transmission or whatever. After all, you think that all his beliefs will be epistemically correct! Now suppose you ask me *why* Matt believes *this here* car is a good deal in a tone of voice that makes it clear that what you are asking for is an epistemic justification of his belief rather than, for example, its causal etiology. There are many ways I might respond. But one way I might permissibly respond (given Explanation–Justification Connection) is by telling you that Matt is epistemically justified in thinking it is a good deal because if he believes that, he'll be more likely to make the sale and so earn a commission, which would make him better off.

I suppose you'd look askance. You might (this is the queasy epistemologist's reaction) simply think that I have failed to cite anything capable of justifying Matt's belief in any case. But here's a different diagnosis of what has gone wrong (or perhaps simply a diagnosis of the queasiness): what I have done is cite something that should make you *extraordinarily suspicious* of the very idea that Matt is used-car reliable. How reliable can he be if what he believes is justified on the grounds that so believing will promote his interests? It does no good at this stage for me to insist that this *just is* Matt's being epistemically correct about used cars – you will presumably not care. Precisely what Matt's case shows is that the facts that purportedly ground being epistemically correct have come unstuck from the kinds of things that can be cited in justifications for agents' beliefs *without simultaneously undermining our judgments of who constitutes a reliable informant.*

This last point is *the* point. The idea is not that epistemic instrumentalism has misidentified the grounds of epistemic correctness because those grounds *couldn't possibly* be the grounds of some kind of correctness or other that we might call "epistemic correctness". The idea is that epistemic instrumentalism has misidentified the grounds of a kind of correctness *whose job it is to flag reliable informants* and that we can know this because we can always cite explanatory grounds in our justifications but, if epistemic instrumentalism is correct, we can't.

The Functionalist Challenge 95

Reversing course, there are some materials that saws simply cannot be made of, given what saws are *for*; this does not mean we can't make a saw-shaped thing out of such materials and begin sawing away with it – it simply means that what we will have is not plausibly a well-made saw. Back the other direction, there are some explanatory grounds that epistemic correctness simply cannot be made of, given what epistemic correctness is *for*; this does not mean we can't make a first-order epistemic theory-shaped thing out of such explanatory grounds and begin evaluating away with it – it simply means that what we will have is not plausibly a well-made *first-order epistemic theory*.

To have things as clear as possible, here is the argument all laid out in one place:

1. If G is the explanatory ground of the k correctness of A's φ-ing, then it is always k-ly acceptable to cite G in a k justification of the k correctness of A's φ-ing. (Explanation–Justification Connection)
2. The fact that it is epistemically correct for A to φ is grounded by the fact that A's φ-ing promotes A's well-being. (First-Order Epistemic Instrumentalism)
3. So, it is always epistemically acceptable to cite the fact that A's φ-ing promotes A's well-being in an epistemic justification of the epistemic justification of A's φ-ing. (1 & 2)
4. For a kind of correctness k a function of which is F: if citing G in a k justification for φ-ing interferes with the ability of k thought and talk to F, then citing G is k-ly unacceptable in that k justification for φ-ing. (No Interference)
5. A function of the kind of correctness that is *epistemic* correctness is to flag reliable informants. (Minimal Functional Criterion)
6. So, if citing the fact that A's φ-ing promotes A's well-being in an epistemic justification for φ-ing would interfere with the ability of epistemic thought and talk to flag reliable informants, then citing the fact that A's φ-ing promotes A's well-being is epistemically unacceptable in that epistemic justification for φ-ing. (4 & 5)
7. Citing the fact that A's φ-ing promotes A's well-being in an epistemic justification for φ-ing can sometimes interfere with the ability of epistemic thought and talk to flag reliable informants. (Interference)
8. So, citing the fact that A's φ-ing promotes A's well-being in an epistemic justification for φ-ing can sometimes be epistemically unacceptable in an epistemic justification for φ-ing. (6 & 7)

(3) and (8) contradict one another. So something must have gone wrong. (3) follows from (1) and (2), (6) follows from (4) and (5), and (8) follows from (6) and (7). I have explained why I think (1) is in effect a truism about the connection between explanation and justification and why (4)

is overwhelmingly plausible, given the idea that some kind of correctness is functionally defined. Chapter 4 was devoted to defending (5): having as its functional role the role of flagging reliable informants is how we distinguish *epistemic* correctness from other kinds of correctness, given the maximally many (or at least many many) different kinds of possible correctness. And I have just given an illustrative case in which (6) is true and explained the general mechanism at work in that case: the explanatory grounds of epistemic correctness have come systematically unstuck from what kinds of things can serve in epistemic justifications without simultaneously undermining the ability of judgments of epistemic correctness to do what they are for, namely, flagging reliable informants.

That leaves (2): first-order epistemic instrumentalism. And that is what I think we should give up. But as I will now explain, giving up first-order epistemic is perfectly fine. We should not think of epistemic instrumentalism as a *first-order* epistemic theory in any case. As we have just seen, as a view about what is epistemically correct, it is not in good shape. At best, it is in a stalemate, via the Goldilocks Problem, with other competing first-order epistemic theories. At worst, it is a complete nonstarter, via the Functionalist Challenge I just outlined.

But epistemic instrumentalism should not be understood as a first-order epistemic theory concerning why and when things are epistemically correct; instead, it should be understood as a second-order epistemic theory concerning why and when facts about epistemic correctness *matter*. As we will see, as a view about this latter topic, epistemic instrumentalism is doing *great*.

Notes

1 One idea might be that adequate moral justifications require the thought that the agent acted, as it's sometimes put, "from duty" rather than simply "in accord" with duty. And it's plausible that the former (being morally justified) requires the agent's mental state to be a certain way, whereas the latter (being morally correct) does not. Hence, there might be more that can be cited in favor of the former than can be cited in favor of the latter. For discussion, see Markovits (2010), King (2020a), Arpaly (2002), King (2020b), and Singh (2019, 2020).
2 For discussion, see Hooker (2010), Eggleston (2013), Wiland (2007), Railton (1984), and Paakkunainen (2017).
3 For example, see the discussion in Railton (1984).
4 As further evidence, this is exactly how (Railton 1984), an avowedly self-effacing consequentialist, sees things.
5 Smith is not the only one to think this. Compare Wiland (2007), Erik (2002), and Bykvist (2007). This idea, that the function, purpose, or point of deontic thought and talk is to guide choice with respect to choosable events, is not at all the same idea as the idea that the point of *morality* is to do this. On the latter idea, see the very useful discussion in Smyth (2017).
6 For the argument, see especially the discussion in section 4 of Sharadin and Greve (2021).

References

Arpaly, Nomy. 2002. "Moral Worth." *Journal of Philosophy* 99 (5): 223. https://doi.org/10.2307/3655647.

Bykvist, Krister. 2007. "Violations of Normative Invariance: Some Thoughts on Shifty Oughts." *Theoria* 73 (2): 98–120. https://doi.org/10.1111/j.1755-2567.2007.tb01193.x.

Eggleston, Ben. 2013. "Rejecting the Publicity Condition: The Inevitability of Esoteric Morality." *Philosophical Quarterly* 63 (250): 29–57. https://doi.org/10.1111/j.1467-9213.2012.00106.x.

Erik, Carlson. 2002. "Deliberation, Foreknowledge, and Morality as a Guide to Action." *Erkenntnis* 57 (1): 71–89. https://doi.org/10.1023/A:1020146102680.

Fricker, Miranda. 2007. *Epistemic Injustice: Power and the Ethics of Knowing*. Oxford: Oxford University Press.

Hannon, Michael. 2019. *What's the Point of Knowledge?: A Function-First Epistemology*. New York, NY: Oxford University Press.

Hooker, Brad. 2010. "Publicity in Morality." *Ratio* 23: 111–117.

King, Zoë A. Johnson. 2020a. "Praiseworthy Motivations." *Noûs* 54 (2): 408–430. https://doi.org/10.1111/nous.12276.

King, Zoe Johnson. 2020b. "Accidentally Doing the Right Thing." *Philosophy and Phenomenological Research* 100 (1): 186–206. https://doi.org/10.1111/phpr.12535.

Markovits, Julia. 2010. "Acting for the Right Reasons." *Philosophical Review* 119 (2): 201–242. https://doi.org/10.1215/00318108-2009-037.

McKenna, Robin. 2014. "Normative Scorekeeping." *Synthese* 191 (3): 607–625. https://doi.org/10.1007/s11229-013-0293-1.

Paakkunainen, Hille. 2017. "Can There Be Government House Reasons for Action?" *Journal of Ethics and Social Philosophy* 12 (1): 56–93. https://doi.org/10.26556/jesp.v12i1.213.

Railton, Peter. 1984. "Alienation, Consequentialism, and the Demands of Morality." *Philosophy and Public Affairs* 13 (2): 134–171.

Rysiew, Patrick. 2012. "Epistemic Scorekeeping." In *Knowledge Ascriptions*, edited by Jessica Brown and Mikkel Gerken, 270–293. Oxford: Oxford University Press.

Sharadin, Nathaniel. 2019. "Consequentialism and Moral Worth." *Utilitas* 31 (2). https://doi.org/10.1017/s0953820818000146.

Sharadin, Nathaniel, and Rob Van Someren Greve. 2021. "Is Deontic Evaluation Capable of Doing What It Is For?" *Journal of Ethics and Social Philosophy* 19 (3). https://doi.org/10.26556/jesp.v19i3.843.

Singh, Keshav. 2019. "Acting and Believing under the Guise of Normative Reasons." *Philosophy and Phenomenological Research* 99 (2): 409–430. https://doi.org/10.1111/phpr.12497.

———. 2020. "Moral Worth, Credit, and Non-Accidentality." In *Oxford Studies in Normative Ethics, Vol. 10*, edited by Mark Timmons, 156–180. Oxford: Oxford University Press.

Smith, Holly M. 1986. "Moral Realism, Moral Conflict, and Compound Acts." *Journal of Philosophy* 83 (6): 341–345. https://doi.org/jphil198683659.

———. 2018. *Making Morality Work*. Oxford/Great Britain: Oxford University Press.

Smyth, Nicholas. 2017. "The Function of Morality." *Philosophical Studies* 174 (5): 1127–1144. https://doi.org/10.1007/s11098-016-0746-8.

Wiland, Eric. 2007. "How Indirect Can Indirect Utilitarianism Be?" *Philosophy and Phenomenological Research* 74 (2): 275–301. https://doi.org/10.1111/j.1933-1592.2007.00018.x.

Williams, Bernard. 1976. "Persons, Character, and Morality." In *Moral Luck: Philosophical Papers 1973–1980*, edited by James Rachels, 1–19. Cambridge University Press.

Wolf, Susan. 2012. "'One Thought Too Many': Love, Morality, and the Ordering Of." In *Luck, Value, and Commitment: Themes from the Ethics of Bernard Williams*, edited by Ulrike Heuer and Gerald Lang, 71–92. Oxford: Oxford University Press.

7 Second-Order Epistemic Theory

7.1 Introduction

I have just argued that epistemic instrumentalism fails as a first-order epistemic theory. I have also said that it is a mistake to understand it as a first-order epistemic theory. Rather than conceiving of it as a first-order epistemic theory that attempts to identify the explanatory grounds of epistemic correctness, we should understand epistemic instrumentalism as a *second*-order epistemic theory that attempts to identify the explanatory grounds of *epistemic authority*. In this chapter, I explain what I mean by a second-order epistemic theory and by epistemic authority. In the next chapter, I outline epistemic instrumentalism as a second-order epistemic theory and extoll its virtues. Its virtues suggest that, being so long ignored, it has been incorrectly ignored; later on (Chapters 9–10), I offer a debunking diagnosis of its unpopularity. The result is a natural, straightforward view. First, what is a second-order epistemic theory anyway?

7.2 Authoritative and Formal Correctness

Recall from much earlier that there are maximally many (at the very least, many many) different kinds of correctness. It is morally correct to keep your promise. It is assassin-ly correct to buy quieter shoes. It is 8chanly correct to believe that Nancy eats children. It is not epistemically correct to believe Nancy is a cannibal. And so on.

In Chapter 4, we talked about how to differentiate epistemic correctness from the many kinds of correctness there are. There, I said that we could appeal to the *functional earmarks* of epistemic correctness in order to distinguish it from other perhaps nearby kinds of correctness. And in the last chapter, we put that view about the function, purpose, or point of evaluation in terms of epistemic correctness to work in explaining what goes wrong with epistemic instrumentalism as a view about the explanatory grounds of epistemic correctness.

But there is a further, important difference between some kinds of correctness that we have been glossing over and mostly ignoring throughout

DOI: 10.4324/9781003096726-7

the discussion so far. There are a number of different ways we can put the intuitive idea, but one way to put it is to say that some kinds of correctness, at least some of the time, *matter*, and others, at least most of the time, do not matter: ordinarily at least, it *really matters* what, epistemically speaking, it is correct for you to believe, whereas it *does not* really matter what, 8chanly speaking, it is correct for you to believe. Can we say more?

We can begin by following the long-standing tradition of saying it in quotes or italics but differently. Some kinds of correctness, we can say, are *binding* (Knight and Johnson 1994; Pinkard 2007; Tiffany 2012; de Ridder 2014; Mason, forthcoming). Some kinds of correctness have *force* (Kornblith 1993; Hardimon 1994; Railton 1999; Greaves and Wallace 2006; Wedgwood 2006; Finlay 2007; Easwaran 2011; Franklin 2013; D'Arms and Jacobson 2014; Woods 2016; Collins 2017; Lindeman 2017; Comesaña 2020; Schmidt 2021). Some exert *pressure* (Kolodny 2005; Calhoun 2009; Copp 2015b). Some kinds of correctness are sometimes *grippy* (Brandom 2002; Kukla 2002; Anderson 2003; Wong 2008; Matt Bedke 2011; Sylvan 2016; Peter 2019). Some kinds of correctness have *normative strength* (Gowans 2002; Gert 2003, 2007, 2008; Sampson 2015). Some are *robustly normative* (McPherson 2011). Some correctness carries *weight* (Darwall 2003; Chang 2004; Behrends 2015; Zöe Johnson King 2019). Some correctness has *oomph* (Joyce 2005; Southwood and Eriksson 2011; Copp 2015a; Sylvan 2017; McPherson 2018; Wodak 2019). Some kinds of correctness are *prescriptive* (Papineau 2013). I have resorted to ostensive definition by italicized metaphor. Let's at least settle on terms.

By far, the most common way to refer to the thing we are interested in here is by distinguishing between "normative" and "nonnormative" kinds of correctness, where the former, but not the latter, are supposed to be the ones that *matter* or have *grip*. Here, I aim to avoid this way of speaking, since the idea of "normativity" carries a range of different baggage depending on the person using it. Instead, I will use the locution "authoritative correctness" to refer to the kind of case that merits italics and "formal correctness" to refer to the kind that does not.[1] Correspondingly, I will say that it is "authoritatively *k*-ly correct" for an agent to φ or that it is "formally correct" for them to do so, and sometimes, I will refer to "*k* authority" as shorthand for the feature that *k* correctness is supposed to have.

Naming things does not get us too far. Can we do better than italics; can we unpack the metaphor?

7.3 Pluralism and Monism Redux

To begin, distinguish between two ways of approaching the task of unpacking the metaphorical language of *force*, *grip*, and the like: monistic and pluralist.[2] According to *monists* about authority, there is a single notion, authority, that travels across different kinds of correctness. In other words, authority as exhibited by, for example, epistemic correctness is the same as authority exhibited by, for example, moral correctness. And if authority is exhibited by other kinds of correctness, it is this same authority, too. For monists, then, once we have identified what authority is and explained what it takes for a kind of correctness to be authoritative, the notion stays identified and stays explained as we move between different kinds of correctness.

In other words, monists think very same authoritativeness that appears – sometimes at least – to attach to what is epistemically correct is what – sometimes at least – attaches to what is ethically correct, to what is prudentially correct and, depending on our view of matters, to what is assassinly correct (if it ever turns out that what is assassinly correct is authoritatively assassinly correct). And so, on this view, if we can explain why it is that *this* kind of correctness is authoritative, we will have explained why *all* the kinds of correctness that are authoritative are so. Hence, we can approach our explanatory project monistically: we can try and give an account of authority such that it explains authority whenever it occurs. Authority is authority is authority.

According to *pluralists*, there are many (perhaps, many, many) non-identical notions of authoritativeness. These notions might resemble one another – we can shelve them in the same aisle – but explaining the authoritativeness of one kind of correctness does not entail that one has thereby explained authoritativeness *whenever* it occurs. In other words, the kind of authoritativeness that epistemic correctness sometimes exhibits is not necessarily exactly the same as the kind of authoritativeness ethical correctness sometimes exhibits or that prudential correctness sometimes exhibits or, for that matter, the same as the authoritativeness that assassin correctness might sometimes exhibit. Hence, we should approach our explanatory project *pluralistically*: we should try to give an account of the specific authority at issue such that it satisfactorily accounts for that kind of authority when it occurs. Epistemic authority is not ethical authority is not prudential authority.

Here, I am interested in epistemic authority. But my being interested in epistemic authority *qua* epistemic authority, as opposed simply to *qua* authority clearly depends on adopting a pluralistic theoretical approach. And that is what I will do. What this means is that I am going to treat *epistemic* authority as the kind of thing we can at least attempt to explain without simultaneously explaining (say) ethical authority or the authority of aesthetics or whatever. In other words, the thought is that we can say why it is that epistemic correctness is authoritative, when it is, without also committing ourselves to anything in particular about why it is that some other kinds of correctness might exhibit their own peculiar kind of authority when *they* do. Let me say just a couple things about why I find pluralism more attractive than monism in the present context.

My primary reason for preferring to run a small shop is that as far as I can tell the phenomenon of authority we can meaningfully point to *in advance of an explanation for it in particular cases* seems to me *far* too diverse to merit the thought that it is the same thing, everywhere, across all the different domains in which something like that phenomenon seems to arise.[3] We have already mentioned a few such domains: ethics, epistemology, prudence. There seems to be something obviously right about the thought that correctness in these domains, whatever it comprises, oftentimes *matters*, is *grippy, forceful, prescriptive*, or whatever other italicized way of putting things you like. Is there something also obviously right about the thought that the kind of mattering that *moral correctness* enjoys is the same as the kind of mattering that *prudential correctness* or *epistemic correctness* enjoys? No.

This does not mean that it will not turn out, when all the arguments are in, that there's a single notion here. (Maybe it turns out, once all the data are in, that there's a single physical cause of Alzheimer's.) My observation that our pre-theoretical grip on the phenomenon does not merit the monist thought is of course not – and not intended as – an argument against monism. (The observation that our pre-theoretical grip on symptomatic Alzheimer's does not merit the thought that there's a single physical cause thereof is not a piece of data that there is not.) It is instead the observation that, in my view, we are not entitled to monism prior to offering an explanation for authority. (It is instead the observation that, in my view, we are not entitled to think there's a single physical cause of Alzheimer's prior to canvassing all the data.)

Equally, you might think, we are not *thereby* entitled to pluralism. Perhaps we should simply be agnostic between the two approaches. Fair enough. But notice that steadfast agnosticism between the two approaches is, in effect, to adopt the pluralistic theoretical approach, which is all I'm interested in here. For, if you aren't sure whether all instances of authoritative correctness are exhibiting the very same kind of authority, the thing to do is explore each one to see whether, as it happens, it's the same as all the others.

Back to my parenthetical analogy, if you don't know whether all cases of Alzheimer's are caused in exactly the same way, the thing to do is to explore each known case and see whether, as it happens, it's caused in exactly the same way as all the others. Here, I'm simply not interested in diagnosing all the patients – which is to say, instances of authority; instead, I'm interested only in offering up what I think is the best diagnosis of – er, explanation for – *epistemic* authority. Maybe it turns out this diag – ... *explanation*, works in other cases too. So much the better. I take no stand on that possibility here (although I do say a bit more about this possibility in Chapter 11).

My second reason for preferring the pluralist approach to matters – and this is really just another way of putting the same point – is that it is (perhaps *distressingly*) easy to generate the intuition that, at least some of the time, some kinds of correctness are authoritative, at least for some agents. For instance, it is aesthetically correct for Gauguin to go to Tahiti to paint.[4] It *really matters* from the aesthetic point of view that he go to Tahiti. That is presumably in part because it will make his art aesthetically better. Remember how we metaphorically gestured at the relevant notion: authoritative correctness appears *grippy*; it is *forceful*; it *exerts pressure*. All these things are true when it comes to aesthetic correctness and Gauguin's trip to Tahiti. It is "important" for him to go.[5]

Of course, there is another kind of correctness that perhaps has some authoritative flavor too: it is *not* ethically correct for Gauguin to abandon his family. It is *really* not ethically correct for him to do so. But why think the former, aesthetic kind of authority is *exactly the same thing* as the latter, ethical kind of authority? Sure, both are *grippy*; both *bind*. But gecko's feet are grippy and bind, and duct tape grips and binds. Sure, both have *force*; both have *oomph*. But stomach punches have force and oomph, and sick bass beats do, too. These notions – sticky feet and tape, punches and beats – might rhyme, but they are not simply identical.

One thing you might want to do is simply reject the thought that aesthetic authority is *genuine* authority. But again, prior to an account of authority monistically understood, why do that? (Prior to a single causal story about Alzheimer's, why say this is not *really* Alzheimer's?)

Monists will therefore need to insist on treating aesthetic authority on a par with ethical authority on a par with epistemic authority on a par with prudential authority and so on. This flattens the landscape. Of course, there are obviously in fact differences between the way aesthetic, ethical, epistemic, prudential, legal, or, for that matter, assassin, correctness actually strikes agents. Monists will then need to explain (away) those differences. Again, the usual tack is to end up saying that some apparent forms or instances of authority are specious: for instance, although it might *appear* that someone planning an assassination not just should not but also *really* should not tweet about it, this intuition does not indicate that there is any such thing as the authoritative nature of assassin correctness, even for some small subset of agents, even in some strange circumstances.

Pluralists have it much easier, since pluralists can happily admit a range of different kinds of authoritativeness, each with its own peculiar properties and features. Authority, according to pluralists, is a kind of family resemblance notion. That is why, although we get the sense that epistemic authority is not *precisely* like legal authority, which, in turn, is not *precisely* like ethical authority, each exhibits a range of sometimes overlapping, convergent features.[6]

If you are not convinced by this that pluralism about authority is true, that is fine – this is not meant to be an argument against monistic approaches. Instead, it is intended to explain the pluralist approach going forward; in this book, I aim to be interested only in *epistemic* authority. And so I focus, going forward, on the explanatory project associated with that notion in particular.

7.4 Epistemic Authority Explanatory Principles

We still have not said anything about how to unpack the metaphor. But I have said I will be approaching things focused on the notion of epistemic authority in particular, rather than the idea of authority quite generally. So, let's dig into the idea of epistemic authority.

Suppose the following is true: It is epistemically correct for Senator Joshua Hawley to believe that Biden won the election. Then, we know that Hawley is making an epistemic mistake if he fails to believe Biden won the election. Our first-order epistemic theory is our account of what explanatorily grounds this fact about what it would be epistemically correct for Mr. Hawley to do. So far, so good.

We have also said that, intuitively at least, facts about what it is epistemically correct to do – such as for Hawley to believe Biden won – *matter*: it is not just correct for him to so believe; it is also *authoritatively* correct for Hawley to believe Biden won the election. What's the "authoritatively" doing here?

One idea would be that attaching "authoritatively" to epistemic correctness transforms the nature of epistemic correctness altogether in much the same way as attaching "Zarrow" to "shuffle" transforms the nature of the shuffle altogether. (A shuffle is a way of randomizing cards. A Zarrow shuffle is not a shuffle; it is a *false* shuffle.) This is a mistake. When it is true that it is authoritatively epistemically correct for Hawley to believe Biden won the election, what we have is not some new claim about what it is epistemically correct for Hawley to do, namely, that it is *authoritatively epistemically correct* for him to believe Biden won the election.

Let me emphasize this point. What it is epistemically correct for an agent to do under some circumstances is determined by whatever grounds epistemic correctness. Our best first-order epistemic theory tells us what that is. Perhaps we are evidentialists. Then, what it is epistemically correct for, for example, Hawley to believe about Biden's election, is determined by what the (or perhaps Hawley's) evidence supports believing. And when we add that it is *authoritatively* epistemically correct for Hawley to so believe, we are not in any way making a claim the truth of which is determined by *those* explanatory grounds. We are making a *further* claim the truth of which is determined by whatever the explanatory grounds of *epistemic authority* are supposed to be. What we have, then, are two ideas. On one hand, it is epistemically correct for Hawley to believe Biden won. And on the other hand, epistemic correctness is in this case authoritative.

Here is another way to put the same point: as we have seen (Chapter 2), a kind of correctness is given by the standards that determine what would be required in order for some doing to count as correct of that kind. But the idea that a kind of correctness is authoritative is not the idea that there is some *new standard*, some new kind of correctness. Instead, it is the idea that, however this is to be explained, the relevant kind of correctness *matters*. So it goes with epistemic correctness and its authority.

I will call this idea, that authoritative epistemic correctness is not some new kind of correctness, namely, authoritative epistemic correctness, the *factoring account*.[7] According to the factoring account, it is possible to *factor* the claim that it is authoritatively epistemically correct for A to φ into two component parts: first, that it is epistemically correct for A to φ and, second, that epistemic correctness is on this occasion authoritative. The truth of the first claim is determined by our best first-order epistemic theory. The truth of the second is determined by ... some other theory.

Hawley's is a case in point. Our evidentialism, if we accept it, explains why it is epistemically correct for Hawley to believe Biden won. The fact that it is *authoritatively* correct for him to do so is explained by ... some other theory. What theory?

Our first-order epistemic theory offers an account of the explanatory ground of epistemic correctness. Our *second-order* epistemic theory, then, is what offers us an account of the explanatory ground of *epistemic authority*. In parallel with our approach to first-order epistemic theory, we can say that our second-order epistemic theory attempts to tell us what *F* is in the generic:

> The fact that it is authoritatively epistemically correct for A to φ is grounded by *F*.

A couple of quick remarks. When I first introduced the relevant notion of grounding I said that, unless otherwise specified, when I said "grounds" I would be using it to mean "completely grounds" rather than "partially grounds." Here is a case in which I need to specify otherwise. The reason for this is obvious.

Earlier, I said that authoritative epistemic correctness is not some novel kind of correctness; instead, authoritative epistemic correctness is epistemic correctness *that is authoritative*. What this means in the present case is that the fact that it is authoritatively epistemically correct for A to φ is *partially* grounded by whatever facts our first-order epistemic theory says explanatorily grounds epistemic correctness. In Hawley's case, the fact that it is authoritatively epistemically correct for A to φ is partially grounded by, for example, his evidence. The remainder of the ground of authoritative epistemic correctness is whatever explanatorily grounds the *authority* of the epistemic correctness. When I talk about second-order epistemic theories offering accounts of the grounds of authoritative epistemic correctness, I will be talking about their offering accounts of *this partial ground in particular*. In other words, the F in

> the fact that it is authoritatively epistemically correct for A to φ is grounded by F

should be taken to be limited to the (second-order) *grounds of authority* rather than also, in part, comprising the (first-order) explanatory grounds of correctness.

Now, you might think (we will see some views think something like this later) that the *very same thing* explanatorily grounds both the facts about epistemic correctness and facts about the authoritativeness of epistemic correctness. That is a possibility we will have to take seriously. And, of course, that's a familiar possibility from other cases of grounding explanations. The very same thing grounds, and so explains, the fact that the Mets just lost and the fact that the Mets' loss was *so lopsided*.

Despite this possibility of doing double work, I assume we can separate in our thinking about the issue the question of what grounds the *authority* of the epistemic correctness and what grounds the *epistemic correctness*. At least, we can do so on the assumption that the one does not *always* track the other – more on this in just a bit. In effect, this way of speaking amounts to a terminological choice.

Speaking of terminological choices: it will sometimes be convenient to have a way to refer to a particular second-order epistemic theory's account of how to fill in F. Following the practice outlined in Chapter 3 in the case of first-order epistemic theories, I shall refer to such principles as a theory's Epistemic Authority Explanatory Principle, or EAEP for short. So, for instance, suppose someone claimed the following:

> Divine Command: The fact that it is authoritatively epistemically correct for A to φ is grounded by the fact that God commands A to φ.

I would then refer to this principle as Divine Command's EAEP. Intuitively, a theory's EAEP specifies whatever it is you need to *add* to the explanatory grounds of epistemic correctness in order to get epistemic authority. According to Divine Command theorists, what you need to add is, as the name suggests, a divine command.

So, what account should we give of F? To begin to answer this question, we need to say more about what epistemic authority actually *is* – what the phenomenon is supposed to be. We have gestured at it (it is the *oomphy* kind of epistemic correctness), but it will be helpful to say some more specific things. I start to do that in the next two sections. There, I outline what I will call the *minimal conception* of epistemic authority by identifying two basic features of authoritative epistemic correctness. Corresponding to these two features, then, I will lay out two minimal criteria of adequacy that a successful explanation for the (minimal conception of) epistemic authority must meet. More on this in just a moment. Before that, let me remind you of something we encountered in thinking about *first*-order epistemic theorizing, in our thinking about the explanatory grounds of epistemic correctness.

You will remember that, when it comes to epistemic correctness, the fact that two theories agree on the *extension* of epistemic correctness does not entail that they are not competitors. This is because first-order epistemic theories, as should be familiar by now, are attempts to identify the explanatory grounds of epistemic correctness. And what we do is *read off* the extension of epistemic correctness from the explanatory grounds thereof.

Here, I simply flag the point that a symmetrical fact is true in *second-order* epistemic theorizing. I will say more about this later on, but it is important to keep it in mind. Second-order epistemic theories purport to tell us what the explanatory grounds of the *authority* of epistemic correctness are. What this means is, first, that two theories that agree on the *extension* of epistemic authority do not thereby fail to count as competitors. And, second, it means that we *read off* the extension of epistemic authority from the explanatory grounds thereof. As I said, I will say more later on. Now it is time to say more about what epistemic authority is supposed to be.

7.5 The Minimal Conception of Epistemic Authority

In this section, I outline what I call the *minimal conception of epistemic authority*. The minimal conception is minimal: it aims to draw some firm, but quite broad lines around what we mean by the idea that epistemic correctness is authoritative. In so doing, the minimal conception puts in place a relatively easily satisfied but nevertheless genuine criterion of explanatory adequacy for any attempt at explaining such authority.

7.5.1 Potential Psychological Impact

Let's return for the moment to our friend Senator Hawley. It can help us catch on to the relevant notion of epistemic authority to think about *our* position with respect to Hawley under certain circumstances. Suppose we say to Josh (we at least *begin* on a friendly, first-name basis): "Josh, I know you have seen the election results, and you have been briefed on the security of the election, and so, given all of the evidence, it is epistemically correct for you to believe that Biden won." Again, I take us to be thereby committed to thinking that our friend, the junior senator from Missouri, would be in some way making an epistemic mistake if he were to believe Biden lost, that he should so believe, and so on. Suppose we then see Josh in the well of the Senate decrying the stolen presidency. We might bell him: "Josh, look: maybe you did not understand. It is not just that it is epistemically correct for you to believe Biden won, it is that it is *authoritatively* epistemically correct for you to believe Biden won." Of course, this will not have any effect.

But what are we thereby trying to convey to the increasingly insufferable senator by adding the "authoritatively"? It cannot just be that he epistemically should believe Biden is president; we – and he – already know this. We are trying to *add something* – something that indicates that, as we put it earlier, epistemic correctness in this instance is *oomphy, forceful, grippy, binding*, and so on. But in what does the "bindingness" consist?

Here is one half of my minimal proposal. What all these metaphors have in common is the implication that we think *authoritative* epistemic correctness, as compared to merely formal correctness, must have at least a *potential psychological impact* on the relevant agent. Put otherwise, it cannot be the case that it is *authoritatively* epistemically correct for an agent to φ and simultaneously that it is *impossible* for the fact that it is epistemically correct for the agent to φ to have any psychological impact at all on the agent for whom it is epistemically correct that they φ. This, then, is the first feature of epistemic authority, minimally construed: epistemic authority entails potential psychological impact. I will address concerns in just a moment. Let me first say a couple of things to qualify the claim.

This idea, that epistemic authority entails potential psychological impact, is *extremely weak* in four related ways. First, it does not say *what kind* of psychological impact the fact that something is epistemically correct is required to potentially have on agents in order for it to count as authoritatively epistemically correct. Second, it only requires that the psychological impact of the fact of epistemic correctness be *potential* rather than actual. Third, it does not specify the *mechanism* by which the fact that something is epistemically correct must be potentially psychologically impactful on agents (nor does it say that this mechanism is always the same). Finally, it is only entailment in one direction; it may be that there are cases of potentially psychologically impactful epistemic correctness that do not count as *authoritative* epistemic correctness.

Despite being weak in these four ways, I think the idea that epistemic authority entails potential psychological impact captures something extremely important – something absolutely essential – about the idea of epistemic authority. It is not clear to me what it would mean for it to be true that it is *authoritatively* epistemically correct for an agent to (say) believe some proposition but for it simultaneously to be true that the fact that it is epistemically correct for the agent to believe that proposition is incapable *in principle* via *any mechanism* of having *any kind* of psychological impact on the agent governed by the authoritative requirement.[8] I think if you describe a case of epistemic correctness like that, what you have thereby described is a case of epistemic correctness that is paradigmatically merely formal and not authoritative.

I confess it is very difficult to see how to argue for this claim beyond iterating examples, which I will not do. Here is our dialectical situation. We pre-theoretically have the sense that facts about what it is *k*-ly correct for agents to do sometimes matter, at least for some *k*s. *Moral* correctness seems like one of these *k*s. But so, too, does *epistemic* correctness. I have said we should treat these ideas as separable, and so in the present instance, we are trying just to get a somewhat firmer grip on what it means to say that epistemic correctness at least sometimes matters in this sense. Call this way of mattering "being authoritative". Here is the present suggestion, in a nutshell: whatever explains why it is that facts about epistemic correctness sometimes matter in this way or are authoritative, it had better at least *allow* that those facts about epistemic correctness are in principle potentially psychologically impactful on agents. Otherwise, I claim – and on behalf of which I have no further argument to offer – we have entirely lost the sense in which these facts about epistemic correctness matter.

The following can be extremely misleading, and so I hesitate even to mention it. But it can also be extremely helpful if we are careful. I will try to be careful. You can think of this restriction on epistemic authority as a cousin – not a *close* cousin, a kissing cousin – of what usually gets called a *resonance constraint* in debates over agential well-being. There, the idea is that any plausible account of the constituents of agential well-being will require that those constituents of agents' well-being be at least *capable* of being the object of various conative pro-attitudes on the part of the agent. The idea, there, is that something does not count as good *for* an agent unless it is at least *possible* for that thing to be, to put it *very roughly*, enjoyed by the agent: it has to, in some way, be capable of *hooking up* (in a positive way) to their psychology.[9] In other words, things that are good for an agent have to be able to "resonate" with that agent.

I am not suggesting here that authoritative epistemic correctness is subject to a resonance requirement. But the two ideas rhyme. I am suggesting that making sense of the idea that there can be a difference between correctness that matters in the way epistemic correctness manifestly sometimes does and correctness that does not matter (e.g., in the way tuesdayical correctness manifestly does not) requires thinking that part of *what it is* to be authoritative is to be capable, in some way, of *hooking up* to agents' psychologies *in one way or another*. As I said, this can be misleading. If you feel misled, ignore the last two paragraphs.

This, then, is a characteristic of epistemic authority. But if I am correct about this characteristic of epistemic authority – that it always entails potential psychological impact – then we can quickly make out a natural criterion for an adequate explanation of the phenomenon of epistemic authority corresponding to this idea, namely, that any such explanation must itself account for the fact that agents cannot be *in principle* psychologically indifferent to authoritative epistemic correctness. This is the criterion of adequacy on explanations of epistemic authority that I will call

> Potential Psychological Impact: The fact that it is authoritatively epistemically correct for A to φ is grounded by F only if F grounds potential psychological impact of the fact that it is epistemically correct for A to φ.

Potential Psychological Impact represents our first criterion of adequacy for an explanation of epistemic authority. I will turn to the second feature of epistemic authority, and the corresponding second criterion of adequacy for an explanation thereof, in just a moment. Let me first try to set aside a couple remaining concerns you might have about Potential Psychological Impact.

First, I have said that because epistemic authority entails potential psychological impact, an adequate account of the explanatory grounds of epistemic authority must also capture the explanatory grounds of the potential psychological impact of authoritative epistemic correctness. You might object to tying the two together in this way.

For, it is not always true that when X entails Y an adequate account of the explanatory grounds of X requires an adequate account of the explanatory grounds of Y. For instance, being born in the United States entails that I am a US citizen.[10] But an adequate account of the explanatory grounds of my being born in the United States not only need not amount to an adequate account of the explanatory grounds of my US citizenship, but it also need not even mention those grounds or, for that matter, even acknowledge the existence of this latter fact *in any way*. It could instead appeal only to facts concerning (say) how people felt like behaving on certain days, the standard gestation period for humans, and the famous unreliability of US-based passenger airlines.

Perhaps you think the situation when it comes to epistemic authority is like that. Although being authoritatively epistemically correct entails being potentially psychologically impactful, we can explain the former fact without in any way even acknowledging – let alone offering up a theory that would even in part explain – the latter fact. But this is not correct. The reason we can divorce the two explanations in the birthright citizenship case is that the two facts are only connected via an arbitrary (legal) principle, Section 1 of the Fourteenth Amendment to the Constitution. Not so in the case of the potential psychological impact of authoritative epistemic correctness. Instead, in this case, the idea is that part of *what it is* to be a case of authoritative epistemic correctness is to be potentially psychologically impactful. Being born in the United States does not partly constitute US citizenship: the former is a geographical–reproductive–biological–historical matter, whereas the latter is entirely a legal matter. By contrast, the thought here – the very thing that drove our intuitions about epistemic authority and psychological impact – is that the potential psychological impact of some case of epistemic correctness, in part, *constitutes* the authoritativeness of that case of correctness. Hence, an explanation of authoritativeness will comprise, in part, an explanation of that impact.

A second kind of worry about the idea of potential psychological impact goes like this: the claim that cases of authoritative epistemic correctness are ones to which the agents subject to them cannot be in principle psychologically indifferent is belied by cases of apparent potential psychological indifference to *other kinds* of plausibly authoritative cases of correctness, such as cases of authoritative *moral* correctness. For instance, and famously, it at least appears possible for an agent to be faced with (say) the fact that it is authoritatively morally correct for them to keep their promise and for them to be *in principle* completely incapable of being psychologically impacted by this fact.[11] But I have just said that this *is not* possible in any case of authoritative *epistemic* correctness. What gives?

I have two responses. The first is to insist, again, that we approach things as pluralists. I am not interested, in this book, in comparing competing explanations for, and so conceptions of, *moral* authority. And I do not think, as monists do, that authority is authority is authority. Instead, I am open to the possibility that epistemic authority is – in principle at least, *quite* – different from moral authority. Of course, there are similarities between the two; they resemble one another. But we cannot know, before commencing our investigation, whether everything that is at least intuitively true of one kind of authority is necessarily true of the other. So, even if it turned out that we were committed to thinking that it *was* possible to be in principle completely psychologically indifferent to authoritative moral correctness, this would not entail that we must think it was possible to be in principle completely psychologically indifferent to authoritative epistemic correctness. In other words, there might not be a corresponding Potential Psychological Impact criterion of adequacy for an explanation of authoritative moral correctness. And this would not be probative with respect to the existence of that criterion of adequacy in the case of epistemic authority.

Moreover (and this is my second response), it is not clear that we *do* think this is true even in the moral case. In other words, there very plausibly *is* a Potential Psychological Impact criterion in the moral case. We can see this by noticing that one common complaint about purported explanations of moral authority is that they fail to meet an *exactly analogous* explanatory criterion of adequacy. For instance, here is Christine Korsgaard making this point, in a somewhat different way, in the course of discussing the "normativity" (authority) of morality:

> When we use moral concepts [e.g., moral correctness], then, we use them to talk about matters which for us are important in very deep,

> strong, and profoundly practical ways. ... [T]he practical and psychological effects of moral ideas set a criterion of explanatory adequacy for a theory of moral concepts. Our theory of moral concepts must contain resources for explaining why and how these ideas can influence us in such deep ways.
>
> (Korsgaard 1996, pp. 11–12)

Potential Psychological Impact is, in effect, the epistemic analogue of this criterion of adequacy for explaining moral authority. And it is not a modern invention; as Korsgaard herself notes, Hume's complaint against certain forms of rationalist explanation of morality was precisely that they failed to meet it.[12]

As a final way of heading-off concern, notice that an explanation of how it is that authoritative epistemic correctness has a potential psychological impact is not the same as an explanation of why it *should have*, or whether we *want that it has*, such a psychological impact. The latter is a (partial) *justification* of epistemic authority; a justification of epistemic authority, in part, explains why it is that the psychological impact of which epistemic correctness is potentially capable is (at least sometimes) *legitimate*, or *appropriate*. In this book, I am not interested in this justificatory project. Let me briefly explain why.

The way to understand this last idea, that the potential psychological impact authoritative epistemic correctness has is somehow *legitimate* or *appropriate* is *as a further claim about correctness*: it is the claim – putting things deliberately awkwardly – that it is correct for epistemic correctness to be potentially psychologically impactful. But if that is (*ahem*) correct, then in investigating this claim we are simply doing first-order theory of one sort of another. Properly, the claim would be that it is k-ly correct for epistemic correctness to be potentially psychologically impactful. And we are then entitled to ask all sorts of questions about the relevant k; moreover, we can go on to ask a kind of second-order question about *this* claim corresponding to the question I *am* interested in investigating here, namely, what explains why it is true (if it is true) that it is *authoritatively* k-ly correct for epistemic correctness to be potentially psychologically impactful. And then, of course, we shall be off down a similar road as the one we were headed down several paragraphs back, before we were diverted. Perhaps k authority is the same kind of thing as epistemic authority; perhaps it is something different. Perhaps the kind k *just is* the kind *epistemic*. If that is correct, then it might be that our best first-order epistemic theory is self-ratifying in some sense: it is epistemically correct that epistemic correctness is potentially psychologically impactful. Or perhaps not.[13]

None of that interests me here. What I am interested in is what explains the authoritative nature of (at least some cases of) epistemic correctness. What I have said is that at least part of what it is to be authoritative in the

Second-Order Epistemic Theory 113

relevant sense is for epistemic correctness to be potentially psychologically impactful: that is the criterion of adequacy for an explanation of epistemic authority that Potential Psychological Impact reflects. Offering such an explanation does not involve *justifying* the potential psychological impact authoritative epistemic correctness has.

Again, although I have warned that it can be misleading, the analogy with ethics can be helpful in this context. As we saw earlier, it is widely thought that, at least most of the time, authoritative ethical correctness is subject to a Potential Psychological Impact condition: for ethical correctness to be authoritative is (in part) for it to have a potential psychological impact of one sort or another. But it is also widely accepted that this fact, that authoritative ethical correctness is potentially psychologically impactful, does not immediately *legitimate* the authority of ethics, and moreover, that an explanation of the potential psychological impact of authoritative ethical correctness does not thereby amount to a legitimation thereof. Instead, the *justification* of the authority morality is a separate project.[14]

Perhaps the easiest way to remind ourselves of this fact is to notice that a certain group of philosophers are *skeptics* about the legitimacy of authoritative ethical correctness – they think, in other words, that it is not the case that authoritative ethical correctness *should be* potentially psychologically impactful. In fact, such philosophers sometimes deploy their very explanation of the potential psychological impact of authoritative ethical correctness – say, that such impact has an evolutionary payoff – in delegitimizing the authority ethics exhibits – say, by pointing out that something's having evolutionary payoff is a poor foundation for legitimacy in a number of ways.[15] So, again, we have a case where explaining authority (and along the way explaining psychological impact) does not entail offering a justification.

One last item. Maybe you disagree. Maybe you think that the very idea of authority – *of any sort* – always entails legitimacy. So, it is a misnomer not only to say that (say) epistemic correctness is authoritative but also to say that epistemic correctness might not be "legitimate" in some to-be-specified sense. I respond: we are not entitled to this conception of "authority" – one according to which it is always everywhere legitimate – prior to an account thereof. Perhaps it will turn out that epistemic authority is always everywhere legitimate (whatever *this*, in turn, means). Again, I am not interested in this question. And the reason we are not entitled to simply assume authority entails legitimacy is that the intuitive data we used to point to the phenomenon of authority does not support it. Recall, we had mostly metaphors for authority to do with *force*: some correctness is *grippy, binding, strong, forceful*; some *exerts pressure*. But none of these merely intuitive metaphors plausibly entails the existence of something that entails legitimacy.[16]

In any case, if you think the fact that some cases of epistemic correctness are authoritative entails that epistemic correctness is also (again, in some to-be-specified-sense) *legitimate*, then you are using "authority" in a different way than I am, and I claim it is not a way we are entitled to use it in the present context, where what we are after is an explanation for epistemic authority.

So, that is our first feature of what I am calling the *minimal conception* of epistemic authority: authoritative epistemic correctness is always potentially psychologically impactful. And corresponding to this feature of epistemic authority, we have a criterion that an adequate explanation of epistemic authority must meet, namely, Potential Psychological Impact. In the next section, I outline a second feature of the minimal conception and a corresponding second criterion.

7.5.2 Usually Authoritative

We know that all cases of authoritative epistemic correctness are potentially psychologically impactful. As we saw, this is a feature of epistemic authority *per se*: part of what it is for epistemic correctness to be authoritative is for it to have a potential psychological impact. But *which* cases of epistemic correctness are, in fact, authoritative? In other words, can we say something about the *scope* of epistemic authority?

Set aside the possibility that *no* cases of epistemic correctness are ever authoritative; I address that view – skepticism about epistemic authority quite generally – later in this chapter (Section 7.6). That leaves two broad possibilities about the relationship between the fact that it is epistemically correct for an agent to φ and the fact that it is authoritatively epistemically correct for the agent to φ:

> Always Authoritative: In all cases, if it is epistemically correct for A to φ, then it is authoritatively epistemically correct for A to φ

and the strictly weaker

> Sometimes Authoritative: In at least some cases, if it is epistemically correct for A to φ, then it is authoritatively correct for A to φ.[17]

Which should we accept? Recall, we are trying to do what we can to limn the edges of the phenomenon of epistemic authority so that we can then go on to offer a theoretical explanation of it. So, at this stage, our reasons for accepting one or the other of these two principles connecting what it is epistemically correct for agents to do and what it is authoritatively epistemically correct for them to do must be entirely based on our intuitive grasp of the phenomenon of epistemic authority.

I claim that intuitive grasp clearly delivers Sometimes Authoritative. (Again, set aside rank skepticism about epistemic authority until the next section.) It is easy to generate cases that support Sometimes Authoritative – we have been doing it all along. For instance, it is not just true that it is epistemically correct for me to believe that biking down mountains is dangerous; it is also true that it is *authoritatively* epistemically correct for me to so believe. It is not just true that it is epistemically correct for Vice President Harris to believe her office is in the Eisenhower Executive Office Building; it is also true that it is *authoritatively* epistemically correct for her to so believe: this case of epistemic correctness has *oomph*. (Given what we have said in the last section, we can now say a bit more about what this means, namely, that it has a potential psychological impact.) In any case, that should not be controversial; absent rank skepticism about epistemic authority, at least *some* cases of epistemic correctness are presumably cases of authoritative epistemic correctness.

The only question, then, is whether we can go further than Sometimes Authoritative. One way to go further would be to accept Always Authoritative. We should not accept Always Authoritative. At least, we should not accept it *prior to a theory of epistemic authority*. It may turn out that, given our best explanation of epistemic authority, all cases of epistemic correctness turn out to be cases of authoritative epistemic correctness.[18] But we are not licensed in assuming this is true at the present stage. It should be clear why this is so, but let me elaborate.

Being a case of authoritative epistemic correctness is, as we have seen, not the same thing as being a case of epistemic correctness. (Compare: being a case of authoritative 8chan correctness is not the same as being a case of 8chan correctness. Being an elegant scientific theory is not the same as being a scientific theory. Being a ridiculous politician is not the same as being a politician.) The extension of epistemic correctness is determined by our best first-order epistemic theory – our theory that explains why it is that agents epistemically should do whatever they epistemically should do. The extension of *authoritative* epistemic correctness is determined by our best second-order epistemic theory – our theory that explains why it is that epistemic correctness is authoritative, when it is. You might want a second-order theory that delivers Always Authoritative; fair enough. But you cannot simply assume it is true *prior to offering such a theory*. And capturing that claim certainly cannot be a criterion of adequacy on a second-order epistemic theory.

Perhaps this seems like special pleading. After all, I have appealed to the thought that epistemic correctness is authoritative while ostending at the notion of authority throughout the discussion in this chapter. But the intuition to which I appealed was that epistemic correctness is *sometimes*, even *often* or *almost always* authoritative and that this intuitive authority epistemic correctness sometimes exhibits contrasted with the cases of (say) formal 8chan correctness and formal assassin correctness. These commonsense intuitions are decidedly *not* the same as the claim that epistemic correctness is always everywhere authoritative – that is, authoritative under all circumstances, over all agents, in all cases, no matter what.

The former is a commonsense intuition: sometimes at least, it *really matters* what, epistemically, it is correct to do. The latter is a recherché philosopher's intuition. In the present context, prior to an account of epistemic authority, we cannot simply assume the latter.

This does not mean we cannot go *a bit* further. I think we can. The intuitive data with which we begin are not just that epistemic correctness *sometimes* matters in the way authoritative correctness matters but also it is that epistemic correctness *often* or *most of the time* matters. This is among the intuitive datum I appealed to in ostending at the difference between authoritative and formal correctness, and it is hard to know how to further motivate it as a fixed point in our theorizing about epistemic authority. One thing that can help is to notice that denying it would involve what looks like a radical revision to our ordinary conception of epistemic correctness. Learning that it is epistemically correct to do something just is not (usually, at least) like learning that it is assassinly or 8chanly correct to do that thing. Unlike assassin correctness (for me and I assume for you, at least most of the time), the fact that it is epistemically correct to do something carries *weight*; at least, *usually* it does: it *usually* has that distinctively authoritative flavor.[19]

Epistemic correctness is, intuitively, at least *usually* authoritative. We have good reason for accepting the following:

> Usually Authoritative: Usually, if it is epistemically correct for A to φ, then it is authoritatively correct for A to φ.

Of course, this goes further than Sometimes Authoritative, but it is *extremely* vague. What does "usualness" require? Certainly occurring more often than not. If I am not in my office more than 50 percent of weekdays, it is clearly incorrect to say I am *usually* in my office on weekdays. Beyond that obvious threshold for being usual, it is difficult to say anything precise. But we do not need to say anything precise here. Our second-order epistemic theory will tell us why it is that epistemic correctness is authoritative and, in doing so, tell us *which cases of epistemic correctness, in fact, are*. What Usually Authoritative says is that any such second-order explanation of epistemic authority must be one that delivers the result that, usually at least, epistemic correctness is authoritative. *How* usual it will turn out to be will depend, then, on what theory we end up accepting.

Usually Authoritative helps us draw the lines around the conception of epistemic authority to be explained – what I am calling the *minimal conception* of epistemic authority. In particular, the minimal conception of epistemic authority is one that has the following feature: usually, epistemic correctness is authoritative. In this way, Usually Authoritative represents a kind of constraint on an adequate explanation of epistemic authority. In the simplest kind of scenario, an explanation of epistemic authority that delivers the result that epistemic correctness is authoritative *only quite rarely* will be inadequate precisely because it violates Usually Authoritative.

More cautiously, Usually Authoritative puts a constraint on our explanation of epistemic authority *in combination with whatever first-order epistemic theory we accept*. For notice that the content of the relevant first-order epistemic theory will play a role in determining whether Usually Authoritative is true, for any given second-order explanation of epistemic authority.

Think of things like this. We have an intuition, captured by Usually Authoritative, that epistemic correctness is usually *authoritative* epistemic correctness. Our second-order epistemic theory had better deliver that result, on pain of failing to be an explanation for epistemic authority in any case. But what delivering this result will actually amount to will depend, in large part, on the relevant first-order epistemic theory we accept. For, if we accept a first-order epistemic theory according to which epistemic correctness has *this* extension, then "usually" will mean *this*, and if we instead accept a first-order epistemic theory according to which epistemic correctness has *this other much different* extension, then "usually" may mean *this other much different* thing entirely. (Everybody thinks meetings are usually a waste of time. But what accounting for their so being will require will depend, in large part, on what we think counts as a meeting.) I say more about this relationship between our first- and second-order theorizing later on (Chapters 9–10).

So that is our second characteristic of what I am calling the *minimal conception* of epistemic authority: epistemic correctness is usually authoritative. And corresponding to this characteristic of epistemic authority, we have a criterion that an adequate explanation of epistemic authority must meet; namely, it must be compatible with Usually Authoritative.

7.5.3 Recap

Let me recap. We began with an intuitive gesture at the idea that some kinds of correctness, at least some of the time, *matter*: ethical correctness seems often to be like this, and so, too, does epistemic correctness. It at least often *really matters* what, epistemically speaking, it is correct to do. Or anyway, that is the thought. How should we understand this thought?

In order to give some content to the question, we need *some* idea of what epistemic authority comprises. I have offered what I called the *minimal conception* of epistemic authority. The minimal conception of epistemic authority is minimal: it says that epistemic authority exhibits at least two characteristics; first, authoritative epistemic correctness is potentially psychologically impactful, and second, usually at least, epistemic correctness is, in fact, authoritative. Corresponding to these two characteristics of the minimal conception are two criteria of adequacy on an explanation of epistemic authority, namely, Potential Psychological Impact and Usually Authoritative.

As we will see very soon, meeting these two criteria of adequacy is not all that onerous; it is a low bar that most explanations – and certainly all plausible explanations – can easily clear. The point of articulating them is not to weed down the field of competing explanations for epistemic authority; instead, the point is to give us a somewhat firmer grip on our intuitive sense of what epistemic authority comprises.

Can we do better than the minimal conception of epistemic authority? Not at this stage. We grasp the relevant kind of authoritativeness by long, close, and frequent acquaintance. Being so long acquainted, we can also sense its conspicuous absence – think of the lack of authoritativeness 8chan correctness exhibits. What we want is a *theory* of the authoritativeness of epistemic correctness. The way to give that theory is to explain why epistemic correctness is authoritative when it is and so also explain why epistemic correctness is merely formal when it is. Think of things like this. We grasp friendship by long, close, and frequent acquaintance with it. And we keenly sense its absence. But that does not mean we know *what friendship really is*. That requires a theory of friendship. The way to give that theory is to explain why the things that are friends are friends and why things that are not friends are not friends.

You might want more to be getting on with. You might want further examples of authoritative as opposed to merely formal correctness, you might want more details about the nature of epistemic authority, or you might want both. But at this stage, you cannot have either. The explanation for epistemic authority we end up with will determine what it is correct to say epistemic authority in the end actually is and, importantly, *when*, in the end, it actually is, that is, when epistemic correctness is actually authoritative. The intuitive grip I here assume we all have on the phenomenon – the minimal conception – is exactly as much as we can expect *prior to a theoretical account of the phenomenon*. Again, think of things like this: it is not fair to ask for a detailed account of the phenomenon of friendship, or an articulation of who, if anyone, is as a matter of fact Stephen Miller's friend absent an account that explains why it is that some things are some other thing's friends and other things are not those other thing's friends. So I do not have more to say, at this point, about the nature of epistemic authority. That will have to wait for my story about why it is that epistemic correctness is authoritative, when it is. I am going to begin to lay out that explanation in more detail in the next chapter.

Before that, let me address a remaining preliminary issue.

7.6 Skepticism about Authoritative Correctness

You might be a skeptic about the idea that correctness, including the kind of correctness I called "all-things-considered" correctness (and about which I expressed skepticism myself earlier on), ever *really matters* – you might be skeptical that correctness can carry any special weight or can be, as we are putting it, authoritative. If so, then you will be a nihilist about authority. Nihilism about authority can be hyperlocal, local, or global.

Hyperlocal nihilism about authority is the result of skepticism concerning the authoritativeness of a particular case of a particular kind of correctness. For instance, you might agree in a particular case that it is epistemically (or ethically or k-ly) correct for an agent to φ but think that, *in this particular case*, it is not the case that it is *authoritatively* epistemically (ethically, k-ly) correct for the agent to φ.[20] If you think this, you will be a hyperlocal nihilist about epistemic (ethical, k) authority: you are a *nihilist* because you think in this particular case of epistemic (ethical, k) correctness there is not any authority; your nihilism is *hyperlocal* because it is restricted to this particular case of epistemic (ethical, k) correctness.

Hyperlocal nihilism about even a *wide* range of cases of epistemic authority is no barrier to the project I am engaged in here. For, as we have seen, the intuition with which we began is simply that, usually, epistemic correctness is authoritative. It may turn out that a range of particular cases of epistemic correctness are not authoritative. This will depend, as we have discussed, on the particular explanation for epistemic authority that we end up thinking is best. For that explanation of epistemic authority will also deliver an *extension* for epistemic authority: it will tell us not just *why it is* that epistemic correctness is authoritative, but it will also tell us *when it is* that it is authoritative. (It will also depend, as I mentioned at the end of the section before last, on the *pairing* between our second- and our first-order epistemic theories, since it is the pairing that in the end tells us what "usually" amounts to.) But it is compatible with many such second-order explanations (and, for that matter, many potential pairings therewith) that, many times (although, of course, not *usually*), epistemic correctness is not, in fact, authoritative.

Local nihilism about authority is driven by skepticism concerning whether *any* of the cases of correctness of some particular kind are ever authoritative. For instance, suppose you settle on some first-order epistemic theory. You might go on to think that it is *never* true that it is *authoritatively* epistemically correct for an agent to do what it is epistemically correct for them to do. Then, you'd be a local nihilist about epistemic authority. You are a *nihilist* because you think that there is *no such thing* as epistemic authority; your nihilism is *local* because it is restricted to this particular evaluative kind, namely, the epistemic. Usually, local nihilism about authority is paired with an error theory that purports to explain why it is that we are misled into thinking the relevant evaluative kind is (at least on occasion) authoritative.[21] I will say something about how to think about local nihilism in relation to this project in just a moment. First, let's get the final kind of skepticism on the table.

Global nihilism about authority is driven by skepticism concerning whether any correctness of any kind is ever authoritative; it is nihilism about the very *idea* of authoritativeness. Like local nihilism about authoritativeness, global nihilism is usually paired with an error theory that attempts to explain the appearance of authoritativeness for at least some kinds of correctness – notably ethical and epistemic correctness.[22]

Unlike hyperlocal nihilist views (compatibly with Usually Authoritative), local nihilism about *epistemic* authority and global nihilism about authority *per se* really are barriers to engaging in the project I am interested in here. In what follows, I simply assume that global nihilism about authoritativeness is not warranted. This is not because I am certain that it is not; instead, this is because I am certain there is no hope, given the constraints of this book, of convincing any global nihilists to move their position, even a bit. I also assume, at least out the outset, that we should not be local nihilists about epistemic authority. But I hope to arrive in the end at a position that at least some of those who might otherwise be skeptical about the idea of epistemic authority can accept. Of course, local nihilism about epistemic authority can be driven by global nihilism about authority *per se*. If that is true, then, as I say, best put down the book. But I think local nihilism about epistemic authority can also often be the result of dissatisfaction with purported explanations thereof, so insofar as this book is, in part, an attempt to offer what I think of as a natural, satisfying explanation of epistemic authority, it can help ameliorate the drive toward local skepticism about that notion. But whether this is so is for skeptics to judge. and that judgment should wait until we have my preferred explanation in hand.

7.7 Conclusion

First-order epistemic theories attempt to specify the explanatory grounds of epistemic correctness. What it is epistemically correct to do sometimes really *matters*: epistemic correctness, sometimes at least, is authoritative in a way that not all other kinds of correctness appear to be. *Second-order* epistemic theories attempt to specify the grounds of the *authority* of epistemic correctness. They try to tell us why it is, and so when it is, that epistemic correctness matters.

This idea, that epistemic correctness is authoritative, that it matters, is notoriously difficult to pin down. But we can at least accept a minimal conception of epistemic authority according to which epistemic authority exhibits two characteristics. First, being authoritative entails being potentially psychologically impactful, and second, usually, at least, epistemic correctness exhibits this authority.

Because it is supposed to be part of *what it is* for epistemic correctness to be authoritative that it is potentially psychologically impactful, any satisfactory explanation for *why it is* that epistemic correctness is authoritative will need to take account of this fact; it will need to explain why it is that authoritative epistemic correctness has a potential psychological impact. And because we know, from the armchair, that epistemic authority, whatever its nature, is something at least *usually* attends epistemic correctness, any adequate explanation of the former notion will need to be compatible with this fact. Hence, we have two criteria of adequacy – albeit, *apparently very minimal criteria* – on second-order epistemic theories.

Various kinds of nihilists about authority are in turn welcomed to the project (hyperlocal nihilists), encouraged to read on and save their skepticism to the end (local nihilists), and encouraged to pick up a different book altogether (global nihilists).

In the next chapter, I explain how (and why) to be an epistemic instrumentalist about epistemic authority.

Notes

1. Cf. McPherson (2018), Baker (2017), Woods (2018), and Maguire and Woods (2020).
2. With apologies for reusing terms, recall that in Chapter 1, I distinguished between monism and pluralism about *kinds of correctness*; here, I'm distinguishing between monistic and pluralist approaches to *authority*.
3. Baker (2017, 2018) makes a similar point.
4. Cf. Williams (1981).
5. Williams (1981).
6. Cf. Tiffany (2007).
7. Not to be confused with the *factoring account* of what it is to have, or possess, a reason. For discussion, see Lord (2010), and Schroeder (2011).
8. Baker (2017, p. 579) makes a similar point: "it can seem that there is no 'force' a normative system could possess, save the impact it has on agents' psychologies."
9. For example, Railton (1986a, p. 9) puts the resonance constraint like this:

    > what is intrinsically valuable for a person must have a connection with what he would find in some degree compelling or attractive, at least if he were rational and aware. It would be an intolerably alienated conception of someone's good to imagine that it might fail in any such way to engage him.

    For further discussion, see Dorsey (2017) and Sobel (2009, 2016).
10. Roughly. The actual text is "All persons born or naturalized in the United States, and subject to the jurisdiction thereof, are citizens of the United States and of the State wherein they reside." ("U.S. Constitution – Fourteenth Amendment" n.d.).
11. This is sometimes how the so-called amoralist or knave is defined. For critical discussion, see Railton (1986b).
12. Korsgaard (1996). Again, this is a similar sort of complaint leveled by so-called subjectivist accounts of well-being, against objectivist views, that they cannot explain why someone's good must resonate with her. For discussion, see Dorsey (2017).
13. A quick aside. Interestingly, many first-order domains, even if the kinds of correctness associated with them are plausibly sometimes authoritative in one sense or another, are not self-ratifying in the sense that they say, from within their own domain of evaluation, *pay attention to me*. For instance, most first-order *aesthetic* theories do not include something like: it is aesthetically

correct for agents to do what it is aesthetically correct that agents do. However, there is some pressure, especially in formal epistemology, to try and give such accounts. The debate over whether there can be a nonpragmatic justification for, for example, Bayesian updating, is the result of such pressure. See Joyce (1998), Easwaran and Fitelson (2012), and Meacham (n.d.).
14 Again, Korsgaard (1996) is especially clear about this point.
15 For example, Street (2006), and Stich (2012).
16 We are all familiar with the idea that *authoritarian* governments might sometimes be wielding illegitimate political authority. Despite sometimes being illegitimate, such governments inarguably possess authority. Perhaps that is all just homonymy, but I doubt it.
17 More carefully, for some A and for some φ such that A it is epistemically correct for A to φ, it is authoritatively epistemically correct for A φ. This is cumbersome and unpretty; I assume the meaning in Sometimes Authoritative is clear.
18 Spoiler: this will *not* turn out to be the case. See Chapter 8.
19 Remember, we are assuming that local skepticism about epistemic correctness is not in the offing. See Section 7.6 for discussion.
20 This kind of hyperlocal nihilism is what fans of the notion of authoritative all-things-considered correctness use to motivate their conception of all-things-considered correctness, as earlier in the passage from Maguire and Woods: "I know that I ought, as a ticket inspector, to give this impoverished person a ticket, but is it really the case that I ought to do so?" (Maguire and Woods 2020, p. 226).
21 For instance, Mackie (1977), Olson (2014), and Joyce (2001) are all local nihilists about moral correctness who go on to defend moral error theory. *Epistemic* nihilism and the corresponding error theory has proven *much* less popular; it is defended as a part of a *global* nihilism and corresponding global error theory (see the following discussion) by Streumer (2017).
22 A global or comprehensive error theory is defended by Streumer (2017).

References

Anderson, Joel. 2003. "Autonomy and the Authority of Personal Commitments: From Internal Coherence to Social Normativity." *Philosophical Explorations* 6 (2): 90–108. https://doi.org/10.1080/10002003058538742.

Baker, Derek Clayton. 2017. "The Varieties of Normativity." In *The Routledge Handbook of Metaethics*, edited by Tristram McPherson and David Plunkett, 567–581. New York: Routledge.

———. 2018. "Skepticism about Ought Simpliciter." *Oxford Studies in Metaethics* 13: 230–252.

Bedke, Matt. 2011. "Passing the Deontic Buck." In *Oxford Studies in Metaethics, Volume 6*, edited by Russ Shafer-Landau, 128. Oxford: Oxford University Press.

Behrends, Jeff. 2015. "Problems and Solutions for a Hybrid Approach to Grounding Practical Normativity." *Canadian Journal of Philosophy* 45 (2): 159–178. https://doi.org/10.1080/00455091.2015.1047684.

Brandom, Robert B. 2002. *Tales of the Mighty Dead: Historical Essays in the Metaphysics of Intentionality*. Cambridge, MA: Harvard University Press.

Calhoun, Cheshire. 2009. "What Good Is Commitment?" *Ethics* 119 (4): 613–641. https://doi.org/10.1086/605564.

Chang, Ruth. 2004. "Putting Together Morality and Well-Being." In *Practical Conflicts: New Philosophical Essays*, edited by Peter Baumann and Monika Betzler, 118–158. Cambridge, UK: Cambridge University Press.

Collins, Stephanie. 2017. "Filling Collective Duty Gaps." *Journal of Philosophy* 114 (11): 573–591. https://doi.org/10.5840/jphil20171141141.
Comesaña, Juan. 2020. "The Normative Force of Unjustified Beliefs." In *Being Rational and Being Right*. Oxford: Oxford University Press. https://doi.org/10.1093/oso/9780198847717.003.0007.
Copp, David. 2015a. "Rationality and Moral Authority." *Oxford Studies in Metaethics* 10. https://doi.org/10.1093/acprof:oso/9780198738695.003.0006.
———. 2015b. "Social Glue and Norms of Sociality." *Philosophical Studies* 172 (12): 3387–3397. https://doi.org/10.1007/s11098-015-0562-6.
D'Arms, Justin, and Daniel Jacobson. 2014. "Wrong Kinds of Reason and the Opacity of Normative Force." *Oxford Studies in Metaethics* 9. https://doi.org/10.1093/acprof:oso/9780198709299.003.0009.
Darwall, Stephen. 2003. "Desires, Reasons, and Causes." *Philosophy and Phenomenological Research* 67 (2): 436–443. https://doi.org/10.1111/j.1933-1592.2003.tb00300.x.
Dorsey, Dale. 2017. "Why Should Welfare 'Fit'?" *Philosophical Quarterly* 67 (269): 685-24. https://doi.org/10.1093/pq/pqw087.
Easwaran, Kenny. 2011. "Bayesianism I: Introduction and Arguments in Favor." *Philosophy Compass* 6 (5): 312–320. https://doi.org/10.1111/j.1747-9991.2011.00399.x.
Easwaran, Kenny, and Branden Fitelson. 2012. "An 'Evidentialist' Worry about Joyce's Argument for Probabilism." *Dialetica* 66 (3): 425–433. https://doi.org/10.1111/j.1746-8361.2012.01311.x.
Finlay, Stephen. 2007. "Responding to Normativity." In *Oxford Studies in Metaethics, Volume 2*, edited by Russ Shafer-Landau, 220–239. Oxford: Clarendon Press.
Franklin, Christopher Evan. 2013. "A Theory of the Normative Force of Pleas." *Philosophical Studies* 163 (2): 479–502. https://doi.org/10.1007/s11098-011-9826-y.
Gert, Joshua. 2003. "Requiring and Justifying: Two Dimensions of Normative Strength." *Erkenntnis* 59 (1): 5–36. https://doi.org/10.1023/A:1023930108900.
———. 2007. "Normative Strength and the Balance of Reasons." *Philosophical Review* 116 (4): 533–562. https://doi.org/10.1215/00318108-2007-013.
———. 2008. "Michael Smith and the Rationality of Immoral Action." *The Journal of Ethics* 12 (1): 1–23. https://doi.org/10.1007/s10892-007-9023-6.
Gowans, Christopher W. 2002. "Practical Identities and Autonomy: Korsgaard's Reformation of Kan's Moral Philosophy." *Philosophy and Phenomenological Research* 64 (3): 546–570. https://doi.org/10.1111/j.1933-1592.2002.tb00160.x.
Greaves, Hilary, and David Wallace. 2006. "Justifying Conditionalization: Conditionalization Maximizes Expected Epistemic Utility." *Mind* 115 (459): 607–632. https://doi.org/10.1093/mind/fzl607.
Hardimon, Michael. 1994. "Role Obligations." *Journal of Philosophy* 91 (7): 333–363. https://doi.org/10.2307/jphil199491719.
Joyce, James M. 1998. "A Nonpragmatic Vindication of Probabilism." *Philosophy of Science* 65 (4): 575–603. https://doi.org/10.1086/392661.
Joyce, Richard. 2001. *The Myth of Morality*. Cambridge, UK: Cambridge University Press.
———. 2005. *The Evolution of Morality*. Cambridge, UK: Bradford.
King, Zöe Johnson. 2019. "We Can Have Our Buck and Pass It, Too." *Oxford Studies in Metaethics* 14. https://doi.org/10.1093/oso/9780198841449.003.0008.

Knight, Jack, and James Johnson. 1994. "Aggregation and Deliberation: On the Possibility of Democratic Legitimacy." *Political Theory* 22 (2): 277–296. https://doi.org/10.1177/0090591794022002004.

Kolodny, Niko. 2005. "Why Be Rational." *Mind* 114 (455): 509–563. https://doi.org/10.1093/mind/fzi509.

Kornblith, Hilary. 1993. "Epistemic Normativity." *Synthese* 94 (3): 357–376. https://doi.org/10.1007/bf01064485.

Korsgaard, Christine M. 1996. *The Sources of Normativity*. Cambridge, UK: Cambridge University Press.

Kukla, Rebecca. 2002. "The Ontology and Temporality of Conscience." *Continental Philosophy Review* 35 (1): 1–34. https://doi.org/10.1023/A:1015111212268.

Lindeman, Kathryn. 2017. "Constitutivism without Normative Thresholds." *Journal of Ethics and Social Philosophy* 3 (XII): 231–258. https://doi.org/10.26556/jesp.v12i3.220.

Lord, Errol. 2010. "Having Reasons and the Factoring Account." *Philosophical Studies* 149 (3): 283–296. https://doi.org/10.1007/s11098-009-9359-9.

Mackie, John Leslie. 1977. *Ethics: Inventing Right and Wrong*. London; New York: Penguin Books.

Maguire, Barry, and Jack Woods. 2020. "The Game of Belief." *Philosophical Review* 129 (2): 211–249. https://doi.org/10.1215/00318108-8012843.

Mason, Elinor. Forthcoming. "Sexual Refusal: The Fragility of Women's Authority." *Hypatia*.

McPherson, Tristram. 2011. "Against Quietist Normative Realism." *Philosophical Studies* 154 (2): 223–240. https://doi.org/10.1007/s11098-010-9535-y.

———. 2018. "Authoritatively Normative Concepts." *Oxford Studies in Metaethics* 13: 253–277. https://doi.org/10.1093/oso/9780198823841.003.0012.

Meacham, Christopher J. G. n.d. "Can All-Accuracy Accounts Justify Evidential Norms?" In *Epistemic Consequentialism*, edited by Kristoffer Ahlstrom-Vij and Jeff Dunn. Oxford: Oxford University Press.

Olson, Jonas. 2014. *Moral Error Theory: History, Critique, Defence*. Oxford: Oxford University Press.

Papineau, David. 2013. "There Are No Norms of Belief." In *The Aim of Belief*, edited by Timothy Chan. Oxford: Oxford University Press.

Peter, Fabienne. 2019. "III – Normative Facts and Reasons." *Proceedings of the Aristotelian Society* 119 (1): 53–75. https://doi.org/10.1093/arisoc/aoz002.

Pinkard, Terry. 2007. "Sellars the Post-Kantian?" *Poznan Studies in the Philosophy of the Sciences and the Humanities* 92 (1): 21–52.

Railton, Peter. 1986a. "Facts and Values." *Philosophical Topics* 14 (2): 5–31. https://doi.org/philtopics19861421.

———. 1986b. "Moral Realism." *Philosophical Review* 95 (2): 163–207. https://doi.org/10.2307/2185589.

———. 1999. "Normative Force and Normative Freedom: Hume and Kant, but Not Hume versus Kant." *Ratio* 12 (4): 320–353. https://doi.org/10.1111/1467-9329.00098.

de Ridder, Jeroen. 2014. "Epistemic Dependence and Collective Scientific Knowledge." *Synthese* 191 (1): 37–53. https://doi.org/10.1007/s11229-013-0283-3.

Sampson, Eric. 2015. "Against Scanlon's Theory of the Strength of Practical Reasons." *Journal of Ethics and Social Philosophy* 3: 1–6. https://doi.org/10.26556/jesp.v9i3.179.

Schmidt, Sebastian. 2021. "Epistemic Blame and the Normativity of Evidence." *Erkenntnis*, 1–24. https://doi.org/10.1007/s10670-021-00430-9.
Schroeder, Mark. 2011. "What Does It Take to 'Have' a Reason?" In *Reasons for Belief*, edited by Andrew Reisner and Asbjørn Steglich-Petersen, 201–222. Cambridge: Cambridge University Press.
Sobel, David. 2009. "Subjectivism and Idealization." *Ethics* 119 (2): 336–352. https://doi.org/10.1086/596459.
———. 2016. *From Valuing to Value: A Defense of Subjectivism*. Oxford: Oxford University Press.
Southwood, Nicholas, and Lina Eriksson. 2011. "Norms and Conventions." *Philosophical Explorations* 14 (2): 195–217. https://doi.org/10.1080/13869795.2011.569748.
Stich, Stephen. 2012. *Collected Papers, Volume 2: Knowledge, Rationality, and Morality, 1978-2010*. Oxford: Oxford University Press.
Street, Sharon. 2006. "A Darwinian Dilemma for Realist Theories of Value." *Philosophical Studies* 127 (1): 109–166. https://doi.org/10.1007/s11098-005-1726-6.
Streumer, Bart. 2017. *Unbelievable Errors: An Error Theory about All Normative Judgments*. Oxford: Oxford University Press.
Sylvan, Kurt. 2016. "Epistemic Reasons I: Normativity." *Philosophy Compass* 11 (7): 364–376.
———. 2017. "Responsibilism Out of Character." In *Epistemic Situationism*, edited by Mark Alfano and Abrol Fairweather, 153–157. Oxford: Oxford University Press.
Tiffany, Evan. 2007. "Deflationary Normative Pluralism." *Canadian Journal of Philosophy* 37 (5): 231–262. https://doi.org/10.1353/cjp.0.0076.
———. 2012. "Why Be an Agent?" *Australasian Journal of Philosophy* 90 (2): 223–233. https://doi.org/10.1080/00048402.2011.605792.
"U.S. Constitution – Fourteenth Amendment." n.d. Accessed October 23, 2021. https://constitution.congress.gov/constitution/amendment-14/.
Wedgwood, Ralph. 2006. "The Normative Force of Reasoning." *Noûs* 40 (4): 660–686. https://doi.org/10.1111/j.1468-0068.2006.00628.x.
Williams, Bernard. 1981. *Moral Luck: Philosophical Papers 1973-1980*. Cambridge: Cambridge University Press.
Wodak, Daniel. 2019. "Mere Formalities: Fictional Normativity and Normative Authority." *Canadian Journal of Philosophy* 49 (6): 828–850. https://doi.org/10.1080/00455091.2018.1433795.
Wong, David B. 2008. "Constructing Normative Objectivity in Ethics." *Social Philosophy and Policy* 25 (1): 237–266. https://doi.org/10.1017/S0265052508080096.
Woods, Jack. 2016. "The Normative Force of Promising." *Oxford Studies in Normative Ethics* 6: 77–101.
———. 2018. "The Authority of Formality." *Oxford Studies in Metaethics* 13. https://doi.org/10.1093/oso/9780198823841.003.0010.

8 Second-Order Epistemic Instrumentalism

8.1 Introduction

We have seen what first-order epistemic instrumentalism looks like. Recall, you are an epistemic instrumentalist about epistemic correctness if you accept the following:

> First-Order Epistemic Instrumentalism: The fact that it is epistemically correct for A to φ is grounded by the fact that A's φ-ing promotes A's well-being.

And we have canvassed the various problems with this view. I argued that the Goldilocks Problem results in a stalemate between the instrumentalist and her critics. More troubling was the new challenge I outlined, what I called the Functionalist Challenge. According to the Functionalist Challenge, the problem with first-order epistemic instrumentalism is not that it either over- or under-generates cases of epistemic correctness (rather than getting them *just right*). Instead, the problem with first-order epistemic instrumentalism is that it *changes the subject entirely*: whatever kind of correctness first-order epistemic instrumentalism is meant to be an account of, it cannot possibly be an account of *epistemic* correctness. We know this because the point, purpose, or function of epistemic correctness is to serve in our practice of flagging reliable informants. But the things that epistemic instrumentalism identifies as the grounds of epistemic correctness, when cited in justifications of epistemic correctness, interfere with the ability of those evaluations to play that role. In effect, if epistemic correctness were, in fact, what epistemic instrumentalism says it is, it would not be capable of doing what it manifestly is in the business of doing. So epistemic instrumentalism is a failure as a first-order epistemic theory.

Now, when I first introduced first-order epistemic instrumentalism, I dived right in. I deliberately failed to offer any reason for thinking that first-order epistemic instrumentalism is a view that anyone would ever come up with, let alone a view that someone might accept. I just laid it

DOI: 10.4324/9781003096726-8

out and started banging away at the view and the problems with it. But let's step back and ask the obvious questions: Why *would* anyone be tempted by first-order epistemic instrumentalism? Why think that what it is epistemically correct for agents to do depends in some way on what would make them better off?

The answer, I think, has two parts. First, I think *second-order* epistemic instrumentalism (of the sort I lay out later) is an extremely natural view to take about how to explain epistemic *authority*. Second, if you have a certain kind of view about how to do your epistemic theorizing, then you will think the only way to arrive at this natural second-order epistemic instrumentalism is via accepting *first*-order epistemic instrumentalism. Hence, you might go in for the latter because of the naturalness of the former. And then, on encountering all the problems with the first-order view, you will be inclined to reject the second-order view too. But I think that is babies and bathwater; let's just be second-order epistemic instrumentalists. In this chapter, I am going to begin talking through these ideas in detail, beginning with the claim that second-order epistemic instrumentalism is an extremely natural view to take about how to explain epistemic authority.

8.2 Epistemic Instrumentalism's Epistemic Authority Explanatory Principle

You will be a *second*-order epistemic instrumentalist if you accept:

> Second-Order Epistemic Instrumentalism: The fact that it is authoritatively epistemically correct for A to φ is grounded by the fact that A's φ-ing promotes A's well-being.

According to second-order epistemic instrumentalism, the *authority* of epistemic correctness is explained by the promotive connection between agents' doing what is epistemically correct and their being better off. This view, I think, is a natural, straightforward view to have about the explanation for the authority of epistemic correctness. I do not attempt to offer anything like a deductive argument in its favor. Instead, in the next several sections, I outline why I think we should find this view so immediately attractive. Before that, let's very quickly get *adequacy* out of the way.

8.3 The Adequacy of Instrumentalism

Recall our two criteria of adequacy any explanation for epistemic authority must meet. First, any explanation for epistemic authority must also explain why it is that cases of epistemic authority are potentially psychologically impactful. That is the criterion I called Potential Psychological

Impact. Clearly, second-order epistemic instrumentalism meets this criterion, given a straightforward, uncontroversial assumption.

The uncontroversial assumption is of course that facts about what promotes agents' well-being are capable of having a psychological impact. Given the extremely weak condition Potential Psychological Impact comprises, it is undeniably true that epistemic authoritativeness will be potentially psychologically impactful if second-order epistemic instrumentalism is true. But recall, we want our second-order epistemic theory not just to guarantee that cases of authoritative epistemic correctness *have* a potential psychological impact; we also want it to *explain* that impact. So does second-order epistemic instrumentalism itself explain why epistemic authoritativeness is always potentially psychologically impactful? Yes.

For notice, it is not as if the explanatory grounds cited in second-order epistemic instrumentalism are somehow only accidentally linked to what explains the potential psychological impact of authoritative epistemic correctness. Instead, precisely what epistemic instrumentalism thinks explains authority also explains that potential impact, namely, facts about what promotes agential well-being. Given the uncontroversial assumption that such facts are capable of having a psychological impact, we get our result. So much for the first criterion.

What about Usually Authoritative? You will recall that this criterion says that an adequate for epistemic authority will deliver the result that, usually, epistemic correctness is authoritative. Hence, it precludes an "explanation" of epistemic authority according to which very few cases of epistemic correctness are ones that matter. Does second-order epistemic instrumentalism meet this criterion? Yes.

Being epistemically correct is not the same thing as being authoritatively epistemically correct. So we have the potential for the two to come apart. Usually Authoritative says that your account of what it is for epistemic correctness to be authoritative had better not make it the case that they come *too far* apart. But how far apart they can in principle come of course depends not just on what second-order epistemic theory you accept – it does not just depend on your explanation for epistemic authority. It depends, too, on what *first*-order epistemic theory you accept – it depends on your explanation for epistemic *correctness*. This is because the extension of epistemic correctness is *read off* from the explanation thereof, and Usually Authoritative says that you'd better deliver the result that at least *usually* cases of epistemic correctness *so understood* are authoritative.

Whether or not a second-order epistemic theory is therefore capable of meeting Usually Authoritative turns on what first-order epistemic theory we accept. So you might think that we cannot evaluate how well second-order epistemic instrumentalism does with respect to this criterion of adequacy without antecedently accepting some first-order epistemic theory (I discuss this idea in more detail in the next chapter). But I have just said it clearly meets that criterion, and I have not said what first-order epistemic theory we are assuming is true.

What's going on? Here is the thing: we can point out – and second-order epistemic instrumentalists should be eager to point out – that epistemic instrumentalism will deliver the result that, usually, cases of epistemic correctness will be cases of *authoritative* epistemic correctness *almost no matter what first-order epistemic theory we accept*. For the record, I actually think something a bit stronger than this is true. I think that epistemic instrumentalism will meet Usually Authoritative given *any* (rather than almost any) first-order epistemic theory. That is because I think there are, in addition to the kind of functionalist restrictions we discussed in Chapter 4, restrictions on what counts as a first-order epistemic theory that tie them closely enough to truth, or accuracy to guarantee that what it will be epistemically correct to do will, usually at least, be the kind of that that promotes agential well-being. This is because, as we have seen (Section 5.5), having true beliefs and accurate representations is exactly the kind of thing that promotes one's well-being. But we do not need anything quite so strong here. Here, we just need the idea that second-order epistemic instrumentalism will meet Usually Authoritative given the acceptance of any of the *plausible* extant first-order views.

There are two ways to show that this is true. The first is by iterating plausible extant first-order epistemic theories and showing that epistemic instrumentalism meets Usually Authoritative given the truth of those first-order epistemic theories. For instance, we could begin this process like so: if we are evidentialists, then second-order epistemic instrumentalism will clearly meet Usually Authoritative. For the overwhelming majority of cases of believing in accord with one's evidence will be cases in which doing so promotes one's well-being. And then we would go on to other first-order epistemic theories: if we are reliabilists, then … and so on. If someone introduces a new first-order epistemic theory, we can put it on the later base. My claim is that the result of this iterative process will be that all the plausible first-order epistemic theories, when paired with second-order epistemic instrumentalism, deliver the result that, usually at least, epistemic correctness is authoritative.

The second way to make this explicit is somewhat easier, since it does not require working through all the possible plausible first-order epistemic theories, pairing them up with second-order epistemic instrumentalism, and seeing how things turn out. But it takes a bit of explaining. Here is the idea. Instead of the onerous iterative process, we can simply remind ourselves of the Goldilocks Problem with *first*-order epistemic instrumentalism. One half of that problem, recall, was that there were intuitively cases in which the explanatory grounds first-order epistemic instrumentalism identified as the explanatory grounds of epistemic correctness were *absent* but in which epistemic correctness was *present*. But those cases were, as we saw, *extremely rare*. That is why it was the *Goldilocks* Problem, and

130 Second-Order Epistemic Instrumentalism

the charge was that the first-order epistemic instrumentalism did not get things *just right*. It was not the Massively In Error Problem with an attending charge that first-order instrumentalism got things *horribly completely wrong*. The Goldilocks Problem is a problem of or at the margins.

But that means that even *opponents* of first-order epistemic instrumentalism agree that the explanatory grounds it identifies for epistemic correctness, namely, promoting agents' well-being, generate an extension for epistemic correctness that *pretty much though perhaps not exactly* matches their preferred extension therefor. They *must* agree to this because first-order epistemic instrumentalists have spent a lot of time persuasively arguing for its truth. As we saw, the way they do that is by pointing out that most of the time believing truly promotes agential well-being, believing in accord with the evidence does so, too, and so on and so on. But here's the thing: second-order epistemic instrumentalism adopts *the very same grounds* as first-order epistemic instrumentalism. What it says is that those grounds explain the *authority* of epistemic correctness rather than epistemic correctness itself. But this means that even opponents of *second*-order epistemic instrumentalism must agree that the extension of epistemic authority, as given by second-order epistemic instrumentalism, will *pretty much though perhaps not exactly* match the extension of epistemic correctness, *whatever that turns out according to them to be*. And they must agree to this because *first-order* epistemic instrumentalists have done the work persuasively (although not intentionally) arguing for its truth. But this amounts to agreeing that second-order epistemic instrumentalism will meet Usually Authoritative, since Usually Authoritative in effect is the requirement that one's extension for epistemic authority *pretty much though perhaps not exactly* (i.e., *usually*) match the extension of epistemic correctness.

To be clear, here's how the argument goes:

1. First-order epistemic instrumentalism delivers an extension for epistemic correctness via its account of the explanatory grounds of epistemic correctness. (Definition of first-order epistemic instrumentalism)
2. Opponents of first-order epistemic instrumentalism agree that first-order epistemic instrumentalism delivers an extension of epistemic correctness that is *almost but not exactly right*. (The Goldilocks Problem)
3. Second-order epistemic instrumentalism delivers an extension for epistemic authority via its account of the explanatory grounds of epistemic authority *and* second-order epistemic instrumentalism adopts the same explanatory grounds as first-order epistemic instrumentalism. (Definition of second-order epistemic instrumentalism)
4. Second-order epistemic instrumentalism's extension for epistemic *authority* will *almost but not exactly* match opponents of epistemic instrumentalism's preferred view about the right *extension* for epistemic correctness. (1–3)

5. Hence, even opponents of epistemic instrumentalism should admit that second-order epistemic instrumentalism meets Usually Authoritative. (4 & definition of Usually Authoritative)

This idea, that second-order epistemic instrumentalism does well by Usually Authoritative independently of any particular commitments in first-order epistemic theorizing is something I return to in Chapter 10, in the course of diagnosing the relative unpopularity of the view. Here, I want to move on.

It is not worth all that much to meet our two criteria of adequacy: they set very low bars. But second-order epistemic instrumentalism has a lot of other things to be said in its favor. In the remainder of this chapter, I will say some of those things.

8.4 The Immediate Appeal of Second-Order Epistemic Instrumentalism

I think second-order epistemic instrumentalism should strike us as immediately appealing. To see how immediately appealing the epistemic instrumentalist view is, first recall what *promotion* and *well-being* are supposed to be in this context.

Agents' well-being is their personal good – their *welfare*. I have not said anything specific concerning the constituents of agential well-being. That is a task I leave to a different set of philosophers or at least for a different time. But I have said that, in order to have relatively uncontroversial and intuitive to work with, we can treat desire-satisfaction as a constituent of agential well-being such that, if an agent desires P, they are better off when P than when not-P. Intuitively, if you want a piece of chocolate, then, *ceteris paribus*, you are better off getting the chocolate than not getting it.

Similarly, I have not committed to a robust theoretical view of promotion in this book. In other coauthored work, I have defended such a view. But here we do not need anything sophisticated here. We can continue to understand promotion as a simple probabilistic increase relative to a natural baseline, such that an agent's φ-ing *promotes* their well-being just in case (and because) the likelihood that A's well-being improves given that they φ is greater than the likelihood that A's well-being improves given that they do not φ.

As we saw, *first*-order epistemic instrumentalism inherits *heaps* of trouble from connecting epistemic correctness to promoting agents' welfares in this way. The Goldilocks Problem is the standard worry. My Functionalist Challenge also exploits the purported connection: it is because facts about agents' welfares cannot serve in justifications for epistemic correctness without interfering with the role, purpose, or point of evaluating things in terms of epistemic correctness that we have, I argued, reason to be suspicious of first-order epistemic instrumentalism.

But as a view about the explanatory grounds of epistemic *authority*, this apparent weakness with the view – that its explanans comprises facts about promoting agents' well-being – becomes its strength. There are a couple of ways to illustrate this. Here is one: remember the way we gestured, intuitively, at the thought that epistemic correctness is (sometimes at least) authoritative. We said that, like moral correctness, epistemic correctness appears to sometimes be *grippy* or *forceful* or that, like moral correctness, it seems to *matter*. But here is something we all already accept: agents' well-being matters. And agents' well-being, usually at least, has a kind of *grip* or *force* over agents whose well-being it is. When I learn that something contributes or fails to contribute to my well-being, I am not usually simply indifferent to this fact, and my lack of indifference is not, I take it, mysterious or idiosyncratic.

Of course, it is *possible* to think that agential well-being does not matter *at all* in any fashion whatsoever. But that is always a result of more general skepticism about the claim that anything matters – broad nihilism. Let me emphasize how uncontroversial this idea that agents' well-being is the kind of thing that matters should be. I have not said that it is the *only* thing that matters. Plenty of other things might also matter! I have not said how important agents' well-being is supposed to be. Perhaps among all the things that matter it is the least important! I have not said what the correct explanation is for why agents' well-being matters. Perhaps it matters because of its relation to some other thing that matters! Unless we are going in for global nihilism, we are going to think that agents' well-being matters in one way or another.

But remember, what we want from our second-order epistemic theory is an account of why it is that epistemic correctness at least sometimes matters. And what second-order epistemic instrumentalism says is that epistemic correctness matters in a familiar, natural way: by connecting up to agents' welfare, to what makes agents better off. Natural as that connection is, second-order epistemic instrumentalism is an extremely natural view to have about what explains the authority enjoyed by epistemic correctness. In effect, epistemic correctness matters because it is (instrumentally) connected to something else that uncontroversially matters.

I think it makes sense to press the point. It is inarguable that doing what is epistemically correct is on almost every occasion – more on this hedge later – in agents' interests. And not just a *little bit* in their interests. *A lot of bit* in their interests. To see this, just notice how much of agents' well-being being promoted depends on their believing what it is intuitively epistemically correct to believe.

We have not said what first-order epistemic theory is correct, but suppose it is one of epistemologists' favorites. Take *evidentialism* first. Then, roughly, what it is epistemically correct for an agent to do on any given occasion is for her to believe in accord with her evidence. But in general believing in accord with the evidence is *wildly promotive* of agents'

Second-Order Epistemic Instrumentalism 133

well-being. It helps agents achieve *all kinds* of things they care about; they can, by according their beliefs to the evidence rather than ignoring their evidence better plan routes to work, better plan on what the weather will be like, better plan on avoiding snakes than encountering them – quite generally, they can *better plan*. It is no mystery why this would be. Plans based on true belief are *ceteris paribus* better for planning than those based on false beliefs, and beliefs based on evidence are *ceteris paribus* more likely to be true than those based on ... well, almost anything else. And planning on ways to achieve what they care about is if not, as some philosophers have it, the *only* thing agents do, then at the very least it is an extremely large part of what agents do![1] Hence, insofar as the authority of what it is epistemically correct to do is thought to depend, as epistemic instrumentalism says it depends, on what promotes agential well-being, it is no surprise at all that epistemic correctness is authoritative.

Similar remarks go for *whatever* first-order epistemic theory we pick. Take a much more recent arrival on the scene: epistemic Kantianism. According to epistemic Kantians, what it is epistemically correct for an agent to do on any given occasion, very roughly, is for them to behave in whatever way respects the truth.[2] Of course, the epistemic Kantian owes us some story about what is supposed to be involved in respecting the truth. The details can get messy here, but there are some unfussy things we can say, such as that *believing* the truth is usually a way of respecting the truth and that *suspending judgment* can sometimes be a way of respecting the truth.[3] Whatever the epistemic Kantian ends up saying, precisely, it will definitely turn out to be the case that respecting the truth is *hugely promotive* of agents' well-being. It helps agents achieve reptile-avoidance and umbrella-carrying for exactly the same kinds of reasons just adduced, namely, that respecting the truth (in whatever specific guise this ends up taking) is good for planning.

Or, take a much less popular also relative newcomer: Daniel Singer's truth-loving epistemic consequentialism. According to Singer (2021), what it is epistemically correct to do is whatever it is that would conduce to the greatest available balance of true beliefs to false beliefs. Again, it's a short step to the thought that an agent's φ-ings being epistemically correct, so conceived, will be φ-ings that make her extraordinarily better off.[4]

8.5 The Ubiquity of Second-Order *K* Instrumentalism

Here is a way of driving home this point about the naturalness of the view. I have been saying "natural," but I might have said that epistemic instrumentalism is the *default* view to have about epistemic authority. Recall our division among different kinds of correctness. Throughout we have been concerned with explaining *epistemic* correctness, and now we have moved on to explaining the *authority* epistemic correctness usually enjoys. But there are, as we know, maximally many (at least: many many) different kinds of correctness. And some of these kinds of correctness, at least some of the time, will also be authoritative in one fashion or another.

In outlining the minimal conception of epistemic authority, I said I was going to approach things as a pluralist and treat epistemic authority as its own distinctive kind of thing to be explained rather than an instance of a more general idea of authority. But I also said that it was clear that the kind of authority exhibited by other kinds of correctness at least *rhyme* with epistemic correctness, even if they do not share all the same features. It is not hard to generate examples of other kinds of correctness that, at least sometimes – perhaps not usually, as in the epistemic case – matter or are authoritative.

For instance, consider the kinds of correctness associated with various games, such as the game of baseball. There are certain things it is basebally correct to do and other things that it is basebally not correct to do. We could do first-order deontic baseball theory if we were so inclined:

> The fact that A's φ-ing is basebally correct is grounded by F.

Presumably, the Fs are going to be facts about the *rules of baseball*. Now, some of the time, in some contexts, it is plausible that baseball correctness is authoritative, by which I mean just that it *matters*, or has a *grip*, or is *oomphy* in much the same fashion as epistemic (or indeed moral) correctness sometimes appear to be. Again, the view is not necessarily that these are the *same notion entirely* but that they at least share some common features. We could therefore try to do *second-order* theorizing about the authority baseball correctness sometimes exhibits:

> The fact that A's φ-ing is authoritatively baseball correct is grounded by F.

We probably will not do this. But we could. Presumably, one thing we would then think is that baseball correctness is only ever authoritative for agents who are *attempting to play the game of baseball*. But then, a natural, straightforward thing to say would be that baseball correctness is authoritative *when and because* it promotes agents' well-being; in particular, it is authoritative when it promotes that part of their well-being (if there is one!) that is tied up with successfully playing baseball. Baseball is not unique. It is natural to give the same kind of instrumentalist explanation when it comes to other games or for kinds of correctness associated not with *games* but with *roles*.[5]

Indeed – and this is my point about it not just being natural but also the default – it can seem like some variant on the instrumentalist explanation is the one we turn to, by default, whenever we want to explain how it is that some standard of correctness, some set of requirements or other, has a grip on us. This is not to say that it is *always* correct, but it is *ubiquitous*.

You might think the known ubiquity of an instrumentalist *style* of explanation does not tell us anything about the unknown quality of the *epistemic instrumentalist* explanation as compared to different kinds of explanation. I disagree. The known ubiquity of a four-wheeled *style* of car tells us something about the unknown quality of the most recent BMW M3 as compared to different kinds of car, for example, the Renault Reliant (an infamous three-wheeler prone to tipping over). It does not mean we shall always want to be driving the M3 (accepting the instrumentalist view), but it does give us reason to take it very seriously as a contender.

8.6 The Naturalism of Instrumentalism

Here is another nice-making feature of instrumentalism: it is naturalist. The idea of naturalism is fraught; it is notoriously difficult to say what, precisely, makes one theory compatible with naturalism, or part of a "natural" worldview. But I do not need to enter that debate in any serious fashion. That is because I am not going to argue that other second-order epistemic theories are *not* natural or are in one way or another *incompatible* with a naturalistic world view. Instead, I am just going to point out how naturalistically respectable second-order *epistemic instrumentalism* is.

Of course, that requires my saying *something* about what being naturalistically respectable amounts to. But I can say extremely uncontroversial things about this. Broadly speaking, a view is naturalistic when it is compatible with our best scientific theories, that is, when it does not explicitly involve any commitment to, or implicitly invoke the existence of, some entities or relations that are incompatible with a broadly scientific worldview according to which everything there is, is either itself a physical entity or reducible thereto and all physical happenings are therefore the effects of interactions between these entities; that is, all causes are physical causes. Such naturalism is not committed to anything about the possibility of reduction from the so-called special sciences to, for example, fundamental physics. All that it says is, roughly, that the whole world is made up of only physical entities, and all the happenings within the world are exhausted by interactions between these entities.[6]

How does epistemic instrumentalism fare with respect to naturalism so understood? Very well, assuming we keep its two important relata, namely, agential doings and their well-being, along with the relevant relation, namely, promotion and naturalistically respectable. But that is trivial to do. There are plenty of accounts of agency and agential well-being that count as naturalist in this sense. For instance, the simple desire-satisfaction model we have been working with is presumably a paid-up naturalist view, on the assumption that desires are themselves capable of being understood naturalistically. And there are, in addition, plenty of accounts of *promotion* that are naturalist. Again, the simple probabilistic model we have been working with is an example. Moreover, and this is important, there is no reason to reach for a *non*naturalist understanding of agential doings, well-being, or promotion simply in virtue of accepting second-order epistemic instrumentalism. The ingredients can clearly be understood in a manner that is naturalistically respectable, and insofar as we care about retaining our naturalist bona fides, there is simply no pressure to look elsewhere. So, second-order epistemic instrumentalism is naturalist.

Maybe you think this is nothing to write home about. After all, I have set the bar very low. Perhaps it is *too* low, such that clearing it is equivalent to walking upright. The thought, then, might be that while it is true on this extremely weak understanding of what it takes to be naturalistically respectable that, perhaps unsurprisingly, second-order epistemic instrumentalism counts as naturalistically respectable, this does not count in its favor or does not count all that much. But that is not true. There are plenty of potential second-order epistemic theories that are not compatible with even this extraordinarily weak understanding of naturalism. Here is one:

> Moorean Epistemic Nonnaturalism: The fact that A's φ-ing is authoritatively epistemically correct is grounded by a realm of *sui generis* nonnatural facts about epistemic authority.

This is a possible view to have about what grounds epistemic authority. It mirrors a familiar Moorean view about *ethical* authority. Whatever appeal even weakly naturalist views have, and I think they have some appeal, this view does not have it.

Anyway, and again, my point here is not to convince you that second-order epistemic instrumentalism does *better* than its competitors on its naturalist scorecard (although I think it does); instead, my point is simply to exhibit the virtues of the view in the course of explaining why I think it is so appealing. One virtue, as I have just explained, is that it is compatible with naturalism, broadly understood.

8.7 The Lamentable Unpopularity of Instrumentalism

Second-order epistemic instrumentalism is adequate, immediately appealing, ubiquitous, and naturalistically respectable. Despite this, epistemologists almost always swipe left. What gives?

I think, broadly, the answer is that it has largely been ignored as a result of a natural but ultimately not all that compelling thought about how to go about second-order epistemic theorizing. As I begin to explain in the next chapter, I think there's a kind of constraint on our second-order epistemic theorizing that can make *second*-order epistemic instrumentalism seem like a nonstarter, given the failures of *first*-order epistemic instrumentalism. Before that, let me say a bit more about where we are in the argument of the book.

First-order epistemic instrumentalism is, like its second-order counterpart, largely reviled. But as we saw, the typical reasoning given for rejecting it leads, inexorably, to stalemate. Instrumentalists will claim to have captured the extension of epistemic correctness, and anti-instrumentalists will give them the incredulous stare. The way to break the stalemate, I have argued, is by noticing that whatever kind of correctness first-order instrumentalism might purport to be an account of, it *cannot* be an account of a kind of correctness the point, purpose, role, or function of which is to flag reliable informants. That is because the grounds first-order epistemic instrumentalism identifies are systematically incapable of serving in various contexts in which we deploy the idea of epistemic correctness without simultaneously interfering with the ability of epistemic correctness to play this role for us. That is what I called the Functionalist Challenge to first-order epistemic instrumentalism. In the face of that challenge, so much for first-order epistemic instrumentalism.

But epistemic correctness, unlike, for example, 8chan correctness, at least sometimes *matters*: it is at least sometimes authoritative rather than merely formal. It is impossible, pre-theoretically, to say what, precisely, this "mattering" amounts to, but we can mark it out by saying that authoritative epistemic correctness is at least always *potentially psychologically impactful* and that *usually*, epistemic correctness is, in fact, authoritative. This minimal conception sets a low bar on second-order epistemic theorizing, but it sets a bar nonetheless. Second-order epistemic instrumentalism, then, is the view that says we should explain the authority of epistemic correctness by appealing to how doing what is epistemically correct promotes agents' well-being. As I just outlined, this view has some appealing features: it is certainly adequate (it clears our low bar), it is immediately appealing, it is ubiquitous, and it is naturalistically respectable.

Where does that leave us? I do not take myself to have offered anything like a strong positive case for accepting second-order epistemic instrumentalism. Instead, what I have done is explain what the view says and how its saying those things represents an answer to the question being asked. As I have said, second-order epistemic instrumentalism is largely neglected or, when it does get an airing, it is simply conflated with first-order epistemic instrumentalism – a view I have said we should be happy to reject. Part of what I do in the next chapter is begin to explain why that conflation has been so widespread.

Here, I am busy setting expectations. In addition to explaining its neglect, you can expect me to explain in more detail why I think second-order epistemic instrumentalism is not liable to variants of the traditional objections facing first-order epistemic instrumentalism. I do that in Chapter 11. You should *not* expect any new positive argument in favor of second-order epistemic instrumentalism. As I have said, the view strikes me as naturally appealing, adequate, and so on; what can be said in favor of it from a theoretical point of view has, I think, just been said.

The argument for its acceptance goes by way of clearing away reasons for not adopting it rather than a direct attack on its competitors. I sketch a few of those competitors in the next chapter, and I inevitably make a few disparaging comments about them in the course of explaining instrumentalism's unpopularity. But I do not undertake to directly criticize them here, in this book.

So, setting aside the additional currency my upcoming diagnosis of its unpopularity lends to the account of second-order epistemic instrumentalism, I take the positive argument in its favor to be largely complete. What remains is to explain why it's so widely rejected. I turn to that now.

Notes

1 Cf. Bratman (1987).
2 Sylvan (2020).
3 Lord (2020) and Sylvan (2020).
4 Don't confuse the claim I'm making here, which is that doing what is epistemically correct makes agents extraordinarily better off, with the claim that this fact is what explains why it is that it is epistemically correct for agents to do such things. That is first-order epistemic instrumentalism. This is second-order epistemic instrumentalism.
5 Cf. Maguire and Woods (2020).
6 Cf. Papineau (1993).

References

Bratman, Michael. 1987. *Intention, Plans, and Practical Reason*. Cambridge, MA: Harvard University Press.
Lord, Errol. 2020. "Suspension of Judgment, Rationality's Competition, and the Reach of the Epistemic." In *The Ethics of Belief and Beyond. Understanding Mental Normativity*, edited by Sebastian Schmidt and Gerhard Ernst, 126–145. Abingdon: Routledge.
Maguire, Barry, and Jack Woods. 2020. "The Game of Belief." *Philosophical Review* 129 (2): 211–249. https://doi.org/10.1215/00318108-8012843.
Papineau, David. 1993. *Philosophical Naturalism*. Oxford: Blackwell.
Singer, Daniel. 2021. "Right Belief." Unpublished manuscript.
Sylvan, Kurt L. 2020. "An Epistemic Non-Consequentialism." *The Philosophical Review* 129 (1): 1–51. https://doi.org/10.1215/00318108-7890455.

9 The Content Constraint

9.1 Introduction

In the last chapter, I laid out the instrumentalist explanation for epistemic authority. According to second-order epistemic instrumentalists, the way to explain the authority of epistemic correctness is via the promotive connection between doing what is epistemically correct and agents' well-being. As I tried to make vivid, the instrumentalist explanation is extremely natural. Given the commonsense ideas that agents' well-being matters and that doing what is epistemically correct (usually) promotes agents' well-being (whatever that turns out to comprise), the instrumentalist explanation for epistemic authority is extremely straightforward. It has other virtues too.

But despite being immediately appealing in this way, second-order epistemic instrumentalism has also proved wildly unpopular among epistemologists. I think second-order epistemic instrumentalism's relative unpopularity has a mostly overlooked and important *methodological* cause. Diagnosing that cause and explaining why the methodology that gives rise to it is not obligatory can, I think, do a lot to clear the way for second-order epistemic instrumentalism's explanation for epistemic authority. At the end of the last chapter, I said I would not be offering any further positive argument on behalf of second-order epistemic instrumentalism. That is strictly correct. But one way to read what I am doing here, and in the next chapter, is as warming up the crowd or tilling the ground or whatever metaphor you prefer for the thought that, if I am right, then it does not really make sense to be as militantly *un*sympathetic to second-order epistemic instrumentalism as most epistemologists have tended to be.

The crowd-warming has two stages. In this chapter, I argue that we should all of us accept an important constraint on our theorizing about how to explain epistemic authority. Then, in the next chapter, I explain how the most common methodology deployed in respecting this constraint makes second-order epistemic instrumentalism look like a nonstarter. Happily, as we will see there, despite being widespread, this methodology is neither obligatory nor, on close inspection, all that useful.

DOI: 10.4324/9781003096726-9

140 The Content Constraint

9.2 Explanations First

As we have seen, first-order epistemic theories offer accounts of the explanatory grounds of epistemic correctness: they tell us why it is that it is epistemically correct for agents to do whatever it is epistemically correct for them to do. And as we have also seen, if we are interested in the question of *what*, as a matter of fact, it is epistemically correct for an agent to do, our answer to this question is determined by our answer to the question of what explains epistemic correctness: first-order *explanation* comes before first-order *extension*.

What about second-order theory? Second-order epistemic theories offer accounts of the explanatory grounds of epistemic authority: they tell us why it is that it is *authoritatively* epistemically correct for agents to do whatever it is authoritatively epistemically correct for them to do. And, as with first-order theorizing about epistemic correctness, explanation precedes extension; if we want to know *which* cases of epistemic correctness are authoritative, then we shall first need some account of what it is that explains epistemic authority.

It is difficult to make sense of the opposing idea – the thought that somehow we could know the extension of epistemic authority prior to an explanation thereof. It would be a kind of unrestricted armchair theorizing about which cases of epistemic correctness are authoritative. But without an antecedent explanation of why it is that epistemic correctness is authoritative, why would we think *this case of epistemic correctness is so*?

Happily, as in the first-order case, I do not know of anyone who disagrees. In second-order epistemic theory, explanation comes before extension. That is the easy, uncontroversial part: explanations always come first.[1]

9.3 First-Order Things First

Here is the somewhat harder part: What about when it comes to first- and second-order theories themselves? Should one of *these* come first? Yes. First-order theory must come first. Or, more carefully, we must first settle on an *extension* for epistemic correctness before moving on to an explanation for the authority of epistemic correctness. And given that, as we just saw, explanation uncontroversially precedes extension in first-order theory, all first-order theory comes before second-order theory. You might already see why this must be so, but let me walk through the argument.

In its broadest form, the argument is simple. We cannot begin to give an explanation for authoritative epistemic correctness without first settling on an extension for epistemic correctness. For without some extension of epistemic correctness, we should lack any explanandum. This is because the extension of what it is *authoritatively* epistemically correct for an agent to do is a not necessarily proper subset of what it is epistemically correct for them to do. And so we clearly need to settle latter before we can settle on an explanation for the former. I will elaborate.

Notice that without some account of *whether* it is epistemically correct for an agent to φ the claim that it is *authoritatively* epistemically correct for the agent to φ is simply not evaluable, let alone explicable. The claim that it is authoritatively epistemically correct for an agent to φ is the claim that epistemic correctness is in this case (resorting to italics) *oomphy* or *binding* in a way that other kinds of correctness (e.g., 8chan correctness) are not. But to evaluate whether this is true, let alone to *explain* it, we need to have already settled whether, in fact, it is *epistemically correct* for the agent to φ. And doing that *just is* offering some extension for epistemic correctness – part of the task of giving a first-order epistemic theory. Given that as we have already seen explanation precedes extension in first-order epistemic theory, *all* first-order epistemic theory precedes second-order epistemic theory.

Here is a second way to make the point. Take two first-order epistemic theories that disagree over the correct explanation for epistemic correctness, such as the following:

> Evidentialism: The fact that it is epistemically correct for A to φ is grounded by the fact that A's φ-ing is supported by A's evidence.
>
> Truth-Loving Epistemic Consequentialism (TLE Consequentialism): The fact that it is epistemically correct for A to φ is grounded by the fact that A's φ-ing conduces to the greatest available balance of true beliefs to false beliefs

Not only do evidentialism and TLE Consequentialism disagree over what *explains* why it is epistemically correct for agents to φ, they will also sometimes (perhaps regularly) disagree over *whether* it is epistemically correct for a particular agent to φ. Consider the following case from Daniel Singer:[2]

> God-Grant: Tony is a scientist interested in getting a grant from a religious organization. Tony does not have sufficient evidence to believe in God, Tony thinks that belief in God is manifestly irrational, and it is in fact true that there is no God. Despite that, Tony discovers that this organization will give him the grant only if it concludes that he is religious. Further, Tony is such a terrible liar that unless he actually gets himself to believe in God they will discover that he is an atheist. Having the grant will enable Tony to come to have many, many important and true beliefs that he would not otherwise be able to have.

According to evidentialism, it is not the case that it is epistemically correct for Tony to believe that God exists. This is presumably because Tony lacks sufficient evidence for the belief that God exists. By contrast, it is at least plausible that according to TLE Consequentialism it is epistemically correct for Tony to believe that God exists.[3] Suppose those are the correct ways to read the verdicts of the two views.

So here we have a bit of substantive extensional disagreement over the content of epistemic correctness. This extensional disagreement has been the subject of much discussion in first-order epistemic theory. Opponents of TLE Consequentialism take the availability of such "trade-off" cases to be decisive evidence that there is something incorrect about TLE consequentialist's explanation for epistemic correctness (Berker 2013a, 2013b). TLE consequentialists, in their turn, wonder why it is that evidentialists fetishize evidence when it does not lead to true belief (Sharadin 2018; Singer 2018; Singer 2021). That dispute does not matter here. What matters is just that the first-order extensional disagreement obviously bleeds through to any attempt to answer our second-order question.

Recall, in our second-order theory we want to know why it is that it is *authoritatively* epistemically correct for a particular agent – Tony – to believe in the way it is epistemically correct for him to believe. But if there is disagreement over *what* it is epistemically correct for Tony to do, then we cannot yet move to the question of *why authoritatively* it is epistemically correct for Tony to so do. If we ask an evidentialist why it is that it is authoritatively epistemically correct for Tony to believe that God exists, they will (after looking exasperated) point us back to their first-order theory that says *this is not what it is epistemically correct for Tony to do*. Equally, if we ask the dual of the question to what will now be an equally exasperated TLE consequentialist.

Compare the following analogous situation. Suppose there is some microphysical particle Q that can have *up* or *down* spin and can appear in physical systems of various sorts. Suppose further that there is dispute among our best physical theories over whether there are any Qs at all in particular physical system S. Then, prior to settling the dispute over *whether* there are any Qs in S, it will not make sense to ask questions about what explains why it is that *all* the Qs in S are Qs with up spin. Of course, we can ask the question *conditionally*: supposing there were Qs in S, what would explain their all being up spin? I will come to a version of that idea for the present case later. The point here is just the – hopefully commonsensical – one that, prior to (at least conditionally) settling the question about *whether* something is the case, we cannot ask questions about why it is the particular way it is without leading to exasperated looks on all sides.

9.4 Can We Instead Explain *De Dicto*?

You might think that we could avoid exasperation by taking the following strategy: instead of looking for an explanation of why it is authoritatively epistemically correct for an agent to φ for some φ such that it is authoritatively epistemically correct for the agent to φ (*de re*), we should go after an explanation of why it is authoritatively epistemically correct for an agent to φ for whatever φ it is such that it is authoritatively epistemically correct for the agent to φ (*de dicto*). (Rather than asking for an explanation of why it is that Qs in *S* are up spin, we might ask why it is that the Qs that are up spin are up spin, wherever they happen to be.)

In Tony's case, the relevant thought goes like this: rather than asking of Tony why it is that it is (not) authoritatively epistemically correct for him to believe God exists, we should ask of Tony why it is that it is authoritatively epistemically correct for him to believe in whatever way it is authoritatively epistemically correct for him to believe. This strategy presumably takes the first-order extensional disagreement between evidentialists and TLE consequentialists out of the picture. And maybe it thereby takes first-order theory out of the picture altogether: maybe we can do our second-order theorizing without first settling our first-order theory.

Unfortunately, this will not do. For, this strategy would require us to settle *which* cases of epistemic correctness are authoritative before settling anything about *why* epistemic correctness is authoritative. We have already discussed why this would be a mistake (Section 7.5.2), but it is an important point, so let me elaborate.

What it is authoritatively epistemically correct for an agent to do is, as we have seen, a not necessarily proper subset of what it is epistemically correct for her to do. So, if we are trying to ask why it is authoritatively epistemically correct for an agent to believe in whatever way it is authoritatively epistemically correct for her to believe, this question is hopelessly empty without some determinate account of the relation between what it is epistemically correct for an agent to believe and what it authoritatively epistemically correct for the agent to believe. That is a mouthful. More prosaically, we cannot meaningfully ask *why* it is that mammals, whichever ones, give live birth if we know that a not necessarily proper subset of mammals give live birth. It is armchair mammalogy meets armchair reproductive biology. One more analogy: we cannot meaningfully ask *why* baseball players, whichever ones, chew tobacco, if we know that a not necessarily proper subset of baseball players chew tobacco. Armchair psychology meets armchair baseball anthropology-cum-sociology.

But then, assuming as we are here that at least *some* cases of epistemic correctness are authoritative, the only principled way to determine the relation between what it is epistemically correct for an agent to believe and what it authoritatively epistemically correct for the agent to believe prior to an explanation for epistemic authority would be to endorse:

> Always Authoritative: In all cases, if it is epistemically correct for A to φ, then it is authoritatively epistemically correct for A to φ.

In other words, whenever we have a case of epistemic correctness, we thereby have an instance of *authoritative* epistemic correctness. It should be obvious why this is the only principled way to determine the relation between what it is epistemically correct for an agent to do and what it is authoritatively epistemically correct for her to do given our present assumptions and prior to an explanation for epistemic authority. As we just saw, we need *some* determinate account of the relation between what it is epistemically correct to do and what it is authoritatively epistemically correct to do in order to meaningfully ask the explanatory question (even *de dicto*). There are only two determinate accounts available: either *all* cases of epistemic correctness are authoritative, or *none* are. We are assuming local nihilism about epistemic authority is false.[4] So all cases of epistemic correctness are cases of authoritative epistemic correctness; that is, Always Authoritative is true.

If we accepted Always Authoritative, then we *could* ask our second-order explanatory question *de dicto*: we could ask why it is that epistemic correctness – *whatever its specific content* – is authoritative. But, and this is the crucial point, accepting Always Authoritative is illicit prior to an explanation for epistemic authority. Whether it turns out to be the case that all cases of epistemic correctness are authoritative is not something we can assume out the outset. Instead, whether this turns out to be so will depend, in part, on the particular explanation of the authority of epistemic correctness that we give. It may turn out that the best explanation for epistemic authority will entail Always Authoritative. But we have no reason for assuming it is true at this stage.

I have already explained why this is so (Chapter 7). But it is repeatedly overlooked. So just to remind you: it is certainly true that, in the course of explicating the phenomenon of epistemic authority, we must assume that at least *some* instances of epistemic correctness are authoritative. And in the course of ostending at the phenomenon of epistemic authority, I (and others) appeal to the intuitive thought that epistemic correctness sometimes – indeed, *usually* – has the distinctive *mattering* we associate with authoritativeness. But these intuitions, that this case of epistemic correctness matters or that this other one matters, do not support anything nearly as strong as Always Authoritative. Instead, as we have seen, they only support Usually Authoritative. But you cannot leverage *Usually* Authoritative into a way of meaningfully asking our second-order explanatory question *de dicto*.

9.5 The Content Constraint

What this means, in sum, is that there is no coherent way of trying to tackle our second-order questions about the explanation for epistemic authority prior to settling our first-order epistemic theory. This is what I will call the

> Content Constraint: In order to evaluate a second-order epistemic theory, we must first settle on some first-order epistemic theory.

Let me be clear. This is a constraint on our theorizing, not a constraint on the world. It is a constraint on our ability to *evaluate* whether and to what extent some second-order epistemic theory does a good job explaining epistemic authority. It is not a constraint on the way the world is. It is not clear what it would even mean to say such a thing, but to avoid confusion, let me be clear that I do not mean to be saying whatever that thing would be. The Content Constraint in effect tells us: if you want to see how well some theory does as a theory that purports to explain epistemic *authority* you have to first settle on some *potential extension* for that authority, namely, a first-order epistemic theory.

As we saw, this is because it is simply impossible to get a grip on what the relevant second-order epistemic theory is even supposed to be saying without some specific content for it to be saying that thing *about*. Again, this is for the reason that second-order epistemic theories are attempts to explain why it is that epistemic correctness sometimes (usually) has a particular feature, namely, that it is authoritative. But in order to evaluate competing explanations for why this might be the case, we need to know *when it is the case*: do not tell me you can explain *why airplanes fly* without some prior theory that delivers the result that *eagles are not airplanes*. So much, I hope, so uncontroversial.

As I explain in the next chapter, what is plausibly the most straightforward, natural way of respecting the Content Constraint yields a methodology that makes second-order epistemic instrumentalism look like an undeniably poor contender. Before that, let me head off three remaining ways of trying to avoid the Content Constraint, that is, the need to settle the extension of epistemic correctness prior to an explanation for the authority thereof.

9.6 Against the Content Constraint

9.6.1 Dogmatic Epistemicism

Perhaps you think it is possible to avoid doing first-order epistemic theory first and second-order epistemic theory second by accepting the following:

> Dogmatic Epistemicism: The fact that it is authoritatively epistemically correct for A to φ is grounded by the fact that it is epistemically correct for A to φ.[5]

In other words, the explanatory grounds of the fact that it is *authoritatively* epistemically correct for an agent to φ is always entirely and exclusively that it is epistemically correct for her to φ.[6] Dogmatic Epistemicism, if true, might appear to preclude the need to do first-order epistemic theory before engaging in second-order theorizing. There are two related problems with this idea.

First, it is theoretically unmotivated. The dogmatic epistemicist is in effect offering a non-explanation; they are simply refusing to engage in second-order theorizing about *why it is* that epistemic correctness is authoritative: it just, in their view, *is*. But this is not only dogmatic; it also is simpleminded. Clearly, some kinds of correctness – it is assassinly correct to sneak up on your victims; it is bachelorettely correct to bare your soul to a stranger – clearly *just do not matter*; they obviously are not (usually or, perhaps, ever) authoritative. The dogmatic epistemicist is not a global skeptic about the very idea of authority; she is not even a local skeptic about the authority of epistemic correctness. Indeed, they presumably agree that epistemic correctness is (as we will see later, *always*) authoritative. They just do not think this fact requires explanation. But, again, this is simpleminded. For, if we simply accept Dogmatic Epistemicism – that is, we accept that epistemic correctness is authoritative without further explanation – then why should we not also accept the following:

Dogmatic Assassinism: The fact that it is authoritatively assassinly correct for A to φ is grounded by the fact that it is assassinly correct for A to φ.

But clearly we should not also accept the Dogmatic Assassinist account of the authority of assassin correctness. I imagine the dogmatic epistemicist saying that this is because assassin correctness is not (ever) authoritative; I agree. The point here is that we are owed an explanation of this fact. And dogmatically pointing to epistemic correctness and saying that *it* is authoritative because epistemic, whereas assassin correctness is *formal* because assassinistic is, well, hopelessly dogmatic.

Note that the dogmatic epistemicist as we are imagining them does *not* go on to appeal to (say) the content of their first-order explanation in their explanation for epistemic authority; in other words, they do not explain the authority of epistemic correctness *via* whatever facts are supposed to explain epistemic correctness itself. It is not as if they simply have the explanatory grounds, as it were, do double duty. That would at least be an *attempt* at engaging in the explanatory project – although, as I suggest in the next chapter, one that does not get us very far. The dogmatic epistemicist *does not explain*: that is why they are *dogmatic*.

Worse and worse, given what I said in Chapter 2 about the conventional differences between kinds of correctness *per se*, there is no route for the dogmatic epistemicist through assigning some sort of higher status to the kind "epistemic" as opposed to the kind (say) "assassin" *qua the kinds they are*. Remember, this does not mean that epistemic correctness is not more important than assassin correctness; I repeat: I agree that it almost always is. What this means is that precisely what we want, and what the dogmatic epistemicist is flatly refusing to give us, is an explanation of this fact.

The second, related problem with the Dogmatic Epistemicism is that it straightforwardly entails:

> Always Authoritative: In all cases, if it is epistemically correct for A to φ, then it is authoritatively epistemically correct for A to φ.[7]

We have already seen why this is problematic: Always Authoritative is an illicit assumption in the present context. As we discussed in the last section, it may be that the best explanation for epistemic authority delivers Always Authoritative. But since the dogmatic epistemicist is flatly refusing without argument to engage in the explanatory project, they have no grounds for insisting on that extensional claim here; recall, their explanation is a *non-explanation*. It is not as if we have been given an explanation for the authority of epistemic correctness that entails that all instances of epistemic correctness are authoritative. Instead, what we have been given is a refusal to explain the authority of epistemic correctness that contains the assertion that all instances thereof are authoritative. And that is not something we have any reason to accept.

There is a way to capture what *might* have been appealing about the dogmatic epistemicist idea. It is to draw our attention, once more, to the fact that *any* complete explanation for epistemic authority is going to require an extension for epistemic correctness. Here is a way to make this explicit. Any complete explanation for the authority of a particular case of epistemic correctness can, as we have seen, in principle be factored into its component explanatory grounds like so:

The fact that it is authoritatively epistemically correct for A to φ is grounded by

(i) whatever facts explain why it is epistemically correct for A to φ.
(ii) whatever facts explain the authority of epistemic correctness (on this occasion).

As we know, when we are after an explanation for epistemic authority, what we are after is an account of (ii). The explanatory question facing second-order theory is not, Why is it epistemically correct for Jon to believe his marriage is ending? Our first-order epistemic theory tells us why (and so *if*) this is the case. Instead, the explanatory question facing second-order theory is, Why is epistemic correctness authoritative on this occasion? Our second-order epistemic theory tells us why *this* is the case, if it is.

What the dogmatic epistemicist gets *correct*, then, is that any explanation of why it is that some particular case of epistemic correctness is authoritative will *in part* require appealing to the idea that, as a matter of fact, it is epistemically correct for the agent to do such and such. But this is just the same idea that we have already accepted, namely, that first-order theory must come first. What the dogmatic epistemicist gets *incorrect* is the idea that this is *all that needs to be said*; in effect, they refuse to engage in the second-order explanatory project (i.e., an account of [ii]) altogether.

9.6.2 Quietism

In the face of these concerns, someone initially tempted by Dogmatic Epistemicism might be tempted to retreat to the following:

> Quietism about Authority: A suitably rich picture of the relationship between mind and world reveals that there is no philosophically interesting explanatory question about why it is that epistemic correctness is sometimes, even usually, authoritative in the way it manifestly is. The felt need for such explanation is either a residue of our inability to grasp the way in which our minds both reflect and structure the independent world with which we engage or (and this might be the same thing), or it is an ineliminable phenomenological aspect of experience for creatures like us that does not merit philosophical theory but instead merits a kind of conceptual therapy.[8]

I have no new reply to this position to offer here. I simply assume, entirely without argument, that the quietist position is not correct. I am interested in theory, not therapy.

9.6.3 What about Ethics?

I have defended the idea that, when it comes to first- and second-order epistemic theory, first-order theory must come first. The reason, just to remind you, is that it is not possible to meaningfully ask and then substantively answer the second-order question about why it is that epistemic correctness is authoritative without some particular view of the explanation for epistemic correctness.

Attentive readers will have noticed that there was nothing about my argument that, in principle, restricted the upshot of the argument to the case of *epistemic* theorizing – as opposed to theorizing about *other* kinds of correctness. This is because the argument proceeded on entirely structural grounds: the problem with trying to do second-order epistemic theorizing first did not have anything to do with the kind of correctness or authority at issue being *epistemic*.

Now add to this the fact that throughout the book I have sometimes leaned on the analogy with other kinds of correctness, especially *ethical* correctness. Although I have said I am approaching things as a pluralist rather than a monist, I have also several times used analogues from the case of ethics to support various claims about the structure and content of epistemic theorizing.

But given that my argument did not depend on anything specific about *epistemic* correctness, and given my willingness to deploy analogous arguments to and from different kinds of correctness, you might think I have dug myself a bit of a hole.

Here is why: you might plausibly think that the symmetrical priority claim simply is not true when it comes to ethical correctness. In other words, it is not true that first-order *ethical* theory must come first. Instead, it is possible to meaningfully ask and then substantively answer the analogous second-order question about why it is that ethical correctness is authoritative without some particular view of what explains ethical correctness. And we *know* this is possible because, manifestly, philosophers have been doing it for more than a few centuries. So something must have gone wrong with my argument.

My response is to retrench. Given what I have said about the structure of first- and second-order theory quite generally it is correct to say that, if first-order *epistemic* theory must come before the second-order explanatory question about epistemic authority, then first-order *ethical* theory must come before the corresponding second-order explanatory question about *ethical* authority. This response means that I then owe an explanation of why it is that a nontrivial amount of second-order ethical theorizing is apparently being done without first settling on first-order ethical theory. Happily, I think there is a straightforward explanation of this fact that exactly fits – indeed helps confirm – what I have said so far.

Recall the strategy, outlined earlier, for *avoiding* the need to do epistemic first-order theory first: we could try to ask what explains the explanatory question *de dicto*: what explains why it is that the instances of epistemic correctness that are authoritative are so, *whichever instances of epistemic correctness end up being authoritative*. As we saw, the problem with this strategy is that it required accepting *some* account of the relationship between epistemic correctness and authoritative epistemic correctness (since we know that the latter is a not-necessarily proper subset of the former). But, on the assumption that at least some epistemic cases of epistemic correctness are authoritative, the only principled way to do this was to accept Always Authoritative, which says that *all* epistemic correctness is authoritative epistemic correctness. And, in the present context, this assumption is illicit: we are not licensed to simply assume, prior to an explanation for epistemic authority, that all epistemic correctness is authoritative.

Now, my official view is that exactly the same thing is true in the case of ethics; just as we cannot assume, prior to a second-order epistemic theory, that all epistemic correctness is authoritative epistemic correctness, we cannot assume, prior to a second-order ethical theory, that all ethical correctness is authoritative ethical correctness. But – and this is the key to accounting for the fact that so much second-order ethical theorizing has been done without *explicitly* adopting some first-order ethical theory – in the case of ethics, there is a large group of individuals who think that the ethical version of Always Authoritative reflects something like a conceptual truth about ethical correctness.[9] According to these people, ethical correctness is in part *defined as* a correctness that is authoritative, always, everywhere, in all circumstances, for all agents. Hence (the idea goes) we can perfectly meaningfully ask the ethical version of our *de dicto* explanatory question, since, prior to any substantive explanatory story for the authority of ethics, we can know exactly what the relationship is between ethical correctness and authoritative ethical correctness – they are coextensive.

There are various ways to cash out and then argue for this idea that ethical correctness *just is* a kind of correctness that is always authoritative. One would be to make an analogue of our functionalist claim about epistemic correctness. You might think that (part of) the role, purpose, point, or function of evaluations in terms of *ethical* correctness is to do something the doing of which requires that ethical correctness always be authoritative. Perhaps the point of evaluations in terms of *ethical* correctness (as opposed to other kinds of correctness) is to mark off behaviors as *really mattering* or *extremely important*, and perhaps that is just what ethical authority amounts to. Then, it would turn out that, on pain of failing to be capable of doing what they are systematically for, all cases of ethical correctness are cases of authoritative ethical correctness. Something like that story might be correct. Here, I take no stand one way or the other on its truth.

I have said that kinds of correctness – ethical correctness, epistemic correctness – are in one sense or another conventionally determined – they are down to *us*, rather than down in some mysterious manner down to the location of the joints in evaluative reality (Chapter 2). What this means is that I must be in principle open to the possibility of convention delivering up a kind of correctness with a particular ambit that is also always everywhere authoritative in the way that many theorists apparently want to insist is the case with ethical correctness. And I *am* open to that possibility; moreover: here, I am not inclined even to argue about whether it is a commitment of our engaging in thought and talk in terms of *ethical* (as opposed to in some way nonethical) correctness that we are engaging in thought and talk about a kind of correctness that is always everywhere authoritative. Maybe that is correct. It is sufficient to explain the fact that so much second-order ethical theory proceeds without first settling first-order ethical theory that *many (perhaps most) people have thought that it is correct*.

What I am inclined to do here is to deny that the analogous claim is correct when it comes to epistemic correctness. It is not that I think we *couldn't* conventionally define up a kind of correctness whose ambit comprised (say) agents' doxastic attitudes and that also was always everywhere authoritative. We could even go on to baptize that kind the "epistemic" kind of correctness, and if we did that, we could then do our second-order epistemic theorizing about the *authority* of epistemic correctness so conceived without needing to first settle anything about the explanation for epistemic correctness. We could do this.

But I think that this simply is not the kind "epistemic" that we actually have and about which we are trying to theorize. In other words, I do not think it is actually a commitment of our engaging in thought and talk about epistemic (as opposed to in some way non-epistemic) correctness that we are engaging in thought and talk about a kind of correctness that is always everywhere authoritative. Whatever you think about the analogous claim in ethics, it simply does not appear to be an obvious *conceptual* error to think that it is epistemically correct for an agent to φ but that it is not the case that it is authoritatively epistemically correct for them to φ. Or anyway, so say I. (More on this in just a moment.)

If this is correct, then we can explain the apparent difference between the approaches to first- and second-order ethical and epistemic theory by appeal to the apparent difference between what kinds of conceptual claims about the relevant kinds of correctness it makes sense to insist on. In the ethical case, it is at least *plausible* that something such as Always Authoritative represents a (necessary?) conceptual truth on the kind of correctness we are attempting to talk about. (Again, I am not saying I accept this view, only that it is at least very plausible – and *widely accepted* – in the case of ethics.) In the epistemic case, this is not the case. It is manifestly possible to think and speak clearly about "epistemic correctness" without being (even implicitly) committed to Always Authoritative.

These are delicate issues, as are all questions about the boundaries of our (manufactured) concepts. But I think my view has the edge precisely in virtue of what makes the issue so delicate. For my opponent is someone who must think a certain kind of conceptual activity *just is not possible* – according to them, you fail to be thinking about what it is epistemically correct for an agent to do if you simultaneously think it is an open question whether it is *authoritatively epistemically correct* for her to do it. That is an almost impossibly courageous claim about the nature of our capacity for certain kinds of evaluative thought and talk. My view is much more cowardly.

Remaining resistance to the view is, I think, largely a product of (unapologetic) Dogmatic Epistemicism or (long-suffering) quietism. These are possible views, but as I have said, both eschew the explanatory project I am interested in here in (different but related) ways that do not reflect what I think of is the real explanatory burden we are under.

9.7 Conclusion

There is universal agreement that, in both first- and second-order epistemic theory, explanation precedes extension. When it comes to the question of first- and second-order epistemic theories themselves, first-order epistemic theory must come first. This is because (roughly), without some explanation for (and so extension of) epistemic correctness, there is no way to meaningfully ask what explains why it is that the epistemic correctness is authoritative. Ways of avoiding this conclusion – either by asking the explanatory question *de dicto* or by simply asserting, in one way or another, that we can do the one without the other, are unsatisfactory. First-order epistemic theory comes first. In the next chapter, I explain how the natural methodology that arises out of an attempt to respect this constraint has made second-order epistemic instrumentalism seem like an especially poor contender.

Notes

1 Kagan (1992) and Sylvan (2018).
2 Singer (2021). Singer adapts the case from Berker (2013a), who, in turn, borrows it from Fumerton (2001), who bases it on cases introduced by Firth and Troyer (1998). See also the discussion in Firth (1981).
3 There are reasons to think TLE Consequentialism does not deliver this result. For instance, see Singer (2021), and Sharadin (2018).
4 For discussion, see Section 6.6.
5 Not to be confused with the "epistemicist" view about *vagueness*, namely, that propositions involving vague concepts have definite truth values. See Williamson (1994).
6 Recall, I am assuming every Authority Explanation will *include* among its explanans the fact that it is epistemically correct for the agent to φ (Chapter 7). The Dogmatic Epistemicist agrees but goes on to claim that *there is nothing more to say*.
7 Proof: Suppose (Dogmatic Epistemicism) the fact that it is authoritatively epistemically correct for A to φ is grounded by the fact that it is epistemically correct for A to φ. Suppose it is epistemically correct for A to φ. Given the factivity of grounding, it therefore follows that it is authoritatively epistemically correct for A to φ. Hence, if it is epistemically correct for A to φ, then it is authoritatively epistemically correct for A to φ (Left-to-Right). Suppose instead that it is authoritatively epistemically correct for A to φ. Given the definition of what it is to be authoritatively epistemically correct for A to φ, it follows that it is epistemically correct for A to φ (Right-to-Left). So, in all cases, if it is epistemically correct for A to φ, then it is authoritatively epistemically correct for A to φ (Always Authoritative).
8 This may be the kind of thing McDowell (2009) has in mind. For critical discussion, see McPherson (2011).
9 This idea is put in a number of different nonidentical ways, but it is perhaps most familiar as the thought that moral correctness is "categorical," "non-optional," or "universal". For discussion, see Korsgaard (1996). For accounts that proceed on the assumption that *if* there is such a thing as moral correctness, *then* it is categorical (in whatever sense), see, for just a few examples, Parfit (2011), Enoch (2011), Scanlon (1998), Scanlon (2014), Cuneo (2007), Brink (1989), and Shafer-Landau (2003).

References

Berker, Selim. 2013a. "Epistemic Teleology and the Separateness of Propositions." *Philosophical Review* 122 (3): 337–393. https://doi.org/10.1215/00318108-2087645.

———. 2013b. "The Rejection of Epistemic Consequentialism." *Philosophical Issues* 23 (1): 363–387. https://doi.org/10.1111/phis.12019.

Brink, David Owen. 1989. *Moral Realism and the Foundations of Ethics*. Cambridge: Cambridge University Press.

Cuneo, Terence. 2007. *The Normative Web: An Argument for Moral Realism*. Oxford: Oxford University Press.

Enoch, David. 2011. *Taking Morality Seriously: A Defense of Robust Realism*. Oxford: Oxford University Press UK.

Firth, Roderick. 1981. "Epistemic Merit, Intrinsic and Instrumental." *Proceedings and Addresses of the American Philosophical Association* 55 (1): 5–23. https://doi.org/10.2307/3131397.

Firth, Roderick, and John Troyer. 1998. *In Defense of Radical Empiricism: Essays and Lectures*. Oxford: Rowman and Littlefield.

Fumerton, Richard. 2001. "Epistemic Justification and Normativity." In *Knowledge, Truth, and Duty: Essays on Epistemic Justification, Responsibility, and Virtue*, edited by Matthias Steup, 49–60. Oxford: Oxford University Press.

Kagan, Shelly. 1992. "The Structure of Normative Ethics." *Philosophical Perspectives* 6: 223–242. https://doi.org/10.2307/2214246.

Korsgaard, Christine M. 1996. *The Sources of Normativity*. Cambridge: Cambridge University Press.

McDowell, John. 2009. "Wittgensteinian 'Quietism'." *Common Knowledge* 15 (3): 365–372. https://doi.org/10.1215/0961754X-2009-018.

McPherson, Tristram. 2011. "Against Quietist Normative Realism." *Philosophical Studies* 154 (2): 223–240. https://doi.org/10.1007/s11098-010-9535-y.

Parfit, Derek. 2011. *On What Matters: Two-Volume Set*. Oxford: Oxford University Press.

Scanlon, Thomas M. 1998. *What We Owe to Each Other*. Cambridge, MA: Belknap Press of Harvard University Press.

——— 2014. *Being Realistic about Reasons*. Oxford: Oxford University Press.

Shafer-Landau, Russ. 2003. *Moral Realism: A Defence*. Oxford: Oxford University Press.

Sharadin, Nathaniel. 2018. "Epistemic Consequentialism: Haters Gonna Hate." In *Metaepistemology: Realism & Antirealism*, edited by Christos Kyriacou and Robin McKenna, 121–143. Cham, Switzerland: Palgrave MacMillan.

Singer, Daniel J. 2018. "How to Be an Epistemic Consequentialist." *Philosophical Quarterly* 68 (272): 580–602. https://doi.org/10.1093/pq/pqx056.

———. 2021. "Right Belief." Unpublished manuscript.

Sylvan, Kurt L. 2018. "Reliabilism without Epistemic Consequentialism." *Philosophy and Phenomenological Research* 3: 525–555. https://doi.org/10.1111/phpr.12560.

Williamson, Timothy. 1994. *Vagueness*. London: Routledge.

10 Bespoke Explanations

10.1 Introduction

Recall, we are under the

> Content Constraint: In order to evaluate a second-order epistemic theory, we must first settle on some first-order epistemic theory.

The most natural, straightforward way to respect this constraint in one's epistemic theorizing is to adopt the following methodology: first, accept some first-order epistemic theory – accept whatever you take to be the best explanation for and so extension of epistemic correctness. Second, do one's second-order epistemic theory – offer an explanation for the authoritativeness of epistemic correctness so understood – that is, as understood in one's antecedently accepted first-order epistemic theory. Then accept the pairing of these two views as one's complete epistemic theory. Easy-peasy.

If you take this approach, then the way to approach one's second-order epistemic theorizing will be by *tailoring* one's second-order epistemic theory to one's first-order epistemic theory; the result will be what I will call a *bespoke explanation* for epistemic authority. A bespoke explanation for epistemic authority is an explanation for epistemic authority expertly tailored to the first-order theory of epistemic correctness that, as it were, you were wearing when you walked in the door.

In this chapter, I have two aims. First, I aim to illustrate the idea behind bespoke explanations with an eye to identifying the process by which they are made and thereby diagnosing the relative unpopularity of second-order epistemic instrumentalism. Being bespoke, there are a lot of them. But many are cut from the same cloth and in the same style. The important point is that the tailoring process – the way in which such explanations are generated – is *almost never* going to result in an epistemic instrumentalist explanation for epistemic authority, hence the relative unpopularity of the view.

DOI: 10.4324/9781003096726-10

This would be a real problem if bespoke explaining were the only way to respect the Content Constraint, or if bespoke explanations enjoyed some advantage sufficient to make us systematically prefer them. But as I explain (this is my second aim), it is *not* a problem. That is because bespoke explaining clearly is not obligatory and bespoke explanations are not (necessarily) always better. The result, if I am correct, is the removal of a long-standing methodological barrier to second-order epistemic instrumentalism's acceptance. In the next chapter, I address two potential problems for second-order epistemic instrumentalism.

10.2 Tailoring Bespoke Explanations

There are myriad bespoke explanations. It is not crucial for my case here that we display the entire line; instead, what I will do is explain the process that gives rise to them – the tailoring – in general terms and then work through an illustrative example.

Broadly, all bespoke explanations for epistemic authority are tailored like so: you enter wearing some particular first-order epistemic theory, and then you pass that style on relatively unchanged to your second-order epistemic theory (maybe you add a few accoutrements here and there). Then, you don the entire outfit and out you go. That is a lot of sartorial metaphor.

Here is the idea, somewhat less metaphorically. The overall plan, recall, is to come up with an explanation for epistemic authority while respecting the Content Constraint – while respecting the requirement that, in order to evaluate the quality of such an explanation, one must accept some first-order epistemic theory or other. And what you have, once you have accepted a first-order epistemic theory, is some account of what explains epistemic correctness – and, importantly, an account that gives some extension therefor. And what you want, when you want a *second*-order epistemic theory, is some account of why it is that epistemic correctness has a *grip* on agents, when it does. But importantly, you do not want just *any* second-order epistemic theory; you want your second-order epistemic theory to *match* your first-order epistemic theory. At the very least, you want a theory that matches sufficiently well so that it delivers on Usually Authoritative.

And so if you begin the process of looking for a second-order epistemic theory by first accepting some first-order epistemic theory, then the range of possible explanations for epistemic authority will be restricted by the content of your first-order epistemic theory. Hence, in crafting a bespoke explanation for epistemic authority, perhaps the most natural thing to do is to first identify the feature that is supposed to explain epistemic *correctness* and then simply *pass that feature through* to one's second-order epistemic theory as the feature that in turn explains epistemic *authority*. That will result in a nicely tailored story, and it is one guaranteed to result

156 *Bespoke Explanations*

in a potentially pleasing sort of *match* between one's first- and second-order explanatory stories.

Here, in case it helps, is an instance of the analogous situation in *ethical* theory. Suppose you impale yourself on Euthyphro's second horn: you are an unrepentant divine command theorist who thinks that divine say-so *explains* (rather than simply extensionally matches) what is ethically correct. And suppose you are now casting about for a second-order theory that explains the *authority* of ethical correctness so construed. The way to tailor such an explanation is to simply *pass through* one's first-order theory to one's second-order theory: it is precisely *divine say-so* that presumably (in your view, at least) explains the authority of ethical correctness. That is how you achieve the basic match between your first-order divine command theory and your second-order story about the authority of ethical correctness. Of course, this will leave *a lot* to be explained: in particular, we will need to hear from you why it is we should think divine say-so (whatever that comprises) is, in fact, the ground of ethical authority – those will be the explanatory accoutrements that complete the look. Then, out you go into the world wearing your ridiculous – but manifestly well-tailored – divine-command theory.

So it goes in epistemic theory. This is *the* method for tailoring a bespoke explanation for epistemic authority: take your first-order theory, pass it through to your second-order theory, and then articulate an account of why it is that the feature identified in your first-order theory is capable of explaining epistemic authority. As we will see in the next section, the method works: you can get extremely well-cut explanations as a result of using it. As I will also explain, you will (almost) never get epistemic instrumentalism. Hence our methodological barrier. But, it turns out, despite being extremely widespread, this methodology is not at all obligatory. And there are good reasons for moving away from it. Hence, no barrier. More on that later. Right now, let's take a look at some finely tailored explanations for epistemic authority.

10.3 Bespoke Explanations for Evidentialists

10.3.1 Preliminaries

It will be useful to work through an example. I am going to walk through the tailoring process for just one first-order epistemic theory: evidentialism. Hopefully it will be clear how you might undertake the process if you begin by accepting a somewhat different first-order epistemic theory. By the end of this discussion, it should also be clear why it is that, almost no matter what first-order epistemic theory you start with, you will never end up with second-order epistemic instrumentalism.

Recall, you are a first-order epistemic evidentialist if you accept:

> Evidentialism: The fact that it is epistemically correct for A to φ is grounded by the fact that A's φ-ing is supported by A's evidence.

What you need, at present, is a second-order epistemic theory that both explains why it is that epistemic correctness is authoritative and, crucially, that matches this first-order theory – at least to the extent that it delivers on Usually Authoritative. As I said, the way to tailor such a bespoke explanation is to take the feature that purportedly explains epistemic correctness – that is, explanatory grounds thereof – and pass it through to one's second-order theory as the explanatory grounds of the *authority* of epistemic correctness.

So, working with evidentialism, we first identify the relevant feature that is supposed to explanatorily ground epistemic correctness; in this case, that is easy: it is *being supported by the evidence*. We have, then, the cut sheet for a bespoke explanation:

> Second-Order Evidentialism: The fact that it is authoritatively epistemically correct for A to φ is grounded by the fact that A's φ-ing is supported by A's evidence.

But this is not all that explanatory, or, putting it another way – it's not much of a *theory*. It is much the same as the ethical divine command theorist simply asserting that divine say-so is what both explains ethical correctness *and* explains the authority thereof. What we require from them – and from our evidentialist here – is, in addition, some story of why it is that the relevant feature – divine say-so or, in this case, *fit with the evidence* – is supposed to be epistemically authoritative. Variations on the broadly evidentialist second-order epistemic theory will then be the result of varying that additional story. It will pay to focus on what such stories might look like on behalf of the evidentialist. First, a quick proviso.

In the last chapter, I criticized dogmatic epistemicism on the grounds that it refused to engage in the obviously meaningful explanatory project of making sense of why it is that epistemic correctness (usually) has a certain kind of authoritative grip on us. It might look like bespoke explanations that are the result of the cut sheet just given for the evidentialist amount to a form of dogmatic epistemicism and so are liable to criticism on the same grounds. But I think that is too quick.

Say what you want about the explanation just offered – and I say quite a bit later – what you cannot say is that it is a straightforward refusal to explain in the way that the dogmatic epistemicist refuses to explain. There is an explanandum – the fit between an agent's evidence and their φ-ing – and the claim, according to the present idea, is that this explanandum somehow explains not just the existence of epistemic correctness but also the *authority* thereof. Whatever we think about the merits of this

158 Bespoke Explanations

explanation, it is not a refusal to explain of the kind the dogmatic epistemicist was engaged in.

But again, there is something correct about the suspicion that the evidentialist cannot simply present this explanation and then *leave it at that*: she is not *done* explaining. She needs, in addition, to say something about why it is that *fitting the evidence* is the kind of thing that is epistemically authoritative – about why it has a *grip* on agents. The components of *this* story are the bulk of the relevant evidentialist explanation. To continue illustrating how the procedure works, let's go through three such stories that evidentialists have offered.

10.3.2 Sui Generis Evidentialism

The most straightforward option is to don

> Sui Generis Evidentialism: Evidence is *sui generis* epistemically authoritative.[1]

You can see why this would do the trick. If you have already got the idea that fitting the evidence is what explains why it is that it is authoritatively epistemically correct for an agent to do what it is epistemically correct for her to do, and you add to this the idea that evidence is *sui generis* epistemically authoritative, you appear to have arrived at a quite tidy explanatory outfit. The outfit is tidy not just because it explains what we were after explaining – epistemic authority – but also because it does so by simply passing through the first-order epistemic theory to the second; that is why, as we just saw, things match up so well in the end. That is the essential nature of bespoke explanations for epistemic authority: they are designed by and for particular first-order epistemic theories.

Now, you might not be much taken with the explanatory outfit you get when you add the evidentialist explanation to the *sui generis* accoutrements. If that is true, I am guessing it is because you are worried about whether the claim that X is *sui generis* authoritative in the end adds anything at all to an explanation of the authoritativeness of X. If I ask you to explain why it is that Oscar lives in a trashcan, and you say that his living in a trashcan is *sui generis*, I will probably be underwhelmed. But my purpose here is not to criticize the particular bespoke explanations offered by, for example, evidentialists. My purpose is rather to illustrate how they arise out of a particular methodology. So I do not pursue this line any further. Instead, by way of continuing the illustration, let me sketch several other options for evidentialists.

10.3.3 Constitutivist Evidentialism

Remember, what we are after is something that fills in the gaps in the bespoke idea that fitting the evidence is what explains epistemic authority.

This can be done, as earlier, in *sui generis* style: if evidence is *sui generis* epistemically authoritative, then (setting aside the worry just noted regarding the explanatory power of *sui generis* claims generally) it is no surprise at all that fitting the evidence exerts epistemic authority over agents. But we can dress things up in different styles too; there are other accoutrements that could complete the evidentialist look. For instance, some evidentialists have offered.

> Constitutivist Evidentialism: Evidence is *constitutively* epistemically authoritative.[2]

Very briefly, the constitutivist idea is that part of *what it is* to be the kind of thing that is within the ambit of the epistemic – paradigmatically, agents' beliefs – is to be the kind of thing that is authoritatively governed by evidence. Let's dig in just a bit via the constitutivist's favorite analogy.

As we have already seen, kinds of correctness proliferate. Take knives. There are lots of different kinds of ways that we can evaluate a knife as being correct or incorrect. It is morally not correct for the knife to be stuck in my arm; it is aesthetically correct for the knife to have a nicer handle; it is prudentially correct for it to be cheaper; it is 8chanly correct that the knife not be sold by the techno-capitalist Satan worshipers secretly running America's largest corporations. You get the idea. Only in some of these ways is it, in one sense or another, correct for a knife to be are ways it is correct for the knife to be *qua knife*; only some ways the knife might be are ways of being such that it is a correct *knife*. Intuitively, this – forgive the expression – knifely correctness – is correctness that attaches to a knife *in virtue of the kind of thing it is*, namely, a knife. Some examples might include that it is knifely correct for a knife to be sharp or that it is knifely correct for knives to keep their edges longer than a day or whatever. You hopefully also get *this* idea. The constitutivist thought, then, is that correctness that applies to things in virtue of the kinds of things they are is somehow special. In particular, correctness that applies to things in virtue of the kinds of things they are is *authoritative*.

Coming back to epistemology: the idea is that *epistemic correctness* when it comes to beliefs is a bit like *knifely* correctness when it comes to knives. Return to Yale Law alumnus and noted riot enthusiast Josh Hawley. There are lots of ways Hawley's beliefs about the election can be right; there are lots of ways that we can evaluate his beliefs as correct or incorrect:

> It is epistemically correct for Hawley to believe Biden won the election.It is politically correct for Hawley to suspend judgment on whether Biden won the election. It is prudentially correct for Hawley to disbelieve that Biden won the election. It is 8chanly correct for Hawley to believe Biden's election victory was the result of a cabal of

Satan-worshiping deep-state Democrats conspiring to overturn the landslide victory of Donald Trump, who will inevitably return in the coming Storm to wash away the corrupt politicians who stand in the way of America's return to greatness.

You get the idea. Only some of these ways it is correct for Hawley's beliefs in one sense or another to be are ways it is correct for those beliefs to be *qua beliefs*; only some ways his beliefs might be are ways of being such that the beliefs are correct *beliefs*. Intuitively, this – forgive the expression – *beliefly correctness* is correctness that attaches to his beliefs in virtue of the kind of things they are, namely, beliefs. Perhaps: It is beliefly correct for Hawley's beliefs to be responsive to the evidence. You hopefully also get *this* idea. The constitutivist idea, then, is that correctness that attaches to beliefs in virtue of the kind of things beliefs are is somehow special. In particular, correctness that attaches to beliefs in virtue of the kind of things beliefs are is *authoritative*. And, it turns out, epistemic correctness *just is* beliefly correctness: that is why epistemic correctness is authoritative. Or anyway, so the story goes.

Let me pause over this constitutivist story for a moment. The constitutivist accoutrement provides an extremely nice illustration of how bespoke explanations work, and it helps illustrate our point about the Content Constraint from the last chapter. Notice first that the constitutivist accoutrement is not available to all first-order epistemic theories. For, if you accept certain first-order epistemic theories, a constitutivist accoutrement will look quite stupid – it simply will not make any sense.

Here is an illustration of that. Suppose instead of being an evidentialist, you are a truth-loving epistemic consequentialist. Then, as we saw in Chapter 3, you will likely think the ambit of epistemic correctness will not only include *almost any φ-ings at all*, including believing, suspending judgment, and their ilk, but *also* include climbing telephone poles, eating sandwiches, making coffee, and so on. But even if we could somehow come up with a way that it is constitutively correct for the activity of eating sandwiches to be, it is *definitely* not going to be the case that this way it is correct for eating sandwiches to constitutively be will be a way that corresponds to or is promoted by the way the epistemic consequentialist says it is *epistemically* correct for eating sandwiches to be.

Remember, the reason the constitutivist accoutrement looks attractive in the evidentialist case is that, according to evidentialists, the ambit of the epistemic is restricted to an agent's doxastic attitudes, such as her beliefs. Because the evidentialist thinks of epistemic correctness as (essentially) involving conformance to the evidence, it is only things that *can* conform to the evidence that *can* be evaluated in terms of epistemic correctness. The constitutivist comes along and points out that (supposedly) it is *beliefly* correct for beliefs to be responsive to the evidence – that is, it is *constitutively* correct for beliefs to be that way. Then, they tell their story about how constitutive correctness is authoritative correctness.[3] What a match! Evidentialist correctness inherits its epistemic authority from the fact that evidentialist correctness turns out to be constitutive correctness, which, in turn, is authoritative.

But again this strategy is simply *crazy* if one has a very different antecedent view of what epistemic correctness comprises. If you think that epistemic correctness is a matter of doing that which produces the greatest available balance of true belief to false belief (as versions of epistemic consequentialism do), then it will not just be an agent's doxastic attitudes that fall within the ambit of the epistemic – it will also be their sandwich-eating and their telephone-pole-climbing and so on. There might be ways that it is constitutively correct for these activities to be (although I doubt it). But to repeat, it is not at all plausible that trying to do that which produces the greatest available balance of true belief to false belief (what it is epistemically correct to do) will produce sandwich-eatings or telephone-pole-climbings that are whatever way it is constitutively correct for such activities to be. (I assume if there is *any* plausible way it is constitutively correct for sandwiches to be, it is something to do with deliciousness or nutrition or whatever. I leave telephone-pole-climbing aside.) So, if you *begin* as an epistemic consequentialist, you will not end up as a constitutivist; you will not even be *tempted* by the constitutivist explanation for epistemic authority – it would be an extremely poor fit for your first-order theory.

One final remark on the constitutivist strategy. Interestingly, this fact, that the constitutivist explanation for epistemic authority only works given certain first-order epistemic theories, especially evidentialism, is well recognized by proponents of explanations for epistemic authority that adopt constitutivist accoutrements. But confusingly, the importance of this fact according to these authors is that it gives us separate, additional reasons for accepting the relevant first-order theory, namely, evidentialism. For instance, Nishi Shah (2006) frames his constitutivist explanation for epistemic authority as an independent argument for evidentialism, so, quite apart from accepting a first-order epistemic theory prior to offering a second-order explanation for epistemic authority, Shah thinks that he has done things in reverse. Of course, given the discussion in the last chapter, we are in a position to see why this is a mistake: first-order theory must come first. Perhaps Shah is trying to explain the authority of epistemic correctness *whatever* its specific content. But if that is correct, then, as we have seen, one of two things must be true. Either he must be assuming Always Authoritative, or his explanation lacks meaningful content. The former, as we have discussed, is illicit at this stage. The latter cannot be the idea.

As before with *sui generis* accoutrements, you might have worries about such constitutivist accoutrements intended to supplement the evidentialist's explanation for epistemic authority. Most obviously, why think that constitutive standards generate the requisite kind of authority? And, relatedly, how should we demarcate the relevant doxastic attitudes (e.g., belief) from their grueish cousins (e.g., *schmelief*) that differ only in how, constitutively, they ought to be?[4] Again, the point here is not to evaluate these explanations on their own merits but instead to illustrate how they arise out of the present methodological attempt to respect the Content Constraint. Let's look at one final possibility.

10.3.4 Veritistic Evidentialism

In broad outlines, this final story attempts to connect fitting the evidence to fundamental epistemic value. The thought, then, is that epistemic correctness (which is a matter of fitting the evidence) inherits its epistemic authority from some relationship epistemic correctness bears to fundamental epistemic value (or values). The idea is that fundamental epistemic value, or values, are the source of authority; what we need to do in our explanation, then, is explain how it is that the feature identified by the relevant first-order epistemic theory (in the evidentialist's case, fitting the evidence) connects up with fundamental epistemic value. If we do that, we will have an explanation for why it is that this feature does not just explain epistemic obligation, but it also exerts authority over agents.

What do I mean by "fundamental" epistemic value? Quite generally, a k value is a fundamental k value in the relevant sense if its being k valuable is not explained by its relationship to any other k values: it is, to put things a different way, nonderivatively k-ly valuable.[5] An example: pleasure, or happiness, is what monistic hedonists think is the only thing (hence monistic) that is fundamentally morally valuable. Its moral value is not derived from its relationship to any other moral values. Instead, pleasure itself is what explains the (derivative, nonfundamental) moral value of (all) other things, such as (say) friendship or justice or ... well, anything you like. The fundamental epistemic values, then, are just whatever values stand (sit?) at the bottom of our epistemic axiology, unexplained by (but perhaps themselves explaining) other epistemic values.[6]

Before we get into more details, here's an analogy for the overall strategy. Suppose I am trying to explain the *practical* authority of the *practical* correctness of (say) intending to φ only if φ-ing promotes the satisfaction of one's desires. One way to do this would be to say that promoting one's desires is *sui generis* authoritative; another would be to say that intentions *constitutively aim at* promoting one's desires. The third option, which I lay out later on behalf of evidentialists in the epistemic realm, would be to say that satisfying one's desires is *practically valuable*, and it is this axiological fact that explains the authority of the fact that it is practically correct to intend in a way that promotes that value. It is a familiar enough idea that values can serve to explain authority in this way: the thought that fundamental moral values stand explanatorily behind the authority of moral correctness is relatively widespread.[7] What we are now after, on behalf of the evidentialist, is the epistemic version of this thought.

So, to make this idea work in the epistemic realm, we need some account of what is supposed to be fundamentally epistemically valuable. Here, again, the evidentialist has options. What's important is that the relevant fundamental epistemic value will need to be something that is plausibly related in some way or other to conforming one's beliefs to the evidence. The most obvious possibility is that the fundamental epistemic value is *truth* (or perhaps the bearers of truth) and that the relation is *promotion*, understood as a matter of *increasing* or *making more likely*. Pretty clearly, conforming one's beliefs to the evidence is a way of making it the case that those beliefs are likely to be true.[8] So, we have our relation – promotion – and our value – truth; call this view the

> Veritistic Evidentialism: Fitting the evidence promotes the epistemic value of true belief.[9]

Again, the strategy here is to explain epistemic authority by connecting the feature identified by the first-order theory as explaining an epistemic correctness (in this case, fitting the evidence) with fundamental epistemic value in some way or other. The idea, then, is that it is because fitting the evidence promotes the fundamental value of true belief that the fact that it is epistemically correct to accord one's belief to the evidence is authoritative.

One more remark, and then we will move on. It is important to note that the veritistic evidentialist story about the *authority* of epistemic correctness is not intended to supplant the standard evidentialist story about the *content* of epistemic correctness; in other words, the first-order epistemic theory with which we began remains untouched. Evidentialists who take the veritistic route to explaining epistemic authority do not thereby give up their view that what explains why it is that it is epistemically correct for agents to φ in any particular case is that their φ-ing conforms to the evidence. Instead, the idea here is that veritistic evidentialists are offering, *in addition*, a second-order epistemic theory intended to explain why it is that conforming to the evidence is something that is *authoritatively* epistemically correct. The authority, according to the veritist, is sourced in the fundamental epistemic value of truth (or true belief).

This is an absolutely *crucial* point to emphasize. Misunderstanding it has led to some distractingly confusing back-and-forth between competing first- and second-order epistemic theories. So while what I am about to say, in large part, repeats what I have already said, I am going to say it again, somewhat differently, in an attempt to ensure it sinks in.

Evidentialism (or any other first-order epistemic theory) consists in an attempt to explain why it is that it is epistemically correct for agents to do whatever it is epistemically correct for them to do. Having settled on that view, if they are interested in the idea of epistemic authority, evidentialists are then on the hook for explaining why it is that epistemic correctness as they construe it is authoritative – in a way that meets our two basic criteria of adequacy, namely, Potential Psychological Impact and Usually Authoritative. That means, roughly, they cannot give the parental "because I said so," and they cannot give an explanation that delivers the result that, as a matter of fact, conforming one's belief to the evidence is not usually authoritatively epistemically correct (although it is epistemically right). But within those two very broad limits, the evidentialist has options.

We have been exploring those options in this section. Crucially – and this is what I am now busy emphasizing – taking up a particular view about what explains the authority of epistemic correctness understood in an evidentialist fashion does not commit the evidentialist to *any further claims at all* about the content of epistemic correctness. So, in the present case of veritism, suppose it turned out that in some particular case, an agent could better promote the epistemic value of true belief by departing from their evidence; maybe it is a version of the God-Grant scenario discussed in Chapter 8. Still, this is neither here nor there for the evidentialist – *even for the evidentialist who offers a veritistic explanation for epistemic authority* – with respect to what it is epistemically correct for the relevant agent to do.

Now, it *may* mean that, in this particular case, the fact that it is epistemically correct for the agent to conform their beliefs to their evidence is not, in fact, authoritative. But, again, this does not mean that what is epistemically correct is thereby somehow otherwise. Remember, the question of what it is epistemically correct for agents to do is settled first, in first-order theory; you do not read epistemic correctness back off the explanation for epistemic authority (or lack thereof). As I said, misunderstanding this point has led to some confusing banter, some of which we will see in the next chapter. So I emphasize it here.

10.3.5 Recap

We just canvassed three bespoke explanations of why it is epistemic correctness is authoritative, given that epistemic correctness is to be explained in an evidentialist fashion, namely, as explained by fit with agents' evidence. There are other possible explanations that match the evidentialist's first-order account, but these are the most straightforward and the most common.

Moreover, there are variations on these explanations that appear to work well for *other* first-order epistemic theories. For instance, it is clear how you might offer a version of, for example, the *sui generis* account for, for example, epistemic coherentism. And it is easy to imagine, say, epistemic Kantians offering a version of veritism that treated *respect* rather than *promotion* as the relevant authority-explaining relation agents' doxastic attitudes bear toward truth.[10]

It would be unworkable, here, to canvass all these possibilities. And anyway, the point here is not to evaluate the plausibility of any given second-order explanation offered by the proponent of some particular first-order epistemic theory. Instead, the point is to illustrate how the tailoring process works. And the point of doing *that* is to show that this tailoring process will almost *never* yield *anything like* second-order epistemic instrumentalism; hence, the relative unpopularity of second-order epistemic instrumentalism. Let me explain.

10.4 Bespoke Second-Order Epistemic Instrumentalism?

First, it is worth remembering that second-order epistemic instrumentalism is perfectly compatible with first-order evidentialism. It is also perfectly compatible with first-order epistemic Kantianism. And epistemic neo-Aristotelianism. And pretty much any other plausible first-order epistemic theory you can imagine. This is something I discussed briefly in Chapter 8 in the course of pointing out that second-order epistemic instrumentalism has an easy time of it with Usually Authoritative. Recall, meeting Usually Authoritative requires delivering the result that, usually at least, epistemic correctness is authoritative. And whether this is so will therefore be a matter *both* of what first-order epistemic theory one accepts *and* which second-order epistemic theory one accepts. We just saw this same point again, in the last section, when we noticed that some second-order epistemic theories, for example, constitutivism, are a particularly poor fit for some first-order epistemic theories.

Not so with second-order epistemic instrumentalism! It is an *excellent* fit: almost no matter what first-order epistemic theory you have got, second-order epistemic instrumentalism is going to be able to deliver on Usually Authoritative. I say "almost": in fact, I cannot think of one where it would fail to deliver the goods. I explained why this is so in Chapter 8.

But I bet you can see what is coming. Despite the fact that second-order epistemic instrumentalism will well-fit almost any first-order epistemic theory in terms of delivering on Usually Authoritative when paired with that first-order theory, it will almost never be the result of *tailoring* an explanation to fit that first-order theory. In other words, it will never be the kind of bespoke explanation you get via the process we just canvassed. This is because, as we just saw, that process works by first taking the explanatory grounds of some first-order epistemic theory and then *passing them through* to one's second-order epistemic theory (and then donning whatever explanatory accoutrements are required). For instance (evidentialists), fit with the evidence grounds epistemic correctness, and, lo! it also (*ahem*, given some assumptions about constitutive correctness or *sui generis* facts or whatever) grounds epistemic authority! Or (epistemic Kantians) respect for the truth grounds epistemic correctness, and, lo! it also grounds epistemic authority! Or (coherentists) coherence grounds epistemic correctness, and, lo! it also grounds epistemic authority!

But given the very real problems with the explanatory grounds appealed to in first-order epistemic instrumentalism as the explanatory grounds of epistemic correctness (Chapters 5–6), you are almost never going to get something equivalent in the case of second-order epistemic instrumentalism. That is, you will not get promoting well-being grounds epistemic correctness; and, lo! it also grounds epistemic authority. Hence, we almost never see second-order epistemic instrumentalism even making a case for itself in second-order epistemic theorizing.

I have been saying "almost" again; here, it really is *almost* never, not *never* ever. That is because there is exactly one first-order epistemic theory where, if you tailor an explanation to match, you will get second-order epistemic instrumentalism. It is (you guessed it) first-order epistemic instrumentalism. But there are vanishingly few first-order epistemic instrumentalists. And again, if I and first-order epistemic instrumentalism's other critics are correct, that is for good reason; either (critics argue) it falls to explain the Goldilocks Problem, or (I argue) it cannot answer the Functionalist Challenge.

In Chapter 8, I outlined why I thought second-order epistemic instrumentalism is a *good explanation* for epistemic authority – at least, for epistemic authority understood in the minimal way I have been understanding it throughout. But it is hugely unpopular. I am now busy explaining why that is. And I am now in a position to state that diagnosis in full. My diagnosis is that in an attempt to respect the Content Constraint, epistemologists have gone about tailoring their second-order epistemic theories to their first-order theories via the process just identified. If you have got to accept some first-order epistemic theory prior to evaluating your second-order epistemic theory (per the Content Constraint), it can seem like the obvious thing to do is take the materials afforded by that first-order epistemic theory and have them do double-duty for you in your second-order epistemic theory, hence bespoke explanations. But first-order epistemic instrumentalism is likely false, either because it fails extensionally (the Goldilocks Problem) or explanatorily (the Functionalist Challenge), hence no second-order epistemic instrumentalism (except for in the case of black swan first-order epistemic instrumentalists).

10.5 Are Bespoke Explanations Somehow Better?

Here is the thing: respecting the Content Constraint does not *entail* tailoring our explanations to fit our first-order epistemic theories. That is just an overwhelmingly natural way to do things. But natural and straightforward as it might be, again, the fact that you must accept some first-order epistemic theory prior to evaluating your second-order epistemic theory does not entail that you must tailor your second-order theory to nicely match your first-order epistemic theory. The question, then, is whether we have any reason to prefer such bespoke explanations to ones that are, as it were, off the rack.

What we want to know, then, is whether bespoke explanations are usually, or maybe even always better in a way that should make us systematically prefer them to non-bespoke explanations. If they are usually better in a way that should make us systematically prefer them to non-bespoke explanations, then second-order epistemic instrumentalism is in genuine trouble. For, recall, evidentialists have, as we have seen, some bespoke options: they could go in for a *sui generis* view, a constitutivist view, a veritistic view – maybe there are some others. They also have a noncustom job: second-order epistemic instrumentalism. If bespoke explanations are largely, or even in small but still meaningful ways better in virtue of being bespoke explanations, then, *ceteris paribus*, the evidentialist can go in for one of those explanations *because it is bespoke*, rather than going in for second-order epistemic instrumentalism. I do not think bespoke explanations are, in fact, better because they are bespoke in a way that should make us systematically prefer them.

There are two ways bespoke explanations might be better in some way because they are bespoke. They might be better in some way *in themselves* because they are bespoke, or they might be better in some way *jointly* with the first-order epistemic theories they are intended to custom fit because they are bespoke. I do not think bespoke explanations are any better in either of these two ways – at least not in a way that should make us systematically prefer them.

10.5.1 Are Bespoke Explanations Better in Themselves?

Bespoke explanations are explanations. So, for them to be better in themselves because they are bespoke is for them to be better *as explanations* because they are bespoke. But we do not have any reason to suppose that is true. We have no reason to think it is true, across the board, that bespoke explanations are better explanations because they are bespoke. In fact, we might have reason to think the opposite is true.

Being better as an explanation of epistemic authority is presumably a matter of bespoke explanations exhibiting more of the so-called explanatory virtues in virtue of being bespoke. But why think that, simply by being well crafted to fit the relevant first-order epistemic theory, such explanations will have more of such virtues, or will exhibit those they have to a greater extent? There is no reason to think this is true.

For example, take "simplicity". It is often thought that simplicity is an explanatory virtue, although it is notoriously difficult to say what, precisely, simplicity as a virtue in explanation amounts to.[11] Let's simply suppose simplicity is a virtue and further, for the sake of argument, suppose both that simplicity is ontological parsimony and that ontological parsimony is *qualitative* parsimony – it is a matter of postulating fewer *kinds* of entities in one's explanations. In effect, simpler explanations do more with less. Do bespoke explanations do better on this score simply *qua* bespoke explanations? Do they necessarily do more with less?

Clearly not. The kinds and number of entities a bespoke explanation postulates in its explanation are almost entirely a function of the kinds and number of entities postulated in the relevant *first-order* epistemic theory it is designed to match. This is because of the process of tailoring: the more different kinds of things involved in the explanatory grounds of epistemic correctness, the more different kinds of things will be passed through to the relevant bespoke second-order explanatory grounds of epistemic authority. But there is no reason to think these will be relatively few; certainly it is easy to imagine cases where there are far more kinds and number of entities postulated by a bespoke explanation than by a non-bespoke explanation.

Take veritistic evidentialism. That bespoke explanation involves several different kinds of entities, including evidence, nonderivative epistemic values, properties such as truth, relations such as promotion, and evidential support. Now take second-order epistemic instrumentalism. That non-bespoke explanation also involves different kinds of entities, including the relation of promotion and agential well-being.

These kinds of comparisons are always a bit suspect, but is the former necessarily simpler in terms of the entities it postulates than the latter? It is not at all obvious that it is. Again, there are delicate counting problems here, but if anything, there are appears to be a few *more* kinds of things postulated by veritistic evidentialism than by second-order epistemic instrumentalism. But my point is not to argue that second-order epistemic instrumentalism is (always) simpler. My point is to cast doubt on the claim that bespoke explanations are themselves, in virtue of being bespoke, always *necessarily* simpler.

Here is a different way of putting the same doubt. The relevant claim here on behalf of bespoke explanations can be understood as an astonishingly bold negative existential. To see this, suppose (and this is quite the supposition) we can somehow measure an explanation's simplicity along a single index of kinds and numbers of entities postulated via a function $S(e)$ that takes you from an *e*xplanation to a real number along the unit interval, with 1 representing the highest degree of simplicity possible for an explanation and 0 representing the least possible degree of simplicity for an explanation. Then, we know that S(epistemic instrumentalism) is *invariant* across changes to the first-order epistemic theory we accept.

This is because the kinds and number of entities postulated by epistemic instrumentalism (which determine S[epistemic instrumentalism]) do not vary along with changes to what first-order epistemic theory we accept. S(bespoke explanation) will, of course, vary; it will vary along with what particular bespoke explanation is on offer, which will, in turn, vary along with what first-order epistemic theory we accept. The particularly bold negative existential we are being asked to accept is that *there does not exist* a bespoke explanation B such that S(B) > S(epistemic instrumentalism). That, I hope you will agree, is simply not credible.

Again, the point is not to argue that bespoke explanations are somehow *worse* because bespoke or that epistemic instrumentalism is always better; it is to argue that bespoke explanations are not necessarily better in terms of being simple because bespoke.

Maybe this is just an artifact of the explanatory virtue of simplicity. It could be that bespoke explanations always do better along some other explanatorily virtuous dimension. I am not optimistic, and what is important here is that we have no reason for assuming this is so at the outset. In fact, despite what I said earlier, I do think there is a strong case that bespoke explanations do *worse* in virtue of being bespoke than second-order epistemic instrumentalism does along a range of dimensions in terms of which we evaluate explanations as better or worse. Although my argument does not depend on its being so, it's worth saying something briefly about why this is.

Sometimes we say that, when it comes to explanations, we care about whether an explanation *predicts* or whether it instead *accommodates* the relevant phenomenon.[12] In the present case, the phenomenon is epistemic authority. It should be clear that bespoke explanations are the *sine qua non* of accommodation: they are precisely theories that are tailored with an eye to accounting for the epistemic authority of epistemic correctness *as the relevant first-order epistemic theory construes epistemic correctness to be*. That, in effect, is what all the talk of "custom-fitting" the second-order epistemic theory to the first-order epistemic theory's account of epistemic correctness amounts to. For example, the second-order explanation I called *sui generis* evidentialism is just the view that you get if you start with first-order evidentialism and attempt to accommodate your second-order explanation to that first-order epistemic theory's story about which things are epistemically correct. Bespoke explanations are in general largely accommodative. Not so with second-order epistemic instrumentalism, which is insensitive in its design to the relevant first-order epistemic theory.

There are delicate issues here. You might not think that "predictive" theories enjoy any systematic advantage over "accommodative" ones or that they do not enjoy that advantage in the present case.[13] But as I said, this is not intended as an argument against any particular bespoke explanation, such as *sui generis* evidentialism, or even as an argument against bespoke explaining *per se*. It is an argument that we do not have any antecedent reason to suppose that such explanations will be better *qua explanations* simply in virtue of being bespoke. If anything, as I have just suggested, we have reason to suspect the opposite. Bespoke explanations are not necessarily better in themselves – that is, as explanations.

Maybe this is too quick. Perhaps bespoke explanations are better as explanations in virtue of enjoying some explanatory virtue other than simplicity or being predictive (rather than accommodative). It would take us too far afield to canvass all the possibilities. And we don't need to do that. This is because my point, here, is not that bespoke explanations fare worse when it comes to a range of explanatory virtues; instead, my point is that there is nothing in the *bespoke* nature of the relevant explanations that gives us any reason to expect them to fare *better*. The one exception, which I turn to now, is when it comes to the theoretical virtue of "unity" or "integration": you might plausibly think that bespoke explanations are better than their non-bespoke counterparts because they are, in one sense or another, more unified. I address this issue now.

10.5.2 Are Bespoke Explanations Better Jointly?

Maybe you are willing to accept that bespoke explanations are not better in themselves because they are bespoke. But you might think that this is because, presumably, bespoke explanations' quality *as explanations* does not really have anything to do with being their bespoke; you can be a hat that is perfectly tailored to fit someone's head *without necessarily being a really great, let alone best possible, hat*. Hence, it was a mistake to look for the advantage enjoyed by bespoke explanations in something to do with their *individual* quality as explanations, such as their relative simplicity or whatever.

Instead, the thought goes, what makes bespoke explanations better is that they are better *jointly* with the first-order epistemic theories they are designed to match. After all, such matching is what they are designed to do! And so (the thought continues) there is something about the overall *explanatory package* you get when you accept a bespoke explanation (as compared to a non-bespoke explanation such as epistemic instrumentalism) together with the relevant first-order epistemic theory that is more attractive than if you accept any non-bespoke explanation together with that first-order epistemic theory.

There is something intuitive about this idea. Take second-order *sui generis* evidentialism as paired with first-order evidentialism:

> Evidentialism: The fact that it is epistemically correct for A to φ is grounded by the fact that A's φ-ing is supported by A's evidence.

> Sui Generis Evidentialism: The fact that it is authoritatively epistemically correct for A to φ is grounded by the fact that evidence is *sui generis* epistemically authoritative.

There is *something* symmetrical going on here. Epistemic correctness is a matter of conforming to the evidence, and the *sui generis* authoritative nature of evidence, in turn, explains epistemic authority. Maybe that symmetry is a Really Good Thing? Similar remarks go for other bespoke pairings:

> Evidentialism: The fact that it is epistemically correct for A to φ is grounded by the fact that A's φ-ing is supported by A's evidence.

> Veritistic Evidentialism: The fact that it is authoritatively epistemically correct for A to φ is grounded by the fact that fitting the evidence promotes the epistemic value of true belief.

The explanation of epistemic correctness, again, is, in large part, mirrored in our explanation of epistemic correctness. It is a kind of *tidy* package. Of course, this is *by design*. Not at all so with the package:

> Evidentialism: The fact that it is epistemically correct for A to φ is grounded by the fact that A's φ-ing is supported by A's evidence.

> Second-Order Instrumentalism: The fact that it is authoritatively epistemically correct for A to φ is grounded by the fact that A's φ-ing promotes A's well-being.

Where did well-being come from? What's all this about promotion? Perhaps a less tidy package, less symmetry.

The present question is whether this tidiness in the overall explanatory package gives us a systematic reason to prefer the bespoke explanations that enable the packages to be so tidy. I do not think it does. Let me explain why.

First, it is worth pointing out that, despite what I just said, I do not think there is anything all that tidy about the bespoke packages. And despite the fact that it is the word I myself have chosen to describe it, I am not entirely sure I understand what tidiness is meant to be in the present context. The idea again is that there is a kind of resonance or symmetry between the two views: evidence in your first order, evidence in your second order. But I confess I do not really find the symmetry all that obvious or the resonance all that, well, resonant. Maybe I just have poor vision or poor hearing.

So, suppose the symmetry and resonance are there. More pressing than the need to convince me that there is in fact something resonant about bespoke explanations as compared to their non-bespoke counterparts is the need to convince me that this resonance is pleasing, that the symmetry is attractive. For the thought is not just that the symmetry is *there* in the case of some explanatory packages but not others but also that it gives us reason to prefer the packages that exhibit it. But this seems to come down to matters of taste. I might prefer the utilitarian jacket to the one that – even by my own lights – better matches my trousers. But maybe I just have poor taste.

So suppose both that the symmetry and the resonance are there *and* that they are attractive and pleasing. Still, we need to be convinced that the relevant attractive symmetries or pleasing resonances are *sufficiently* attractive or *sufficiently* pleasing to give us a reason to systematically prefer the packages of views that enable those symmetries and resonances. For the thought is not just that the relevant symmetry gives us *some* reason to prefer the bespoke explanations to the non-bespoke explanations but also that we have *systematic* reason to prefer the former to the latter. But having systematic reason to prefer the former to the latter would require something quite strong about the reason given by the relevant symmetry – it would require it to be decisive in at least many of the relevant cases.

Now, I have not said a lot about the broader process by which we should be evaluating either first- or second-order epistemic theories in this book, or the explanatory packages that comprise them. Instead, my aim has mostly been to lay out the territory – especially in second-order theorizing – and try to convince you there is some fertile but hitherto fallow ground, namely, second-order epistemic instrumentalism's explanation for epistemic authority. But we are now starting to run up against questions about how to consider the relative merits of second-order epistemic theories considered both individually and jointly with particular first-order epistemic theories. These are difficult questions. They touch on some of the most hotly contested meta-philosophical issues; at the limit, answering them appears to require answering something like the question, What are philosophical theories such as the ones considered here even *doing*? I have some views on this, but heading off in that direction would *definitely* be heading far afield.

Recall, our focus here is supposed to be on the question of whether bespoke explanations are usually, or maybe even always better, in a way that should make us systematically prefer them to non-bespoke explanations. But I think we can admit that bespoke explanations are usually or maybe even always better by comprising part of more tidy explanatory packages without also being committed to the thought that this should make us systematically prefer them to non-bespoke explanations. And I think we can do this without delving too deep into any too-controversial ideas about how to consider the relative merits of first- and second-order epistemic theories or the explanatory packages they jointly comprise.

This is because, even if we admit that, in part, comprising a bespoke explanation contributes to a pleasing symmetry and that the relevant kind of pleasingness is a reason to prefer the relevant package, there is no reason to think this kind of pleasing symmetry will regularly be a *decisive* reason in favor of accepting a package comprising a bespoke as compared to a non-bespoke explanation.

In other words, it is possible to think that always everywhere bespoke explanations, in virtue of being bespoke, comprise explanatory packages that are better *by way of being tidier* than do non-bespoke explanations without also simultaneously thinking that it never makes sense to go in for something a bit messier. Tidiness, whatever it comprises, and whatever the explanation for why we should care about it, is only plausibly one desideratum among many. There can be reasons to take the parka even when you are wearing a three-piece. In saying this, I align myself with a long tradition of treating theories' exhibition of various explanatory virtues, such as tidiness ("unity", "integration") as *pro tanto* contributors to the overall plausibility of the views. Loveliness is a guide to likeliness, to be sure,[14] but there are manifestly many contributors to loveliness.

10.6 Conclusion

I had two aims in this chapter. The first was to complete my diagnosis of the relative unpopularity of second-order epistemic instrumentalism. As we saw in the last chapter, evaluating second-order epistemic theories requires settling on *some* first-order epistemic theory. That is the Content Constraint. As we saw in this chapter, the most natural, straightforward way of respecting this constraint, by tailoring one's second-order epistemic theory to match, or fit, one's first-order epistemic theory, is vanishingly unlikely to yield second-order epistemic instrumentalism. Hence, the relative unpopularity of second-order epistemic instrumentalism.

My second aim was to explain why the naturalness of this methodology does not serve as a real barrier to accepting second-order epistemic instrumentalism. In the first place, it is not obligatory: there are other ways to respect the Content Constraint. In the second place, bespoke explanations are not (necessarily) better than non-bespoke explanations, such as second-order epistemic instrumentalism, in any way that should make us systematically prefer them.

In the next chapter, I consider two remaining issues facing second-order epistemic instrumentalism.

Notes

1 This is the view adopted by Kelly (2003, 2007). It also appears to be a background assumption in a broad range of evidentialist accounts, such as, for example, Feldman and Conee (1985) and Conee and Feldman (2004). However, see Berker (2013a) for discussion.
2 This is the view taken by Shah (2006), Shah and David Velleman (2005), and Wedgwood (2007), among others. The ethical analogue of this view is defended most famously by Korsgaard (2009).

3 This is a rough overview of the constitutivist idea. In some cases, constitutivists instead claim that what beliefs constitutively should be is *true*. The idea in this case is then that a belief's being responsive to the evidence (the evidentialist requirement) is *the only way* for one's beliefs to be *like that*, that is, true. For a version of this strategy, see Shah (2006), and Shah and David Velleman (2005). For criticism, see Enoch (2006, 2011), Steglich-Petersen (2006), and Sharadin (2016).
4 Enoch (2006, 2011).
5 On the distinction, see Zimmerman (2019), and Chisholm (2005). This is roughly what Korsgaard (1983) calls "final" value.
6 There are important issues here, such as whether our epistemic axiology ought to be monistic or pluralist – that is, whether there is just one or whether there is more than one fundamental epistemic value. I am strongly inclined to the pluralist view, but here I remain officially neutral on this question since it will not matter to the issue I am interested in. For discussion, see the essays collected in Haddock, Millar, and Pritchard (2009).
7 The most straightforward examples of such views are consequentialist in form, for example, Mill (1987) and Sidgwick (1874).
8 Indeed, as accuracy–dominance arguments on the degree-theoretic side of things purport to show, conforming one's credences to the evidence by updating those credences via Bayes' rule *maximizes* expected accuracy in one's credences. For discussion, see Joyce (1998).
9 Feldman and Conee (1985), and Berker (2013a, 2013b, 2015). Of course, it is possible to swap in a difference conception of what is fundamentally epistemically valuable. For instance, you might think that truth (or true belief) is not what is fundamentally epistemically valuable. Instead, you might think that *knowledge* or *understanding* are fundamentally epistemically valuable. For discussion, see Pritchard (2010).
10 Sylvan (2020).
11 For a classic discussion, see Sober (1975).
12 However, as with simplicity, this has proved difficult to spell out, and it is controversial. See White (2003), Lange (2001), and Hitchcock and Sober (2004) for arguments on both sides.
13 Lange (2001).
14 Lipton (2003).

References

Berker, Selim. 2013a. "Epistemic Teleology and the Separateness of Propositions." *Philosophical Review* 122 (3): 337–393. https://doi.org/10.1215/00318108-2087645.

———. 2013b. "The Rejection of Epistemic Consequentialism." *Philosophical Issues* 23 (1): 363–387. https://doi.org/10.1111/phis.12019.

———. 2015. "Reply to Goldman: Cutting up the One to Save the Five in Epistemology." *Episteme* 12 (2): 145–153. https://doi.org/10.1017/epi.2015.3.

Chisholm, Roderick M. 2005. "Defining Intrinsic Value." In *Recent Work on Intrinsic Value*, edited by Rønnow-Rasmussen, Toni and Michael J. Zimmerman, 15–16. Dordrecht: Springer.

Conee, Earl, and Richard Feldman. 2004. *Evidentialism: Essays in Epistemology*. Oxford: Oxford University Press.

Enoch, David. 2006. "Agency, Shmagency: Why Normativity Won't Come from What Is Constitutive of Action." *Philosophical Review* 115 (2): 169–198. https://doi.org/10.1215/00318108-115-2-169.

———. 2011. "Shmagency Revisited." In *New Waves in Metaethics*, edited by Michael Brady, 208–233. New York: Palgrave-Macmillan.

Feldman, Richard, and Earl Conee. 1985. "Evidentialism." *Philosophical Studies* 48 (1): 15–34. https://doi.org/10.1007/bf00372404.

Haddock, Adrian, Alan Millar, and Duncan Pritchard. 2009. *Epistemic Value*. Oxford: Oxford University Press.

Hitchcock, Christopher, and Elliott Sober. 2004. "Prediction versus Accommodation and the Risk of Overfitting." *British Journal for the Philosophy of Science* 55 (1): 1–34. https://doi.org/10.1093/bjps/55.1.1.

Joyce, James M. 1998. "A Nonpragmatic Vindication of Probabilism." *Philosophy of Science* 65 (4): 575–603. https://doi.org/10.1086/392661.

Kelly, Thomas. 2003. "Epistemic Rationality as Instrumental Rationality: A Critique." *Philosophy and Phenomenological Research* 66 (3): 612–640. https://doi.org/10.1111/j.1933-1592.2003.tb00281.x.

———. 2007. "Evidence and Normativity: Reply to Leite." *Philosophy and Phenomenological Research* 75 (2): 465–474. https://doi.org/ppr200775229.

Korsgaard, Christine M. 1983. "Two Distinctions in Goodness." *Philosophical Review* 92 (2): 169–195. https://doi.org/10.2307/2184924.

———. 2009. *Self-Constitution: Agency, Identity, and Integrity*. Oxford: Oxford University Press.

Lange, Marc. 2001. "The Apparent Superiority of Prediction to Accommodation as a Side Effect: A Reply to Maher." *British Journal for the Philosophy of Science* 52 (3): 575–588. https://doi.org/10.1093/bjps/52.3.575.

Lipton, Peter. 2003. *Inference to the Best Explanation*. New York: Routledge.

Mill, John Stuart. 1987. *Utilitarianism and Other Essays*. London: Penguin Books.

Pritchard, Duncan. 2010. *The Nature and Value of Knowledge: Three Investigations: Three Investigations*. Oxford: Oxford University Press.

Shah, Nishi. 2006. "A New Argument for Evidentialism." *Philosophical Quarterly* 56 (225): 481–498. https://doi.org/10.1111/j.1467-9213.2006.454.x.

Shah, Nishi, and J. David Velleman. 2005. "Doxastic Deliberation." *Philosophical Review* 114 (4): 497–534. https://doi.org/10.1215/00318108-114-4-497.

Sharadin, Nathaniel P. 2016. "Nothing but the Evidential Considerations?" *Australasian Journal of Philosophy* 94 (2): 1–19. https://doi.org/10.1080/00048402.2015.1068348.

Sidgwick, Henry. 1874. *The Methods of Ethics*. London: Macmillan and Co.

Sober, Elliott. 1975. *Simplicity*. Oxford: Clarendon Press.

Steglich-Petersen, Asbjørn. 2006. "No Norm Needed: On the Aim of Belief." *Philosophical Quarterly* 56 (225): 499–516. https://doi.org/10.1111/j.1467-9213.2006.455.x.

Sylvan, Kurt L. 2020. "An Epistemic Non-Consequentialism." *The Philosophical Review* 129 (1): 1–51. https://doi.org/10.1215/00318108-7890455.

Wedgwood, Ralph. 2007. *The Nature of Normativity*. Oxford: Oxford University Press. https://doi.org/10.1093/acprof:oso/9780199251315.001.0001.

White, Roger. 2003. "The Epistemic Advantage of Prediction over Accommodation." *Mind* 112 (448): 653–683. https://doi.org/10.1093/mind/112.448.653.

Zimmerman, Michael J. 2019. "Intrinsic vs. Extrinsic Value." In *Stanford Encyclopedia of Philosophy*, edited by Edward N. Zalta, Spring 2019. https://plato.stanford.edu/entries/value-intrinsic-extrinsic/

11 New View, Old Problems

11.1 Introduction

In this penultimate chapter, I deal with a potential worry. I explore whether there are variants on the problems facing first-order epistemic instrumentalism – the Goldilocks Problem and my Functionalist Challenge – that arise for second-order instrumentalism. In the final chapter, I consider whether second-order epistemic instrumentalists might want to abandon the traditional approach to *first*-order epistemic theorizing altogether.

11.2 Goldilocks Problem Redux?

Recall the Goldilocks Problem was a problem faced by *first*-order epistemic instrumentalism, according to which that view either (or both!) over- and under-generated cases of epistemic correctness (rather than getting it *just right*). The idea there was that, because first-order epistemic instrumentalism explanatorily grounded epistemic correctness in facts about what would or would not promote agential well-being, there would be a range of cases in which either it was manifestly *not* epistemically correct to φ but in which doing so would promote agential well-being or where it *was* manifestly epistemically correct to φ but where doing so would not promote agential well-being.

As we saw in that discussion, playing out the problem led to stalemate. Anti-instrumentalists pose a case of one or the other of the two potentially problematic kinds, first-order epistemic instrumentalists explain why their view does not have the problematic extensional result or, at the limit, they explain away the counterintuitive result. Anti-instrumentalists continue to look askance. And so it goes.

This dialectic is familiar. It happens pretty much whenever we have a theory that generates an extension for some phenomenon and where there are some strongly held pre-theoretical intuitions about what the extension of that phenomenon actually is. You might think we are going to have a similar problem, here, for second-order epistemic instrumentalism. But I do not think that is correct.

DOI: 10.4324/9781003096726-11

Again, the problem facing first-order epistemic instrumentalism depended on the existence of a strong intuition that *here in this case*, it is epistemically correct for some agent to φ or that it was *not* epistemically correct for them to φ. As you have probably gathered by now, I myself do not have any strong intuitions about whether this is the case in any given scenario; I tend to let my first-order epistemic intuitions be dragged about by whatever first-order epistemic theory is in the offing rather than the reverse. But plenty of people *do* appear to have (relatively) strong intuitions about whether this or that φ-ing in this or that scenario would be epistemically correct. It was the presence of those intuitions that presumably generated the incredulous stare. And I am happy to admit to being the outlier here and therefore to admit that the relevant intuitions deserve to be taken seriously.

But whatever you think about the quality of our pre-theoretical intuitions about the extension of epistemic *correctness* and thereby about the importance of explaining (rather than explaining *away*) those intuitions, the corresponding dialectic just is not going to arise in the case of epistemic *authority*. As I have already explained, the most we can get from our pre-theoretical intuitions about the idea that epistemic correctness matters, that it has *oomph* or *grip* or is *authoritative*, is the thought that it *usually* does so; that is, the most we can get is Usually Authoritative. You might *want* more pre-theoretically, but, as I have tried to explain, you simply cannot have it.

Here is the reason, put in a somewhat different way than the way I put it in Chapter 5. Take the kinds of examples used to motivate the Goldilocks Problem for first-order epistemic instrumentalism. They are cases where it is *extremely easy and compelling* to say that what it is epistemically correct for an agent to do is one thing but where it is *extremely difficult and not at all compelling* to say that this is because doing so promotes the agents' well-being. For example, you do not need any special philosopher's intuition to think that it is epistemically correct to believe what your evidence indicates is true and that it is not epistemically correct to believe something *because doing so makes you happier*. Fair enough, hence the pressing need to handle the cases on behalf of first-order epistemic instrumentalism.

But in the case of epistemic *authority*, we are dealing with something quite a bit more rarefied. I am happy to think – and second-order epistemic instrumentalists also should be happy to think – that we do not need any special philosopher's intuition to think that being epistemically correct *matters* in a similar fashion as (say) being polite matters, and being assassinly correct does not matter. That is the intuitive grasp on "authority" that we start with, and that is what delivers Usually Authoritative. (After all, sometimes at least, who cares about politeness!) You *would* need a truly exquisite, recherché intuition to arrive at the thought that always, everywhere, without exception, being epistemically correct matters in this way. Again, epistemic authority is something we try to put our finger on, in advance of a theory about it, by way of pointing at cases and by pointing at its analogues in different areas. But none of those pointings delivers the intuition that what we are dealing with here is exceptionless mattering for every case of epistemic correctness.

And that latter intuition is what you'd need to get up and running to generate the symmetrical Goldilocks Problem at the second-order level for the second-order epistemic instrumentalists. For, as we have seen, the second-order epistemic instrumentalist will be able to deliver the result that, almost without exception (and so certainly *usually*), epistemic correctness exhibits authority. *Perhaps* there will be exquisitely refined cases in which, it turns out, according to second-order epistemic instrumentalism epistemic authority, epistemic correctness does not really matter. But, again, that does not do any violence to any strongly held intuitions. In effect, the pre-theoretical second-order intuitions about epistemic authority necessary to generate a version of the Goldilocks Problem for second-order epistemic instrumentalism simply do not exist.

11.3 Functionalist Challenge Redux?

The Functionalist Challenge went like this: evaluations in terms of epistemic correctness are *for* something – we use them to do something distinctive for us. The point, purpose, role, or function of such judgments is to enable us to flag reliable informants. Any conception of epistemic correctness that disables epistemic correctness from doing what it is for is thereby disqualified as a conception of *epistemic* – as compared to some other kind of – correctness. But if first-order epistemic instrumentalism has the correct view about what explanatorily grounds epistemic correctness, that is exactly what happens. For it should always be possible to cite the explanatory grounds of some kind of correctness in a justification of why it was correct in that way to do whatever it was, in fact, correct to do. But it is *not* always possible to cite instrumentalist grounds in epistemic justifications – at least, not without undermining the point, purpose, or function of epistemic correctness. This is because facts about what does or does not promote agential well-being are not tied in any recognizable way to facts about which informants are reliable.

In the face of the Functionalist Challenge, I recommended the instrumentalist change tack – they should offer their view explicitly and entirely as a view about what explains epistemic *authority* rather than epistemic *correctness*. Exploring that possibility is what we have been up to since.

You might think that this problem reappears for the second-order epistemic instrumentalist. After all, the second-order epistemic instrumentalist, like their first-order counterpart, cites facts concerning what promotes agential well-being in their account of the relevant explanatory grounds. Since it was the presence of those facts in the explanatory grounds that gave rise to the problem in the case of *first*-order epistemic instrumentalism, perhaps the presence of those facts will also give rise to a symmetrical problem here, in the case of *second*-order epistemic instrumentalism.

But it was not just the fact that the first-order epistemic instrumentalist included facts about what promotes agential well-being in her account of the explanatory grounds of epistemic correctness that gave rise to the Functionalist Challenge. It was also crucially the facts that (1) evaluations in terms of epistemic correctness have a distinctive functional role to play, namely, flagging reliable informants, and (ii) including facts about promoting agential well-being in the explanatory grounds of such evaluations disabled such evaluations from playing their role. So, in order for a symmetrical problem to arise here, symmetrical claims must be true. In other words, the following would have to be true:

(i) Evaluations in terms of *authoritative* epistemic correctness have a distinctive functional role to play.
(ii) Including facts about promoting agential well-being in the explanatory grounds of such evaluations disables such evaluations from playing their role.

What should we think about each of these claims? I will take them in order.

First, let me say that I am a bit skeptical about whether (i) is true. If it is true, then I am skeptical about whether we can say anything all that precise about it. Although I think we all have at least the minimal conception of epistemic authority, I am not sure it makes sense to think of our thought and talk in terms of epistemic authority as being *for* something in particular. Or if it is for something in particular, I think it will be very difficult to acquire evidence for what that might be. In part, this is because such thought and talk is a uniquely philosophical way of thinking and speaking. For the most part, most of the time, insofar as we talk about epistemic correctness at all, we simply talk about what is or is not epistemically correct.

Now, I think that what is going on here, *usually*, is that we are thinking of things as *authoritatively* epistemically correct (rather than only formally so). (Hence, Usually Authoritative.) But the language of authoritative epistemic correctness is not really a part of our *explicit* conceptual repertoire in the way that epistemic correctness is (and various cognate epistemic evaluative notions are). This makes theorizing about the point, purpose, or function of such thought and talk a bit mysterious.

But I am willing to be convinced that (i) is true. After all, there is plausibly *something* we are trying to do when we italicize our voice, pound our fists, stomp our feet, and then say things such as "he *really* should believe that *P*". Suppose (i) is true. What's the distinctive functional role of evaluations in terms of *authoritative* (as opposed to merely formal) epistemic correctness? The distinctive functional role, whatever it is, must be something to do with the fact that epistemic correctness is supposed to be *authoritative* on the relevant occasion. It cannot simply be that such evaluations are for what evaluations in terms of epistemic correctness are for. Otherwise, there would not be any distinctive point to evaluations in terms of *authoritative* epistemic correctness. So it cannot simply be that these evaluations are for flagging reliable informants, since that (we are assuming) is what evaluating things as epistemically correct is for.

What we are after is something distinctive for evaluations in terms of *authoritative* epistemic correctness to be for. Here is the only thing that seems plausible: such evaluations are *for* flagging – not *reliable informants* but instead *the importance of epistemic correctness*. Indeed, the plausibility of this claim is, in large part, due to how we went about putting our finger on the idea of authoritative epistemic correctness in the first place. Recall our intuitive attempts to gesture at what epistemic authority amounted to: we said that epistemic correctness has *oomph* or *grip* or *mattered*. Plausibly, the point of making such claims is precisely to *mark off* epistemic correctness from other kinds of correctness as *mattering*.

Now, I am not arguing, here, that we should do all our theorizing about authoritative epistemic correctness in terms of this plausible functional role any more than I agreed, in Chapter 4, that we should do all our theorizing about (mere) epistemic correctness in terms of *its* plausible functional role. Instead, what I am suggesting is that, *if* there is something that such evaluations of authoritative epistemic correctness are *for*, what that thing is, is plausibly primarily a matter flagging the importance of epistemic correctness. After all, that is part of how we pick out the concept of authoritative epistemic correctness in the first place, namely, in terms of its flagging the importance of epistemic correctness.

What about (ii)? Is there something about second-order epistemic instrumentalism's account of the explanatory grounds of epistemic authority that would disable such evaluations from playing their distinctive role, construed as flagging the importance of epistemic correctness? No. To see this, remember that the content of epistemic correctness is set by our first-order epistemic theory: this is what determines when and why it is epistemically correct for A to φ. Then, second-order epistemic instrumentalism enters and says that epistemic correctness is (on this occasion) *authoritative*: it *really matters* that A φ, and *this is because A's φ-ing promotes A's well-being*. But there is absolutely nothing about citing facts about what promotes A's well-being that would somehow interfere with the ability of such claims to do what they are for, namely, flag the importance of being epistemically correct on some occasion.

Quite the contrary! As we saw in our discussion of the immediate appeal of second-order epistemic instrumentalism, claims about what does or does not promote agential well-being seem *especially* well suited to flagging importance. We use them *all the time* to do so! (Why should not I smoke? Because you will get cancer. Why *authoritatively* should not I smoke? Because *getting cancer dispromotes your well-being*.)

This does not *decisively* show that no symmetrical Functionalist Challenge appears for second-order epistemic instrumentalism. But I think it goes a long way toward showing how difficult it will be to get such a challenge up and running. For not only will it require some plausible account of what evaluations in terms of *authoritative* epistemic correctness are for, but it will also require showing that including facts about what promotes agential well-being in the explanatory grounds of such evaluations somehow disables such evaluations from playing that role. But, again, as we have seen, epistemic authority is, in large part, a matter of epistemic correctness *mattering*. And, also as we have seen, *promoting well-being* is an incredibly uncontroversial way of things mattering. So it is going to be quite tricky to argue that thoughts about the latter disable thoughts about the former from doing what they are for. Hence, I do not think there is any plausible Functionalist Challenge facing second-order epistemic instrumentalism.

11.4 Conclusion

You might worry that the problems facing *first*-order epistemic instrumentalism are equally problems for *second*-order epistemic instrumentalism. But they are not. The second-order epistemic instrumentalist does not make any claims about the extension of epistemic correctness; so they are not liable to an exact version of the Goldilocks Problem. Moreover, there is no revised version of the problem that we can generate for second-order epistemic instrumentalism. This is because, while it might be plausible that there is some extensional mismatch between first-order epistemic instrumentalism's account of epistemic correctness and our intuitive view about the extension thereof, there's no reason to think that there's a corresponding extensional mismatch between *second*-order epistemic instrumentalism's account of epistemic *authority* and our intuitive view about the extension thereof. Moreover, there is absolutely nothing in the explanatory grounds second-order epistemic instrumentalism cites in its explanation of epistemic authority that somehow disables epistemic authority from doing whatever it is for, assuming it is for something or other, for example, flagging the *importance* of judgments about epistemic correctness.

12 Going Further

12.1 Introduction

I've argued that second-order epistemic instrumentalism is compatible with the truth of a wide range of first-order epistemic theories. This is because, as I've explained, second-order epistemic instrumentalism simply isn't a view about which things are epistemically correct (or why); instead, it is a view about which instances of epistemic correctness are *authoritative* (and why). As a view about the latter, it's strictly compatible with (almost) any view about the extension of epistemic correctness. Second-order epistemic instrumentalism, so understood, is a relatively conciliatory view.

In this final chapter, I consider whether second-order epistemic instrumentalists might want to make themselves less agreeable. In particular, I consider whether they might want to go on offense and claim, contrary to the conciliationist view of matters, that their view is *not* compatible with the ordinary way of understanding first-order epistemic theory. The most promising way of doing this, I argue, is by becoming *epistemic ecologists*.

I'll explain epistemic ecology and the motivation for it by analogy with a recent view defended by Jennifer Morton (2011, 2017) about not *epistemic* but instead *deliberative* correctness. According to Morton, we should be ecologists about deliberative correctness. Morton argues that we should think that there is no stable fact about what deliberative correctness amounts to. Instead, what deliberative correctness comprises varies along with changes to agents' environments and psychologies. If Morton is correct, then first-order theorizing about deliberative correctness ought to look very different than it typically does.

As I explain, the second-order epistemic instrumentalism I've described has all the tools at its disposal to pick up a variant on Morton's view and run with it. I consider whether second-order instrumentalists might be inclined to do so.

DOI: 10.4324/9781003096726-12

12.2 Deliberative Correctness

Let *deliberative correctness* be a kind of correctness we pick out in the following way: it's the kind of correctness that applies to agents' practical deliberations, that is, the activity of practically deliberating over how to answer the question, "What to do?" when those deliberations are done in accordance with a set of deliberative rules or requirements. We can then imagine various competing first-order deliberative theories that aim to tell us what those deliberative rules *are* by filling in principles such as the following:

> The fact that it is deliberatively correct for A to φ in her deliberation concerning "What to do?" is grounded by the fact that φ-ing conforms to rule R.

Intuitively, competing first-order deliberative theories will offer competing views about the rules, norms, or principles that must structure agents' practical deliberations in order for the various things agents might do in those deliberations to count as correct. Which rules "R" comprise will therefore vary along with the relevant first-order view about what correct deliberation requires. For example, one first-order deliberative theory might say that the fact that an agent's deliberation conforms to the rule that says "If you intend E and M is a necessary means to achieving E, then intend M" is a fact that grounds deliberative correctness. Another view might disagree, claiming that manifesting means–ends coherence is *not* a requirement for deliberative correctness.[1] You get the idea.

One quick proviso. Practical deliberation, conceived of in this way as the activity of aiming to answer the question, "What to do?" in accordance with a set of rules or requirements, isn't necessarily something we should think is all that commonplace. In fact, it *isn't* commonplace. Most of what we do we do as a result of a range of psychological processes, not only including what we ordinarily call "habits" but also including the much broader category of decision-making capacities that tend toward being automatic, nonintentional, and subpersonal. There's wide variation among these activities and processes, but the important point at present is their contrast with practical deliberation, so to set them off from the kind of activity I'm interested in, call all these ways of answering the question, "What to do?" nondeliberative processes, or NDPs for short.

You might think, given how central a role they play in our actual decision-making, NDPs have received insufficient philosophical attention. This is especially true, perhaps, if you think of the contrast between practical deliberation and NDPs in terms of the proportion of agential choices that are the result of each. If that's the right way to measure things, it's clear that NDPs are a much more central aspect of agential choice. I think that's entirely fair – I have no quarrel with anyone who wants to insist on the importance of paying philosophical attention to the diverse range of things other than practical deliberation that agents can do in order to make up their minds (or, perhaps better, that agents usually do when they, in fact, make up their minds).

So not everything that involves answering the question, "What to do?" counts as practical deliberation in my sense. Instead, I'm interested here in just this particular – admittedly, probably relatively rare – activity agents engage in when they try to answer the question, "What to do?" in accord with some set of rules, namely, the deliberative rules. Moving on.

The fights between various first-order views about deliberative correctness, understood, again, as a kind of correctness that applies to agents' practical deliberations, are long-standing and ongoing. We can imagine the entire range of such views, from extraordinarily restrictive views that make deliberative correctness difficult to come by to the view that there are only quite minimal requirements one must conform to in order to exhibit deliberative correctness.

12.3 Invariantism about Deliberative Correctness

Despite the wide variation in particular first-order theories of deliberative correctness, these views all share a common assumption. The assumption they share is that the rules governing deliberative correctness, whatever they comprise, are *invariant*: they all accept what I'll call *invariantism* about deliberative correctness. According to invariantism about deliberative correctness, the rules conformance with which grounds deliberative correctness do not vary along with changes to actual agents' psychologies and environments.

In other words, invariantists think that, if it turns out that some particular first-order deliberative theory has managed to tell the right story about which rules are the rules conformance with which entails manifesting deliberative correctness, then this first-order deliberative theory's story will be the right story to tell independently of any variance in what agents' psychologies and environments are like.

Of course, it's entirely compatible with this idea that our *verdicts* regarding deliberative correctness will vary from agent to agent, and from environment to environment. That is because the content of the rules might be sensitive in some ways to agents' psychologies and environments. The idea behind invariantism is that the rules themselves represent fixed points in our theorizing about how it is correct for agents to deliberate. According to the invariantist view of matters, there's just one set of rules that uniquely determine the way it's correct to deliberate, and these rules are themselves invariant across actual changes to facts about the way agents and their environments are. This thought allows that what deliberative correctness comprises on particular occasions might be varied and complex. What it does not allow is that corresponding to both or either of the varied, complex, and diverse psychologies agents possess and/or the varied, complex, and diverse environments agents find themselves, there are a range of different rules conformance with which *grounds* deliberative correctness in those diverse environments and for agents with those diverse psychologies.

It's hard to overemphasize how familiar this invariantist conception of deliberative correctness should be to you. As I said, it's an assumption shared by (almost) all extant views of what deliberative correctness requires. On this way of thinking, our theorizing about correct practical deliberation aims, in part, to uncover and explain the single (perhaps in some way unified) contents of the rules that correctly govern such deliberation. So, for instance, we might argue for accepting some version of a *consistency norm* on agents' practical deliberations, which says that rationality requires an agent to not simultaneously decide on courses of action they believe to be incompatible. The exact details of the relevant rules don't actually matter in the present context; arguments over those details are what fill up the journals. Instead, what matters is that, on the invariantist picture, once we've settled to our satisfaction that some rule R is, in fact, a rule conformance with which grounds deliberative correctness, then we know that R applies to all agents, regardless of specific facts about those agents' particular psychologies and environments. Again, it may be that R does not deliver any specific verdict for some specific agent in some specific circumstances. But, as we might put it, this is not for lack of trying: conformance with R is still understood as *the* determinant of correctness in that agent's deliberation.

(A brief aside: Why emphasize "actual" as I've done? Because it's possible to be an invariantist of the sort I have in mind and to think that the content of the rules grounding deliberative correctness varies across various counterfactual possibilities. For instance, you will remain an invariantist [of the sort we're interested in here] even if you think that had certain facts about agents' psychologies and environments been otherwise than they are, then the rules of deliberative correctness would be different than they, in fact, are. I won't explore this possibility further here, since actual-world invariantism (as we could call it) is the relevant view to have in mind in what follows. Hence, I often drop the "actual" in talking about the invariantist picture in what follows.)

12.4 The Case for Ecologism about Deliberative Correctness

Invariantism about deliberative correctness can seem not just like the default position but also like the only possible position. But it has recently come under forceful attack by a range of philosophers, most notably Jennifer Morton, who argue that the correct picture of deliberative correctness is an *ecological* one according to which the rules conformance with which ground deliberative correctness can and do vary along with differences in agents' psychologies and environments.[2] I'll come to the argument for the ecological picture in just a moment, but for now let's set it up in contrast to the invariantist view.

Recall that invariantism holds that the rules conformance with which grounds deliberative correctness do not vary along with changes to agents' psychologies and their environments. The ecological picture, by contrast, holds that this can and does sometimes happen: it sometimes happens that the rules conformance with which ground deliberative correctness vary along with changes to agents' psychologies and environments.

On the ecological view of matters, then, once we've settled to our satisfaction that some rule R is a rule conformance with which sometimes grounds deliberative correctness, we do *not* thereby learn that conformance with R always everywhere grounds deliberative correctness. Instead, it may be that while R governs *some* agents, it does not govern all. Again, this is because according to an ecological conception of deliberative correctness facts about which rules are the rules conformance with which ground deliberative correctness vary along with facts about agents and their environments.

An example will both help illustrate this unfamiliar view and point the way toward its proponents' arguments in its favor. Here is one lifted from Morton's (2011) discussion of the issue. Consider the following:

> Stability Rule: Rationality requires that, if an agent settles on an intention to E, barring a change in her circumstances or information, she abstain from reconsidering her intention to E in her deliberations.[3]

Now consider two different agents, both with simple sets of needs for food, shelter, and sleep. One of these agents, call her Abundy, lives in an environment of plenty. In such an environment, Abundy does not require long-term stable intentions in order to get what she needs. It's not the case, given Abundy's environment, that constantly revisiting her intentions will preclude her from achieving what she cares about, namely, getting adequate food, shelter, and rest. As Morton points out, it may be that Abundy fails to get what she needs, but that won't be for lack of stability in her intentions.[4] Compare Abundy with Scarcey. Just like Abundy, Scarcey has a simple set of needs, but Scarcey lives in an environment with scarce resources. And so, unlike Abundy, Scarcey's ability to satisfy her basic needs *will* depend on her ability to form stable, long-term intentions. For instance, she will need to, say, plan around competitors' and predators' behaviors in order to acquire sufficient food and adequate rest.[5]

What this example shows is that the usefulness of a specific rule governing agents' deliberately formed intentions can depend, in part, on the environment in which an agent finds themselves. The Stability Rule is a case in point: it usefully governs Scarcey's practical reasoning but is otiose when it comes to Abundy's reasoning about what to do. Morton uses an array of examples such as Abundy and Scarcey's – drawn largely from behavioral, social, and cognitive science research – to motivate the thought that the rules conformance with which comprise deliberative correctness can vary in the way ecologism says they can.

But – and this is not intended as a criticism of Morton's argument, only as an adaptation of it to my present use – notice that the existence of cases such as Scarcey and Abundy, *however prevalent such cases might, might be*, doesn't *by itself* show that we should adopt an ecological view of matters. For pointing out that the *usefulness* of conforming to a specific rule purportedly governing agents' deliberations can vary along with changes to agents' environments doesn't *by itself* entail anything about which rules *as a matter of fact* are the rules conformance with which ground deliberative correctness.[6]

To get *there*, we need to add two claims: first, that deliberative correctness is always authoritative and, second, that the authority of deliberative correctness is in some fashion grounded in usefulness. The first claim goes largely unremarked on in Morton's work, but let me just flag the importance of the idea. If you thought that deliberative correctness only sometimes authoritative, then even if you thought that conformance with some purported rules were only sometimes useful, this wouldn't yet tell you anything about the nature of deliberative correctness as (in)variant *per se, even if you thought that the authority was grounded in usefulness*. For, while it might be true that (say) the Stability Rule isn't useful on this or that occasion, this wouldn't show that it wasn't always a rule governing deliberative correctness unless we also thought not just that such rules' authority was grounded in their utility but also that all such rules were always authoritative. Let's just grant this claim for the time being, in order to finish laying out the view: assume deliberative correctness is always authoritative. I'll return to the analogue of this claim that we're already quite familiar with in the case of epistemic correctness in the following discussion.

The second thing we need is, as I've said, the claim that what grounds the *authority* of deliberative correctness is something about usefulness. In other words, we need to adopt something like *second-order deliberative instrumentalism*:

> Second-Order Deliberative Instrumentalism: The fact that it is *authoritatively* deliberatively correct for A to φ in their deliberation concerning "what to do" is grounded by the fact that A's φ-ing in their deliberation concerning "what to do" promotes A's well-being.

Now, as it happens, and as Morton is quick to point out, *we all do already accept* (something like) second-order deliberative instrumentalism. Practical deliberation just is a kind of process of deciding on an answer to the question, "What to do?" that aims to achieve what one cares about. Unlike controversial second-order *epistemic* instrumentalism, which claims that the "grip" of epistemic correctness on agents depends on epistemic correctness' relationship to well-being, it's completely *un*controversial that the "grip" – whatever it amounts to – that *practical deliberative requirements* have on agents depends on those requirements' relationship to agential well-being.

Put second-order deliberative instrumentalism together with the claim that deliberative correctness is always authoritative and with the observations earlier about Abundy and Scarcey, and we arrive at deliberative ecologism, that is, the view that the rules conformance with which ground deliberative correctness can vary along with changes to agents' (psychologies and) environments. After all, there's simply no reason to think Abundy would do any better from the point of view of her well-being were she to abide by the Stability Rule. Not so, of course, with Scarcey: it's only by, or at least it's arguably *best* by, abiding by the Stability Rule that Scarcey is able to promote her well-being by, for example, satisfying her (relatively simple) needs for adequate food, shelter, and rest. According to the ecological conception of deliberative correctness, the lesson to draw from this example – and others like it – is that the rules of deliberative correctness can *vary*: they can vary (at least) according to the environment in which agents find themselves.

I've said that ecologism is the view that the rules conformance with which ground deliberative correctness can also vary not just with differences in agents' environments but also with differences in agents' psychologies. Let me quickly illustrate the ecologists' case for that idea. To get a sense of that idea, notice that actual human agents are prone to a range of cognitive biases and that different agents are more or less prone to these cognitive biases to greater and lesser degrees. Research on such biases from cognitive science, psychology, and (behavioral) economics suggests that such biases serve as heuristics, or rough-and-ready guides for agents engaged in planning behavior. As before, in the environmental case, we can imagine two agents who differ this time not in their environment but instead in the degree to which they are subject to the relevant biases. And in doing so, we will thereby be imagining agents for whom different deliberative rules are differently useful. Morton's example of this phenomenon is the psychological differences between the way in which different agents might be disposed to discount future rewards.[7] Psychological research shows that actual human agents tend to be *hyperbolic discounters*; that is, they tend to discount future rewards against present gain at a rate in some way proportional to their temporal distance from that reward. Of course, from the point of view of maximizing utility, hyperbolic discounting of any sort is dispromotive of one's well-being. But, again, agents will vary to the degree to which they actually are disposed to discount; hence, different rules governing discounting in deliberation will be differently useful for these different agents in their planning behavior, depending on the degree to which they're subject to this bias. For instance, it can intuitively be (authoritatively) deliberatively correct for agents with particular psychologies to conform to deliberative rules requiring various so-called commitment-devices whereas that would be intuitively (authoritatively) deliberatively incorrect for agents with very different psychologies.[8]

And once more, according to the ecological conception of deliberative correctness, the lesson to draw from examples of this sort is that deliberative correctness should be understood ecologically. The rules conformance with which ground deliberative correctness can *vary*: they can vary not just according to the *environment* in which agents find themselves but also according to the *psychologies* with which those agents are equipped.

To be clear, here is how the argument for deliberative ecologism goes:

1. The usefulness of agents' manifesting the grounds of deliberative correctness (e.g., by conforming to some particular deliberative rule) varies along with facts about those agents' psychologies and environments.
2. The authority of deliberative correctness is explanatorily grounded in the usefulness of manifesting the grounds of deliberative correctness. (Second-order deliberative instrumentalism)
3. Deliberative correctness is always authoritative.
4. So what authoritative deliberative correctness comprises varies along with facts about agents' psychologies and environments. (Deliberative ecologism)

Very briefly, (1) is meant to be supported by examples such as Abundy and Scarcey and the empirical research surrounding, for example, our tendency to engage in hyperbolic discounting. Item (2) is an assumption. As we saw earlier, it's relatively uncontroversial that the way to explain the grip, such as it is, that deliberative correctness has on agents is via its promotive connection to their well-being, that is, its usefulness. Item (3) is also an assumption. It mirrors the assumption I've said we should *reject* in the case of epistemic correctness (although more on this later). Item (4) follows from (1) through (3). For, if the usefulness of conforming to particular deliberative rules varies along with changes to agents' psychologies and environments, and we know both that the authority of deliberative correctness is grounded in usefulness and that deliberative correctness is *always* authoritative, then deliberative correctness *itself* varies along with changes to facts about agents' psychologies and environments. In other words, deliberative ecologism.

Let me make a couple quick remarks before moving to the analogue with epistemic correctness. First, the ecological view is *not* arguing in favor of building exception clauses into our understanding of the rules conformance with which ground deliberative correctness. The idea is not that, on discovering the failure of, for example, the Stability Rule, to be useful in Abundy's circumstances, what we need to do is move to a rule such as the following:

> Stability Rule*: Rationality requires that, if an agent settles on an intention to E, *and if she is in an environment of relative scarcity*, barring a change in their circumstances or information, they abstain from reconsidering their intention to E in their deliberation.[9]

This would be a way of attempting to cleave to the invariantist conception of deliberative correctness. According to the ecological view, this is a mistake. The failure is not that we've so far articulated insufficiently precise invariant rules governing practical deliberation. Instead, the failure is that we've so far adopted an insufficiently nimble understanding of the rules themselves. The rules governing practical deliberation simply aren't a single fixed point the nature of which we tweak in the face of these sorts of examples. Instead, what these examples are meant to do is motivate a view of the rules of practical deliberation and agents' psychologies and environments as being, as we might put it, *dependent variables*: we solve for, and negotiate our understanding of, the former as we learn more about the latter. And it can turn out that there's no unique way of solving this problem: given suitably different agents, or suitably different environments, our understanding of what rules appropriately govern agents' practical deliberations will, in turn, be suitably different. Or anyway, so the ecological account has it.

Second, my aim here isn't to argue in detail in favor of the ecological view. Instead, my aim is just to lay out the view and present a sketch of its proponents' arguments and their motivations for accepting the view. So, if you find yourself thinking that there's more argumentative work to do in order to move us toward accepting the ecological conception, that's a natural response to have. But that work won't interest me here. That's because what I'm interested in, recall, is the connection between the ecological view of deliberative correctness and a potentially more aggressive form of epistemic instrumentalism. I'll turn to that in just a moment.

Before that, let me point out the consequences of accepting deliberative ecologism when it comes to the ambitions of first-order theorizing about deliberative correctness. The consequences should be relatively clear, but they bear emphasis. If ecologism about deliberative correctness is true, then it simply doesn't make sense to engage in disputes over *the* rules of correct practical deliberation. Instead, we should be interested in sussing out the rules for correct deliberation *under different conditions* or *for agents with such-and-such* psychologies. This doesn't mean first-order theorizing about deliberative correctness is somehow *pointless*, but it does mean that a particular kind of fight over the rules for correct deliberation is particularly pointless. Rather than worrying about whether (say) agents should always everywhere have stable intentions or whether there's a wide- or narrow-scope means–ends rule governing deliberation, we should be asking questions about *when it is* that stable intentions are useful, or perhaps *what kinds of agents* are best-served by conforming to narrow- or wide-scope means–ends rules.

12.5 Invariantism about Epistemic Correctness

The situation with first-order epistemic theories, that is, accounts of what grounds epistemic correctness, is exactly analogous to the situation with first-order deliberative theories when it comes to invariantist orthodoxy. There is, as we've seen throughout this book, extremely wide variation in the particular first-order theories of epistemic correctness that various philosophers adduce. Familiarly by now, we have all the following:

> Evidentialism: The fact that it is epistemically correct for A to φ is grounded by the fact that A's φ-ing is supported by A's evidence.
>
> Coherentism: The fact that it is epistemically correct for A to φ is grounded by the fact that A's φ coheres with A's other doxastic attitudes.
>
> Reliabilism: The fact that it is epistemically correct for A to φ is grounded by the fact that A's φ-ing is produced via a reliable mechanism.

But what all evidentialists, coherentists, reliabilists, and so on all assume is that, whatever grounds epistemic correctness is *invariant*: the grounds of epistemic correctness do not vary along with changes to actual agents' psychologies and environments. In other words, it's orthodoxy that, if it turns out that some particular first-order epistemic theory has managed to tell the right story about the explanatory grounds of epistemic correctness, then this first-order epistemic theory's story will be the right story to tell *regardless of what agents' psychologies and environments are like*.

Of course, and importantly exactly as in the case of deliberative correctness, it's entirely compatible with this idea that our verdicts regarding epistemic correctness vary from agent to agent, from environment to environment. That is for the obvious reason that the grounds themselves might be sensitive in some ways to facts about agents' psychologies and environments. An obvious example of this is *reliabilism*, which says that it's facts about the reliability of certain mechanisms that ground epistemic correctness. It's relatively uncontroversial that what "reliability" consists in can vary along with changes to agents' environments. Nevertheless, the invariantist idea is that the grounds represent fixed points in our theorizing about what epistemic correctness comprises. This idea allows that what epistemic correctness comprises on particular occasions might be varied and complex. What it does not allow is that corresponding to both or either of the varied, complex, and diverse psychologies agents possess and or the varied, complex, and diverse environments agents find themselves, there are a range of different grounds of epistemic correctness.

Perhaps even more so than in the case of deliberative correctness, this invariantist conception of epistemic correctness should be extraordinarily familiar. But, as I'm now about to argue, there's a case, analogous to the one Morton makes for deliberative ecologism, to be made for *epistemic ecologism*, that is, the view that the grounds of epistemic correctness can vary along with changes to agents' psychologies and environments. Importantly, as I explain, only second-order epistemic instrumentalists are in a position to avail themselves of this argument. I close by identifying some consequences of doing so; I explain what happens if epistemic instrumentalists go in for epistemic ecologism.

12.6 The Case for Ecologism about Epistemic Correctness

The case for ecologism about epistemic correctness goes, in rough outline, the same way it goes on the side of deliberative correctness. Recall that there the idea was that reflection on the fact that, for example, agents are predictably, systematically, and cognitively biased and limited in certain specific identifiable ways – such as being hyperbolic rather than exponential discounters – militates in favor of thinking that the rules conformance with which comprise deliberative correctness are sensitive to this fact. Given that we tend to be hyperbolic discounters, for instance, it might make sense to think that agents are governed by a deliberative rule requiring them to simply ignore (i.e., discount at 100%) certain sorts of present rewards in their planning behavior.[10] At least, as we saw, we are pressured toward such a position given the two crucial assumptions that deliberative correctness is always authoritative and that the authority of deliberative correctness is explained in an instrumentalist fashion.

We can generate a symmetrical argument here in the case of epistemic correctness, assuming we adopt the corresponding crucial assumptions. Let me first lay out the structure of the argument, and then I'll comment on each part. Here's the version of the argument that mirrors the argument for ecologism in the case of *deliberative* correctness:

1. The usefulness of agents' manifesting the grounds of epistemic correctness (e.g., the evidentialist grounds or the coherentist grounds, etc.) varies along with facts about those agents' psychologies and environments.
2. The authority of epistemic correctness is explanatorily grounded in the usefulness of manifesting the grounds of deliberative correctness. (Second-order epistemic instrumentalism)
3. Epistemic correctness is always authoritative. (Always Authoritative)

4. So what authoritative epistemic correctness comprises varies along with facts about agents' psychologies and environments. (Epistemic ecologism)

Working backward, (4) follows from (1) through (3). I'll return to (3) later. For now, one quick remark: (3) just is what we've been calling Always Authoritative throughout the book. In Chapter 7, I argued that the intuitive starting point for our second-order epistemic theorizing couldn't assume it. Instead, we were only licensed by that intuitive data in thinking that epistemic correctness was *usually* authoritative. Again, I'll return to this later. (2) is, of course, second-order epistemic instrumentalism. That leaves (1): Do we have any reason to think it's the case that whether manifesting the grounds of epistemic correctness is useful varies along with facts about those agents' psychologies and environments?

There's a familiar route to a "yes" and a less familiar, but ultimately, I think more satisfying, route we could take. Start with the familiar route: we can simply point at one half of the Goldilocks Problem. In other words, we can simply advert to a case in which an agent's, for example, conforming their doxastic attitudes to their evidence, isn't useful. If you think evidentialism isn't the right view about what epistemic correctness comprises, we can generate a case for *any other first-order epistemic theory* with one important exception. The exception, of course, is first-order *epistemic instrumentalism*. Setting that to one side, for any purported account of the grounds of epistemic correctness, it will be possible to imagine a case in which the usefulness of an agent's manifesting the grounds so understood will vary along with facts about those agents' psychologies and environments. This is for the simple reason that the grounds of epistemic correctness cited in those first-order epistemic theories (again, with the exception of first-order epistemic instrumentalism) won't include the facts along with which usefulness varies, namely, *agents' psychologies and environments*. As I said, that's the familiar route to (1).

The problem with the familiar route is that it looks like a trick. I don't think it *is* a trick; I think it's perfectly fine. But it appears to rely on our judgments about relatively rare, one-off cases – cases in which, for example, it's not useful to conform one's beliefs to the evidence or to have coherent doxastic states and so on. And that, in turn, invites the kind of (usually not very dialectically helpful) response to arguments that rely on judgments about cases that we're all familiar with.

Hence, we might try a different path; that different path is the epistemic analogue of the one Morton takes in the case of deliberative correctness. Notice that Morton doesn't simply appeal to the fact that, sometimes, it's useful for agents to depart from particular rules conformance with which is meant to comprise deliberative correctness and then *leave it at that*. That would be the analogue of the familiar route we considered earlier. And it would invite the kind of unhelpful response noted before. Instead, Morton points to the fact that there is *systematic* variance in whether conformance with this or that deliberative rule is useful for agents. Is something similar true in the case of epistemic correctness? I think it is.

Notice that agents are not just limited in terms of their practical deliberative abilities – they don't just suffer from particular practical deliberative biases, such as hyperbolic discounting. *Epistemic* agents, like agents in engaged in practical deliberation, are predictably, systematically, cognitively biased and limited in certain specific identifiable ways. For instance, agents have limited cognitive and attentional resources. And this makes a systematic difference to how it is useful for them to comport themselves with respect to their epistemic lives.

We can be more specific than this. There's a large (and continuously growing) body of empirical research on the ways in which it is useful for agents with particular psychologies or who find themselves in particular environments to depart from so-called ideal rationality – in our language to – depart from conceptions of epistemic correctness that are not sensitive to facts about agents' psychologies and environments. For example, take the *representativeness* heuristic as famously described by Kahneman and Tversky.[11] Very roughly, the idea is that when making judgments about the likelihood of uncertain events, it is useful for epistemic agents *like us* to pay more attention to how representative – that is, similar to the relevant parent population and reflective of the process by which it's generated – the event is (or would be) than to how probabilistically likely that event actually is given our actual evidence regarding the frequency or objective probabilistic likelihood. Of course, ordering the subjective likelihood of future events by their representativeness rather than by updating on one's evidence via, for example, Bayes' rule, will lead to outcomes in which agents' beliefs are sometimes systematically false or their partial beliefs – their credences – are systematically inaccurate. It will correspondingly fail to manifest the relevant grounds of epistemic correctness conceived of in the, for example, evidentialist fashion. What's important is that the systematic use of the representativeness heuristic for agents like *us* in our environments is far more useful than it is to, for example, update via Bayes' rule.

I could continue to iterate examples, but I won't. As I said, the literature is vast and growing.[12] There are myriad ways in which it is *systematically* – and not just on this or that one-off occasion – useful for agents to depart from particular conceptions of what epistemic correctness requires. So that is the less familiar, but I think ultimately more satisfying, route to (1); again, there's nothing wrong with the familiar route – but it can help head off complaints about the examples by pointing out how widespread we should think they, in fact, are.

So much for (1). We're already very familiar with (2): this just is second-order epistemic instrumentalism. Now we come to (3): Always Authoritative.

You'll recall that I was at pains to deny that we have any pre-theoretical reason to endorse Always Authoritative, that is, the view that epistemic correctness always exerts its grip on agents. My view has been that whether this turned out to be true would have to depend on what second-order epistemic theory we ended up endorsing. We've ended up with – at least, I've argued we'd be perfectly fine ending up with – a second-order epistemic theory that doesn't *entail* the truth of Always Authoritative. For, as we've seen, it's perfectly compatible with second-order epistemic instrumentalism that, some of the time, it turns out that some of what it is epistemically correct for an agent to do isn't something that it's also authoritatively epistemically correct for them to do. That is what will presumably happen if a non-instrumentalist first-order epistemic theories, such as evidentialism, coherentism, and so on, is true *and invariantism is true*; that is, it's true both that some (non-instrumentalist) particular first-order epistemic theory is right about what grounds epistemic correctness and that those grounds do not vary along with changes to agents' psychologies and environments. For then we'll have exactly the kinds of cases I've been in the business of identifying in this section.

What this means, in effect, is that the range of views available to the second-order epistemic instrumentalist is lightly restricted. They can have one of the following pairs of views:

1. Invariantism + Usually Authoritative
2. Ecologism + Always Authoritative
3. Ecologism + Usually Authoritative

But they cannot have the following:

4. Invariantism + Always Authoritative

The reason they cannot have (4) is precisely because of the argument we've just been canvassing; that argument shows that, together with their second-order epistemic instrumentalism, Always Authoritative leads to ecologism. So, which of (1) through (3) should the second-order epistemic instrumentalist adopt? Clearly, one way to decide things would be to decide whether they should accept Always Authoritative. But I don't think there's any way to do this, given their second-order instrumentalism. That view hasn't added anything to the balance of the reasons either for or against accepting Always Authoritative. And so we're left with respect to Always Authoritative in the same dialectical position we occupied in Chapter 7. What about the remaining choice: between invariantism and ecologism?

I don't have a view on this, but I do have a hunch, or perhaps a preference, which I'll explain in closing. My hunch-cum-preference is that second-order epistemic instrumentalists (will) not go for (1): they will (or I prefer they) be ecologists *whatever comes*. The reason I prefer slash hunch this is that whether you're inclined to go in for invariantism will largely be a function of how important you think first-order epistemic theorizing is; in other words, it will depend in large part on how concerned you are to *get it right* about what epistemic correctness comprises. After all, it's only invariantists who should think that it makes any sense to fight to the academic death over whether, for example, evidentialism or reliabilism is correct. If instead ecologism is true, the nature of the first-order debate changes.

Recall the symmetrical point about deliberative correctness. If ecologism about deliberative correctness is true, then we shouldn't be interested in *the* rules for correct deliberation – we should instead be interested in what works well for different agents with different psychologies in different environments. The same thing goes here, in the case of first-order epistemic theorizing. If ecologism is true, then rather than worrying about whether evidentialism or coherentism or reliabilism or *whatever* is *the* correct account of what epistemic correctness comprises, we should instead worry about what kind of epistemic correctness works well for different agents with different psychologies in different environments, where working well is a function of promoting their well-being. Maybe conformance to the evidence is a good idea *here* but not *there*; perhaps reliability really matters in *this* environment but not *this* one. And worrying about *that* – about what it is that actually promotes agents' well-being – is exactly the kind of thing, it seems to me, that second-order epistemic instrumentalists will (preferably) be inclined to worry about.

Notes

1 Usually, these disputes go on under the guise of disputes about the "norms" of practical reasoning. I'll mostly avoid this way of speaking.
2 Morton (2011, 2017).
3 This is adapted from Morton (2011).
4 Morton (2011, p. 570).
5 Morton (2011, p. 570).
6 Morton herself deploys further arguments. See especially Morton (2011).
7 Morton (2011). Morton borrows this example from psychologist George Ainslie's (2001) work on the topic. The literature on this topic is vast; see the seminal work by Tversky and Kahneman (1974); see also the essays collected in Kahneman, Slovic, and Tversky (1982).
8 On commitment devices, see Gharad et al. (2010).
9 This example is due to Morton (2011).
10 Morton (2011, p. 573). For discussion, see Ainslie (2001, pp. 28–35, referenced in Morton 2011).
11 Kahneman and Tversky (1972).
12 For a particularly nice overview of a range of such examples, see Goldstein and Gigerenzer (2002).

References

Ainslie, George. 2001. *Breakdown of Will*. Cambridge: Cambridge University Press.

Gharad, Bryan, Dean Karlan, and Scott Nelson. 2010. "Commitment Devices." *Annual Review of Economics* 2: 671–698.

Goldstein, Daniel, and Gerd Gigerenzer. 2002. "Models of Ecological Rationality: The Recognition Heuristic." *Psychological Review* 109 (1): 75–90.

Kahneman, Daniel, Paul Slovic, and Amos Tversky. 1982. *Judgment under Uncertainty: Heuristics and Biases*. Cambridge: Cambridge University Press.

Kahneman, Daniel, and Amos Tversky. 1972. "Subjective Probability: A Judgment of Representativeness." *Cognitive Psychology* 3: 430–454.

Morton, Jennifer. 2011. "Toward an Ecological Theory of the Norms of Practical Deliberation." *European Journal of Philosophy* 19 (4): 561–584.

———. 2017. "Reasoning under Scarcity." *Australasian Journal of Philosophy* 95 (3): 543–559.

Tversky, Amos, and Daniel Kahneman. 1974. "Judgment under Uncertainty: Heuristics and Biases." *Science* 185: 1124–1131.

Index

ambit, *see* focal points
Aristotelianism, neo-epistemic 49–50
authoritativeness, pluralism and monism about 100–104

bayesianism 34, 194

coherentism 42, 49–50, 191
concepts, evaluative 9
consequentialism: epistemic 45, 56, 133, 141–142; ethical 40, 79, 85–88
constitutivism 66, 158–162
content constraint 139–151, 154–155, 162, 166, 173
correctness, formal 99–100, 115–116, 118
correctness, kinds of: all-things-considered 21–26; conventionalism and anti-conventionalism about 14–18; maximal pluralism about 12–13; monism about 18–28; restricted pluralism about 13–18
correctness, standards of 11, 28

deliberation 183–196
divine command theory 106, 156
dogmatism 145–148
doxastic attitudes 45, 55–58, 160–162, *see* focal points

earmarks of the epistemic: content-based 58–60; functional 60–64; object-based 54–58
ecological rationality 185–190, 195–196
ecologism, *see* ecological rationality
epistemic correctness, authoritative: always 20–21, 27, 114–115, 143–144, 147, 149–151; described 99–101; minimal conception of 107–117; sometimes 114–116, 137; usually 114, 116–118, 128–131, 144, 155, 157, 164–165, 177, 179, 195
epistemic value 162
error theory, *see* skepticism about authoritative correctness
ethics, *see* morality
etiquette 52–53
evidentialism: first-order 1, 38–39, 42, 45, 49–50, 57, 64, 71, 132, 141; second-order 2, 158–164, 168–171, 191
explanation: bespoke 154–173; de dicto 142–144; first-order 40–41; must come first 140; relationship to grounding 41; relationship to justification 86; second-order 104–107; virtues of 166–173
extension: first-order 38–41, 141–142; mistakes of, *see* goldilocks problem; second-order, *see* epistemic authoritativeness, usually

factoral theories, *see* extension, first order
factoring account 105
focal points 43–46, 55–56, *see* earmarks, object-based
foundational theories, *see* explanation, first order
functional criterion 64–65
Functionalist Challenge 84–96, 126, 131, 137, 178–181
function-first epistemology, *see* earmarks, functional

genealogy, *see* function-first epistemology
genres, *see* correctness, kinds of
Goldilocks Problem 75–80, 129–130, 176–178, 193

instrumentalism, first-order epistemic: defined 72; variations on 70–71
instrumentalism, second-order epistemic: bespoke 165–166; defined 127
interference 89–90
invariantism 184–192, 195–196

justification: moral 85–88; relationship to correctness 33–34; relationship to explanation 85–88; relationship to legitimate authority 113–114

Kantianism, epistemic 133, 171

modal strategy, *see* Goldilocks Problem
morality: and blame 88; as a kind of correctness 35, 37; authority of morality 19, 27, 111–113, 150–151; first-order theories of 58–59; functional role of 90–91; justifications in 85–88; second-order theories of 148–150

naturalism 135–136
nihilism, *see* skepticism about authoritative correctness
nonnaturalism 136
normative, *see* epistemic correctness, authoritative

particularism, epistemic 43–44
pluralism: about kinds of authority, *see* authoritativeness, pluralism and monism about; about kinds of correctness, *see* correctness, kinds of; normative 11

potential psychological impact 107–115, 118, 120, 128, 164
pragmatism, *see* function-first epistemology instrumentalism, first-order epistemic
prediction vs accommodation, *see* explanation, virtues of
promotion 72–74
psychological impact, *see* potential psychological impact

quietism 148

reliabilism 42, 191
reliable informants, *see* earmarks, functional
resonance constraint, *see* potential psychological impact

scarcity, *see* ecological rationality
scope, *see* focal points
self-effacing 88–89
simplicity, *see* explanation, virtues of
skepticism: about all-things-considered correctness 23–26; about authoritative correctness 113, 118–120, 132
special interests, *see* Goldilocks Problem

too few reasons, *see* goldilocks problem
too little correctness, *see* goldilocks problem
too many reasons, *see* goldilocks problem
too much correctness, *see* goldilocks problem
trade-offs 79, 141–142

unity, explanatory, *see* explanation, virtues of

veritism 162–168

well-being 71–80, 109, 128–137, 176–181, 187–189

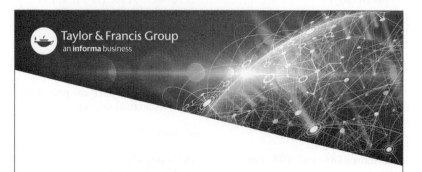

Taylor & Francis eBooks

www.taylorfrancis.com

A single destination for eBooks from Taylor & Francis with increased functionality and an improved user experience to meet the needs of our customers.

90,000+ eBooks of award-winning academic content in Humanities, Social Science, Science, Technology, Engineering, and Medical written by a global network of editors and authors.

TAYLOR & FRANCIS EBOOKS OFFERS:

A streamlined experience for our library customers

A single point of discovery for all of our eBook content

Improved search and discovery of content at both book and chapter level

REQUEST A FREE TRIAL
support@taylorfrancis.com